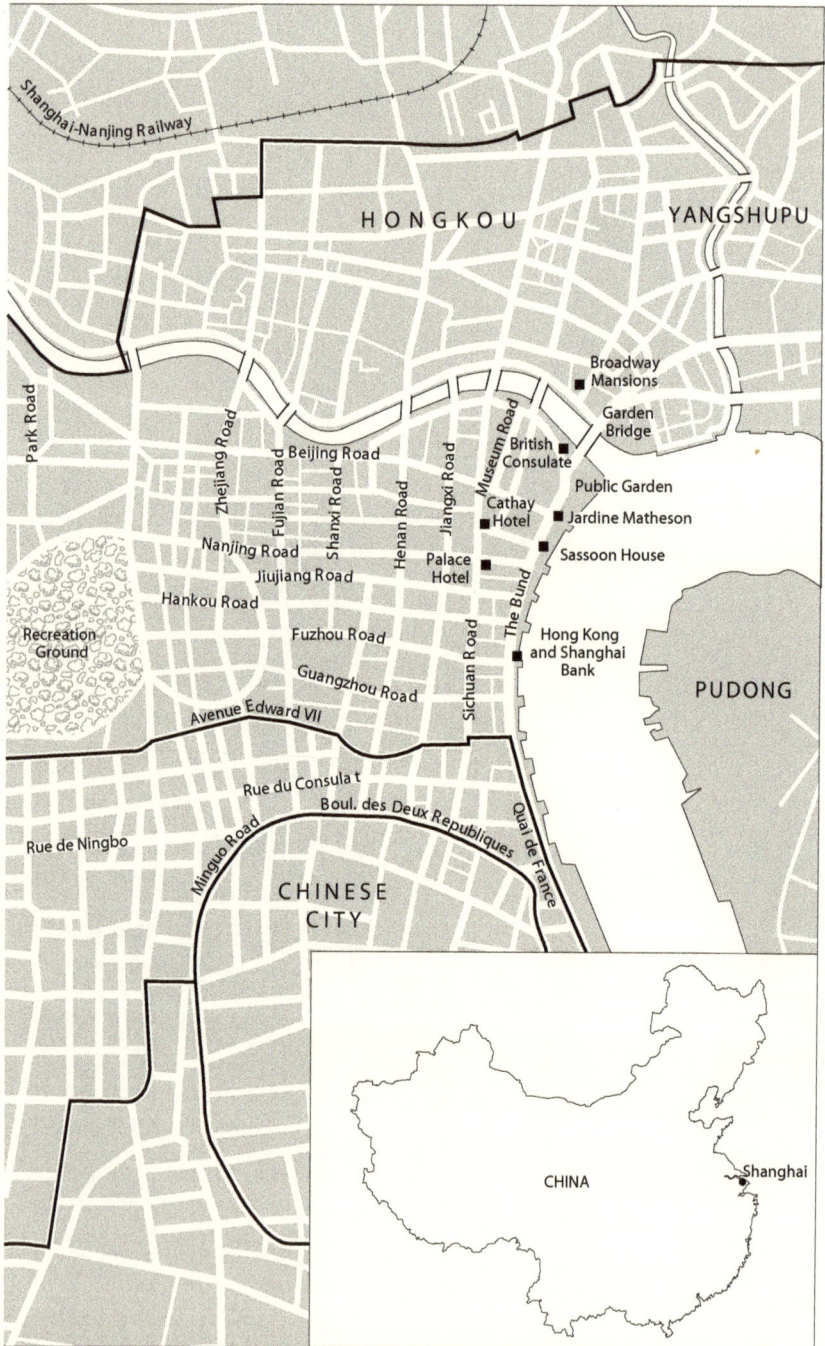

Shanghai-Nanjing Railway

HONGKOU

YANGSHUPU

Broadway Mansions

Garden Bridge

British Consulate

Public Garden

Jardine Matheson

Cathay Hotel

Sassoon House

Palace Hotel

Hong Kong and Shanghai Bank

PUDONG

Park Road

Zhejiang Road

Fujian Road

Beijing Road

Shanxi Road

Henan Road

Jiangxi Road

Museum Road

Nanjing Road

Jiujiang Road

Hankou Road

Recreation Ground

Fuzhou Road

Guangzhou Road

Sichuan Road

The Bund

Avenue Edward VII

Rue du Consulat

Boul. des Deux Republiques

Quai de France

Minguo Road

Rue de Ningbo

CHINESE CITY

CHINA

Shanghai

The Jacquinot Safe Zone

The Jacquinot Safe Zone

Wartime Refugees in Shanghai

Marcia R. Ristaino

STANFORD UNIVERSITY PRESS

STANFORD, CALIFORNIA

2008

Stanford University Press,
Stanford, California
© 2008 by the Board of Trustees of the
Leland Stanford Junior University

Library of Congress Cataloging-in-Publication Data

Ristaino, Marcia R.
    The Jacquinot Safe Zone: wartime refugees in Shanghai / Marcia R. Ristaino.
        p. cm.
    Includes bibliographical references and index.
    ISBN 978-0-8047-5793-5 (cloth : alk. paper)
    1. Sino-Japanese War, 1937–1945—Refugees—China—Shanghai.   2. Shanghai (China)—History—20th century.   3. Jacquinot de Besange, Robert, 1878–1946. I. Title.   II. Title : Wartime refugees in Shanghai.

DS777.533.R45R57   2008
940.53086'9140951132—dc22   2007031058

Printed in the United States of America on
acid-free, archival-quality paper

Typeset at Stanford University Press in 10.5/13 Garamond

For Barbara Ann, G. Gordon, and dear Betty

Contents

Illustrations

Preface

As the research for this work progressed, I was astonished to discover that the French Jesuit Father Robert Jacquinot de Besange's contributions to relief and refugee work in China were almost entirely unknown to American scholars, Chinese researchers, and even to most of the Jesuits I met. His life spanned several decades, countries, communities, and also events central to World War II. During his lifetime, he did receive special recognition for his contributions on several occasions. Nevertheless, the subsequent lack of knowledge of his person and life today seemed to me quite puzzling. Perhaps this deficiency can be partly explained by his untimely death in Berlin in 1946, at a time when the world was still in chaos. The years just after World War II were also a time when China, where he had spent twenty-seven years of his life, was entering a period of civil war, followed by the reclusive and difficult years under Mao Zedong's leadership. Overall, it seems that Father Jacquinot somehow fell into obscurity through no fault of his own.

My discovery of his life and work convinced me that at least Father Jacquinot's main contribution, the establishment of safe zones meant to provide refuge and security for civilian refugees during wartime, needed to be carefully studied and presented. I found that to do justice to the subject required putting his zone concept in the context of his extensive services in the major treaty port city, Shanghai. I needed to illuminate his pastoral work, his extensive relief activities during periods of serious flooding in China, and his acute observations and firsthand experiences gained during the first Japanese attack on Shanghai in 1932. During the second Japanese attack in 1937, Jacquinot was ready with his plan to provide relief and safety to the Chinese who were threatened and in danger.

I was also inspired by the timeliness of the refugee issue. It is obvious that today there are many instances of refugee suffering, hardship, and, sometimes, failure to survive. So many of the sources I read on Jacquinot's work suggested that valuable information might be gained from this early example of refugee protection and care. I share the aspirations of those earlier observers and believe that perhaps his example can be of practical use in meeting the often dire needs of refugees and their communities today. His safe zone concept does appear in the Geneva Convention of 1949, but without any context or explanation as to how his safe zone came about.

The fact of Father Jacquinot's life and work being so little known raises the obvious question as to how I learned about him. I came across Father Jacquinot's name several times in sources I used in researching a previous book, which focused on two other major refugee diasporas, the Jewish and White Russian refugees who found refuge in Shanghai during the first half of the twentieth century. For example, I discovered that Father Jacquinot was the senior chaplain of the Shanghai Volunteer Corps, a respected, quasi-militia organization that included both Russian and Jewish refugee units. I also happened to be well attuned to Jesuit work in China as a result of having done research for the master's degree on another French Jesuit, Joachim Bouvet, who left for China in 1685 and worked at the court of the Kangxi Emperor. My curiosity seemed to have a promising direction, so my interest in studying Father Jacquinot remained strong. As soon as time permitted, I began to research and uncover the fascinating story of his work with Chinese refugees in Shanghai.

Support for the research that resulted in this book was provided by the John W. Kluge Center at the Library of Congress. The Kluge Center grant afforded me the time, office space, and resources to complete my work. In that regard, I am especially grateful to Prosser Gifford who was the director of the center at the time of my grant and a source of inspiration. My colleagues there, Patricia Sieber, Lu Liu, Temur Temule, and Galina Yermolenko, provided a much valued generosity of spirit and friendship, in addition to scholarly guidance. JoAnne Kitching and Mary Lou Reker were unfailing in their assistance and support.

I would like to express my sincere gratitude to the many archivists, librarians, and scholars who helped gain access to material for me at the Library of Congress; U.S. National Archives Military Records Division, College Park; Franklin D. Roosevelt Presidential Library; Shanghai Municipal Archives; Shanghai Municipal Library; Shanghai Academy of Social Sciences; Ministry of Foreign Affairs, Diplomatic Record Office, Tokyo; League of Nations Archives, Geneva; French Ministry of Foreign Affairs Archives at Nantes; Jesuit Archives at Vanves, France; Archives des Pères Jèsuites, Québec; and the University of South Carolina Film Library.

Especially helpful in this regard were Carol Armbruster, Ming Poon, the late Peter Lu, Ito Eiichi, Mi Chu-wiens, John Taylor, Robert Clark, Wang Renfang, Tao Benyi, Atsuta Miruko, Françoise Maxence, Anne-Sophie Cras, Father Robert Bonfils, S.J., Regine Thiriez, Isabelle Contant, Fang Tan, and Greg Wilsbacher. Valuable assistance was ably provided by my research assistant, Bridget Lines.

Scholarly recommendations and suggestions were provided by colleagues such as Robert Bickers, the late Frederic Wakeman, Jr., John Meehan, S.J., Father John Witek, S.J., Pan Guang, Xu Xin, Tess Johnston, Yu Maochun, Yang Daqing, and Frank Joseph Shulman. I am very grateful to Parks Coble for his careful reading of the manuscript and to the other, anonymous, reader who provided useful comments. Assistance with Japanese sources came generously from Cecil Uyehara; with French sources, especially the poetry, from, Jeannine Cap, Marilyn Clemens, and Liliane Willens. Peter R. Dreyer improved the manuscript with his expert editing. Special technical assistance was provided by Robert DeMariano, Elizabeth Timberlake, Tessa Klein, and Kelsey Strampe.

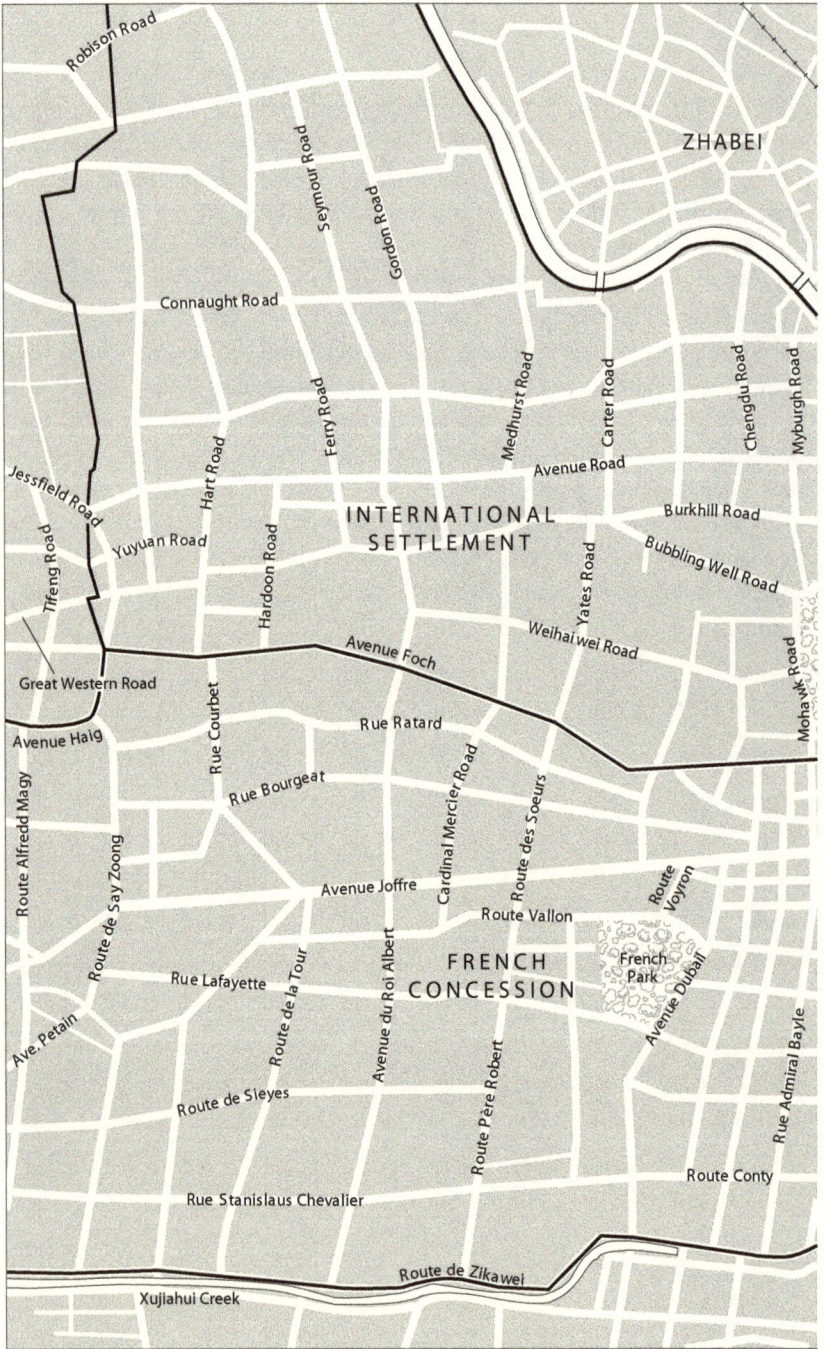

Map of Shanghai in 1937. From Marcia Ristaino, *Port of Last Resort: The Diaspora Communities of Shanghai* (Stanford, 2001), p. xx, based on a map in Harriet Sergeant, *Shanghai: Collision Point of Cultures, 1918–1939* (New York, 1990).

The Jacquinot Safe Zone

Father Robert Jacquinot de Besange, S.J. *The Story of the Jacquinot Zone* (Shanghai, 1939), p. 1.

Chapter One

The Early Years

≈

This study focuses on the humanitarian services of a French Jesuit, Father Robert Jacquinot de Besange, who played a key role in the emerging crisis of urban warfare and refugee handling in Shanghai during World War II. Father Jacquinot came to China in 1913. By the early 1930s, he had recognized the need to provide safety and refuge to victims of the horrendous methods of modern warfare, including aerial bombing in congested urban areas. In the course of his work, he displayed an unusual ability to organize available resources and mobilize official support to deal with the catastrophes that accompanied the Japanese invasion. His greatest accomplishment was the establishment of a protected haven or safe zone for endangered Chinese refugees while a brutal war raged in Shanghai between the Japanese invaders and responding Chinese troops.

It is difficult to write about a truly remarkable individual like Father Jacquinot without seeming to drift into hagiography. Sometimes, an individual's contributions, especially humanitarian ones, are so considerable that they make finding human frailties or evidence of weakness seem like a trivial or token pursuit. One recommended approach is to work with as many and varied sources as possible, with the expectation that not all parties consulted will have a special interest in trying to burnish the subject's image and reputation, and that some will allow her or his more human dimensions to emerge. Achieving a balanced perspective is central to creating an authentic and believable portrait. Even with these goals in mind, however, dealing with an individual showing such spirit and accomplishments made the goal of drawing a balanced portrait more difficult to achieve than it otherwise might seem.

The Sino-Japanese War, which for many Asians was the beginning of World War II, reached Shanghai in August 1937. The Safety Zone (*Anquan qu*) established by Father Jacquinot and his committee became known as the "Jacquinot

Robert Jacquinot de Besange, S.J., in Shanghai, 1937.
Courtesy of Malcolm Roshost.

Zone," and gave protection and survival to at least 300,000 Chinese fleeing from chaos in the wartime city. It is the earliest example in history of a successful response to modern warfare for the protection of civilians in a densely populated metropolis. Father Jacquinot, "the Christian Savior of Shanghai," a Chinese newspaper called him, and the Safety Zone served as models for other refugee protection efforts.[1] In the months and years that followed, the Jacquinot Zone inspired similar zones, with less success in the Chinese capital, Nanjing, but with better results in Wuhan, Canton, and other cities. This study will show that more than 510,000 Chinese were spared almost certain death by the implementation of Father Jacquinot's zone concept in different parts of China.

The Sino-Japanese War, or war of resistance, as it is known in China, lasted for eight years and brought extreme hardship to the Chinese, both urban and rural. It is estimated that almost 100 million Chinese became refugees during the course of the devastating onslaught. Shanghai, China's major industrial and trade center, was directly attacked in August 1937, letting loose a tidal wave of refugees hoping to find refuge in the International Settlement and French Concession. Showing caution regarding these foreign areas, the Japanese made the Chinese-administered areas of the city the focus of the attack, and there the toll of human suffering and property damage was immense. The thriving industrial and port facilities lay in ruins. Besides the enormous loss of life, suddenly becoming a refugee amidst the devastation, without a means of livelihood, dictated a changed life replete with danger, hunger, humiliation, dependency, and loss of opportunity or a sense of future. Of course, there were attempts to deal with these tragic circumstances. The various aid organizations responded and even the Nationalist government, which was still in the early stages of developing a national and comprehensive refugee aid program, began to expand its approach from mainly a local to a more national plan.

Still, it is fair to ask why Father Jacquinot remains unknown to so many: to scholars of Chinese history, war atrocities, aid organizations, and refugee issues, to those who study international organizations and relations, and, most surprising of all, to the Jesuit Order itself. His name has failed to bring recognition by scholars and participants at academic gatherings and was unknown to several Jesuits I contacted. Other important explanations will emerge in the course of this study, but one likely reason is the relative lack of attention given to the lengthy Sino-Japanese War by Western and Chinese scholars alike.[2] Fathoming the simultaneously ongoing struggle between the Communists, especially Mao Zedong, and the Guomindang (Nationalists) under Chiang Kai-shek is given higher priority than scrutiny of the war and its development. Chinese scholars have preferred, at least until recently, to document the rise and leadership of the Chinese Communist Party.

Father Jacquinot was obviously a born diplomat and superb organizer. Tenacious and determined, he was able to gain approval for the refugee zone by bringing together, in the midst of a hot war, the Chinese and Japanese diplomatic and military parties, while also reassuring the presiding foreign interests in this treaty port city. After days and nights of intense negotiations, both sides approved the Zone. Jacquinot then turned his organizational skills to working out plans and programs for the relief and support of the thousands of war refugees in this new area and other parts of the city. Finding ways to finance his refugee operations was obviously essential. Engaging in an early form of shuttle diplomacy, Jacquinot therefore traveled to Japan to meet with the Japanese Foreign Minister, Hirota Kōki, to Chongqing to meet with President Chiang Kai-shek, and to Washington, D.C., where, after a meeting with President Franklin D. Roosevelt, he won approval for $750,000 in support of his refugee camps, a hefty sum during those depressed times.

On returning in June 1940 to a France that was under attack and soon to be occupied, Jacquinot sought to apply his Shanghai experience to the circumstances around Paris, but with different results. His lasting legacy after years of humanitarian work was to be the inclusion of his Jacquinot Zone concept, cited by that name, in the Protocols and Commentaries of the Geneva Convention of 1949, where it is described as a successful example of a neutralized zone for the humanitarian protection of refugees during wartime.

Unfortunately, Father Jacquinot did not live to see this outcome. He died of illness and exhaustion at the age of sixty-eight while serving as head of the Vatican delegation for refugees and displaced persons in Berlin. It is easy to see that this is a remarkable story that needs to be told. What follows is a detailed and, I hope, balanced account of his work, experiences, and accomplishments.

ROOTS

Robert Charles Joseph Emile Jacquinot de Besange was born on March 15, 1878, to François Eugenie Emile Jaquinot and Lesbie Marie Emma Josephine Got. His place of birth was the town of Saintes in the Charente-Maritime département in western France.[3] A market town on the Charente River, Saintes has a long and varied history. It was once occupied by the Romans, as is evidenced by its extensive remaining and well-preserved Roman ruins, including a large amphitheater and triumphal arch, resembling the famous one in Paris, along with two partially restored Romanesque churches dating from the eleventh and twelfth centuries.

Jacquinot's family moved away when it was time for his schooling. He was recognized as a brilliant student during the eight years he spent at the school, Notre Dame du Bon Secours, in the northwestern port city of Brest, on France's Atlantic seacoast.[4] The aristocratic Jacquinot de Besange family, however, is usually associated with the northeastern region of Lorraine, another historic province of France. Besides being the birthplace of Joan of Arc, with whom the Jacquinot family claimed connection, Lorraine was also im-

A modern photograph of the home where Jacquinot was born. Author's photo collection.

portant to the Romans, who regarded it as a passageway between northern and southern Europe. Lorraine, with its main city, Metz, is located in a frontier position on the German border. Germany figured prominently in its history, annexing Lorraine during the nineteenth century and relinquishing control of it only after Germany's defeat in World War I. It was eventually the site of the pivotal Verdun battles and later the Maginot Line. With its frontier position and strong Catholic tradition, Lorraine had an important influence on the young Jacquinot. Father Jacquinot's clear sense of history and religious devotion could not help but be nourished by his early exposure in these various French historic settings.

THE SOCIETY OF JESUS

The Society of Jesus, whose founding was approved in 1540 by Pope Paul III, was the creation of a Spaniard, Ignatius Loyola, and held as a primary doctrinal source his *Spiritual Exercises,* published in 1552. Loyola's book is a kind of handbook of practical guidance to develop man's greatest virtues, his own individual talents. In line with this teaching, the Jesuits in China had a long and remarkable record of becoming skilled linguists and serious scholars of Chinese customs and traditions. This practical and flexible approach led the early Jesuits in China to emphasize their talents in mathematics, the sciences, arts, and culture over teaching complex religious ideas. During their training, they were well schooled in the latest scientific teachings and developments in European mathematics. By winning the respect of the Chinese, who revered learning, for Western science, they hoped in the end to win a place for the Christian religion in China.

During the seventeenth century, the Jesuits had succeeded in placing members of the Society as confessors to Louis XIV and other leading figures of the time. The Society was an aristocracy of intellect and won the respect and confidence of the patrons of the day. Jesuit educational institutions were among the most respected in Europe and concentrated on spreading contemporary knowledge and discoveries in the arts, mathematics, and sciences.[5] In their missionary capacity, the Jesuits presented themselves to the world, not as censors of aberrant Christian thinking, but as men skilled and useful in practical affairs, exponents of the modern, accommodating, and efficient ideal furbished by the seventeenth century. The rise of rationalism and the scientific movement, the belief in human capacities, and the emergence of powerful nation-states precipitated a gradual transition in society, especially in the eighteenth century, to a commitment to Western civilization itself. The Jesuits, in their widely scattered positions, became exponents in the stream of European rationalism, which flowed through the Society of Jesus to many parts of the world, until the Society's suppression in the Catholic countries of Europe and their colonies by 1773.

Official figures report that by the year of Father Jacquinot's birth in 1878, there were 2,464 Jesuits serving in France.[6] Like him, many of them were connected to the old French gentry and enjoyed the favors that came with local privileges and titled backgrounds. This provincial grounding soon extended beyond France, however, as Jesuit service took an outward turn during the first decade of the Third Republic (1870–80). France was entering a period of colonial expansion, developing an empire in Africa and Indo-China. New opportunities for service to the Faith became readily available and eventually attracted 40,000 French to take up duties as missionaries in the far-flung empire. The Jesuits were not to be left behind. They actively trained to serve in these new destinations and soon could count 25 percent of the Order in service as missionaries. In the government's view of these developments, the strong missionary ties would help to bind the Jesuits' talents and energies to the French state, while at the same time adding to French prestige abroad by their important social, educational, research, and pastoral services.

Jacquinot entered the Society of Jesus on September 20, 1894, at the tender age of sixteen, at a time when France was nearing the end of a period of political turmoil, crisis, and scandal. The Third Republic (1870–1940) was still reeling from the trauma surrounding the events of the Paris Commune of 1871, recognized as probably the bloodiest civilian event in modern French history. In addition, the government became embroiled in the frequent and often heated religious and philosophical feuds between the clericals and anticlericals. These angry spasms created an era during which the atmosphere was one of extreme bitterness. Roots of the controversy lay in the new emphasis on "Positivism" as espoused by the leading French philosopher Auguste Comte. According to his teachings, materialism and science became the Church's rivals, with followers eager to replace any aspects of theology and metaphysics, often referred to as superstition, with a faith in science and its social expression, progress.[7]

In part, the Republican fears were that the Church, if not checked, might achieve a stranglehold on politics and especially French education. According to their thinking, in 1850, the Church had achieved a major victory when the French government adopted a Catholic-sponsored reform program known as the Falloux Law. This legislation granted the Church the power to operate secondary schools (*collèges*) in addition to those managed by the French state. Beyond that prospect, it allowed the Church enhanced authority in the running of primary schools. The obvious benefit to the Church was that it would have the opportunity to play a key role in shaping the knowledge, skills, and especially the thinking of the next generation of young French. This possibility was not lost on the Church's opposition. The anti-clerical factions and Republicans became imbued with an intense suspicion of the Church and its orders, especially the teaching orders, of which the Jesuits were the major one.

The outcome of this reaction against Church influence in education was a series of laws enacted starting in 1879, known as the Ferry Laws after their cabinet sponsor, Jules Ferry. The laws had their greatest impact on primary and secondary schools. According to these laws, members of the Catholic teaching orders were to be denied the right to teach in public schools after a five-year transitional period. Catholic teaching orders faced an economic penalty as well. Primary education became compulsory, and because state schools were free, Catholic schools lost those who preferred to avoid paying Church fees.

In the public schools, emphasis was to be placed on providing a broad civic education, aimed at instilling patriotism and loyalty to the French Republic. The bitter debate over these educational reforms only deepened the existing divide and encouraged the arguments of extremists on both sides. It also inspired some who wanted to follow a teaching vocation to consider becoming missionaries and teaching abroad at one of the new mission stations.

This overheated atmosphere became further inflamed by the notorious Dreyfus Affair, beginning in 1894. Briefly summarized, Alfred Dreyfus was a captain in the French General Staff who was arrested and charged with treason. As a Jew and a Republican, Dreyfus was an outsider among the aristocratic and Catholic officers of the General Staff. This helped make him vulnerable to the charges and an easy mark for fabricated evidence against him. As the case wore on, with increasing public awareness of serious irregularities, the personal fate of Dreyfus became something of a side issue. After trial by a military tribunal, he was convicted and sentenced to life on Devil's Island, in French Guiana. What mattered in the case was that the reproofs of a Jewish Republican led to broader condemnations against French Protestants and other Republicans by the military and the Church. In short, the Dreyfus Affair grew into a heated battle between the Catholic Church and the French state. It split the French educated elite into two sides, with the most vocal side exclaiming that the Dreyfus Affair and its fallout was at heart a clerical-monarchist plot to unseat the Republican government.

The Third Republic entered a radical period following the Dreyfus Affair, with government leaders determined to restrict and punish those regarded as a threat to the French state and its ideals. The targeted groups included the Jesuits, who, they believed, were deeply involved in the Dreyfus Affair, and who were usually included as fair game in just about any anti-clerical campaign. To exact their revenge, the Republican deputies passed legislation exiling all religious orders involved in the Dreyfus Affair. The Jesuits and others, having been expelled from France, accepted their fate and set out for new missions in Spain, Indochina, China, the United States, and elsewhere. France's diplomatic relations with the Vatican were broken off in 1904.

Still another major onslaught against the Church and clergy occurred the next year, in 1905, when the French parliament denounced Napoleon's Concordat of 1802, which had been negotiated with representatives of Pope Pius VII. According to that agreement, the state, recognizing that Catholicism was the religion of the "great majority of the people" in France, had allowed for a semi-privileged status for the Church. It legalized the rights of clergy and agreed to pay the salaries of priests and bishops in return for their taking an oath of loyalty to the French government. This peaceful framework for coop-eration and compromise came to an abrupt end in December 1905, however, when the Republican government passed legislation that severed all ties be-tween the Church and state.[8] Members of the clergy were taken off the state payroll, and the state assumed the titles to all Church property. By losing its identification with the state, the Church, of course, suffered diminished pres-tige in the aftermath of this action. Records showing fewer baptisms and more civil marriages document the impact of this legislation marking the official separation of Church and state.

FORMATION OF A JESUIT

The bad blood between the Church and the Republican government had direct repercussions for the young Jacquinot and his chosen vocation. Having been expelled from France, the Jesuits had to find new means of support and other training facilities for the all-important formation for the priesthood. Since its foundation in 1540, the Jesuit Order had required a lengthy and rigorous training program, always based on diverse intellectual, spiritual, and service experiences. What follows is a description of Jacquinot's varied and most important experiences in preparing for the taking of final vows years after ordination. As indicated in the above discussion, Jacquinot's required training program to become a Jesuit could not be undertaken in France. Pro-viding this rather detailed information on Jesuit training is meant to show how well prepared priests like Father Jacquinot were to take up their service in China. Their language skills, knowledge of history, philosophy, and even science, would add to their teaching, pastoral work, and general effectiveness in relating to the communities they served. This is in addition to the discipline and depth of commitment that a priest had to live in order to serve in this Order. It was important preparation for the challenges ahead at this time in history and especially at this time in China.

For most Jesuits, their period of priestly formation usually took about fif-teen years. In Jacquinot's case, his preparation extended to nineteen years, lengthened or at least complicated by the particular circumstance of the Jesuit Order at the turn of the century in France. The Jesuit administrative system was divided into provinces, each under a provincial superior, with a superior general domiciled in Rome holding the pivotal position at the top of the hier-archy. France existed as one of the provinces within this system, but because of the expulsion of the Order, the French province came to occupy the peculiar status of a province-in-exile. These unusual circumstances had the most serious impact on the Jesuit formation programs.

First, it should be noted that not all members of the order were forced to leave France. Those who had been ordained and with final vows for many years and, over those years, had received all the necessary training, could remain in place. The troublesome stipulation was that no additional training of prospective Jesuit priests could take place in France.[9] By necessity, then, Jacquinot's training took place abroad, as it happened, in England and in Belgium. His Jesuit formation required him to undergo what are called the three probations: the first to be fulfilled during the initial weeks after joining the order. Following Loyola's *Spiritual Exercises*, the core of Jesuit training emphasized a systematic form of meditation and contemplation meant to lead one to examine one's conscience and promote better understanding of the cardinal concepts of sin, the life and passion of Christ, and his resurrection and ascension. Of all stages of formation, this is the most "monastic" and regulated. This state lasts two years, culminating in the first vows.

The second probation, usually considered the main part of Jesuit formation, consisted of a rigorous fourteen-year course of study and apostolic work. In this part of the formation program, as a novice, Jacquinot would engage in prayer, reflecting on the Ignatian Exercises, and spend two years learning in depth about all aspects of the Jesuit Order and its lengthy history. Jacquinot received this early training at St. Mary's College in Canterbury, England. Next, two more years, known as the juniorate, were devoted to learning Greek, Latin, the classics, and the humanities. The rigorous language training was necessary for entering the next phase of training, which involved three years of devoted study of Western philosophy. In Jacquinot's case, he undertook this intensive course of study (1898–1901) at the Maison St. Louis, in St. Helier, on the Isle of Jersey in the English Channel.[10]

At this point, Jacquinot had received sufficient training to begin a pastoral phase of the commitments, usually teaching (high school, college, or university) involved in his formation program. This period, known as regency, lasted three more years and involved his service under the supervision of Rev. Father Louis Trégard in Paris from 1901 to 1903. The next period, 1903–4, placed him in Marneffe, Belgium, where he taught the English language to students at St. Joseph's College.[11] For the following year, 1904–5, he was sent to Salisbury, England, as an intern teaching French to English students.[12]

Although Jacquinot had to endure the occasional inconveniences of being forced to take his training outside of France and in English-speaking settings, his experiences actually had fortuitous consequences, for it provided him with a firm grasp of English, a skill that was to stand him in good stead throughout his career, especially when he entered service in English-speaking Shanghai. (Shanghai, of course, was a Chinese city, but as a treaty port, it was dominated by English and French speakers in the foreign International Settlement and French Concession.)

Another foreign assignment before undertaking the final stage of his formal training involved Jacquinot's teaching French at St. Francis Xavier College in Liverpool, England. Then, finally, with all of this service to his credit, he began the last stage in his lengthy pedagogical training. This was the especially intensive, four years (1906–10) of study of theology, during which Jacquinot would continue to live the rigorous and disciplined life of a Jesuit scholastic. He completed his theological studies at the Jesuit theologate at Ore Place, Hastings, in East Sussex, England.[13]

Also during this study period, Jacquinot received more immediate pastoral experience when he was directed to serve as an aide to the clergy in the parish of Rye in Sussex.[14] The tradition was that at the end of the third year of this part of the formation, the prospective Jesuit priest was ready to be ordained. On what must have been a very special occasion, Father Jacquinot was ordained deacon/priest at Hastings, England, in 1909. During the next year, 1910–11, he served at Sainte Croix in Le Mans.

There remained in his broad formation program the third and final probation, the portion of formation known as tertianship, during which the priest could reflect on his journey and renew his commitment to his calling. Lasting one year (1911–12) in Canterbury, England, Father Jacquinot's tertianship began with a 30-day retreat known as the Long Retreat. This retreat period was taken up with more reflection upon and contemplation of the *Spiritual Exercises*. Also included was an intensive review of the Jesuit Constitutions of the Society of Jesus, written by Ignatius himself, readings and discussions with others of the aims of the Jesuit Order, and then serving in pastoral work, such as serving as a parish priest to a congregation of parishioners. During the month-long silent retreat, the Tertian reflects on his many years of experience as a Jesuit since the period of his novitiate when he took his first lengthy retreat.

Father Jacquinot, after his tertianship, was able to return to France and take up pastoral ministry in two different parish locations: Le Mans and Paris, so that from 1911 to 1913, he was finally engaged in active pastoral work in his native France. With all of this spiritual, religious, intellectual, and service exposure and formation brought to a close, the way became clear for taking the ultimate or final vows. These vows had two primary goals: the individual's commitment and service to the Jesuit Order, and, most important, the Jesuit order's incorporating the individual into itself on a permanent basis. Father Jacquinot took his last vows in Paris on February 3, 1913.

In addition to his studies and service commitments, Jacquinot spent several of his summer vacation periods working with underprivileged youth in the poorest sections of Poitiers, a city located southeast of Nantes. He was tall and in robust health. Fernande Monnot, who was baptized and married by Jacquinot during her years living in the Shanghai's French Concession, recalled that his square-cut, reddish beard gave him an imposing presence, often remarked upon by his colleagues.[15] In his later years, his hair and beard turned white, adding to his aristocratic personal bearing. When carrying out his duties, his usual attire was a long black cassock, which made him seem even taller than he was, and an ever-present blue French beret. The overall effect was of one not easily missed or forgotten.

Jacquinot excelled in several sports, often serving as a referee at the frequent soccer games. When he was only watching a game, his booming voice could be heard cheering on his team. What seemed to please his young charges most was his willingness to join the celebrating players in the festivities that usually followed the games. He was also admired as an excellent swimmer, participating in swim meets and other nautical sports and was able to put those skills to work on one important occasion. Nearing the end of the summer camp, he organized a river excursion to reward his assembled group of campers for a successful camp experience. The event almost ended in tragedy. The river current that day was very swift and turbulent, making keeping one's balance on the pitching river craft difficult. On the downside of a roll, some of the campers lost their footing and tumbled into the water. Alerted to the emergency, Jacquinot, fully dressed, threw himself into the river and with great effort succeeded in rescuing the panicked campers. His bravery on this occasion and successful rescue mission became a common subject of conversation at various public occasions in the Poitiers region.[16]

In that same year that he took his final vows, Father Jacquinot learned that his first missionary assignment was to be in Shanghai, China. It is not likely that his top priority was to serve in China. Shortly before he returned to France, during his retreat period, he wrote a personal letter to his provincial superior, which indicates that he expected to meet with the latter to discuss his future assignments after he arrived home. Anticipating the topic of their discussion, Jacquinot raised the subject of his service in China and his future service there. He stated directly that he had no inclination to go to China. Of course, he prefaced this with the statement that he offered himself to the

Maintaining his French identity.
China Weekly Review (Apr. 1938).

order to fulfill whatever mission it had planned for him. He explained that he wanted to work in France and might be of useful service to those who did have a religious calling to serve in China.[17] Aware of the difficulties for the faith in France, he believed he might be useful in helping to strengthen and rebuild the foundations of Catholicism in his home country. Another consideration he noted, likely the key one, was his elderly and ailing mother and the sacrifices she would have to endure if he undertook a lengthy commitment in far-off China.[18] In the end, his clearly stated considerations and reservations were overridden by the order's decision that his full service as a Jesuit priest would begin in Shanghai.

Father Jacquinot seems to have preferred speaking directly to the point, even with his superiors. It was a characteristic often noted by those commenting on his personal style. Described as intelligent, with an ebullient personality, he would receive much praise for being both decisive and personable. Both gentle and zestful, he won a lot of respect for being able to make his point and still garner others' support. Some described him as not being easy in character, but also observed that his heavy involvement in charitable work seemed to

temper his nature over time. Still, his independent nature and superior training sometimes got in the way of his being entirely agreeable to the ways of his
superiors.

Within the territorial jurisdiction of the Jesuit Order abroad, Shanghai was
included in the domain of the province of Paris. Accordingly, Jacquinot was
under the French provincial of the Province of Paris, with its headquarters in
that city at 42 rue de Grenelle.[19] Once in Shanghai, he would live in the Jesuit
community, and his service would be observed and guided by the rector of the
famous Jesuit Université l'Aurore (Aurora University). Completing the peck-
ing order, the vicar apostolic of Shanghai was over all the Catholic religious
communities there, including the Jesuits. Monsignor Augustin Haouisée was
the vicar apostolic of Shanghai from 1915 until 1943. He took his direction
from the apostolic delegate in Nanjing, who outranked the vicar apostolic of
Shanghai. The guidance from Rome was clear and emphasized that Catholic
missionaries serving in China should stand aloof from political matters and
occupy themselves only with matters of religion and the well-being of those
under their care.[20] Father Jacquinot, about to enter this new Shanghai community, was joined by Father de Boynes, S.J., who had taken his final vows
at the same time as Jacquinot. These two young priests made their preparations for departure for service in Shanghai. It would be a long journey by
ship, probably taking anywhere from 23 to 72 days, depending on the ship, its
route, and the weather.

Not long before his departure, what Jacquinot feared most occurred. He
suffered the death of his mother, Madame Jacquinot de Besange (née Got).
Like other aristocratic women of the period, Madame Jacquinot had engaged
in active relief work within her community in Brest. She devoted most of her
energy to the care of poor French children, becoming well known in the Brest
and Metz regions for her energy and service. Her lifework was always a rich
source of inspiration for her son and helped shape his future life and work
choices.[21] His mother's death in 1913 closed an important chapter in his life,
but opened another that would challenge his talents and personal resources.
During his years in China, from 1913 to 1940, he would provide remarkable
and varied services to the Chinese population at all social and age levels.

The two priests were leaving France on the eve of World War I, the war to
end all war, which in just three weeks' time from its starting date on August
4, 1914, would claim the lives of 260,000 French soldiers. At its bitter end,
France was left demoralized and its resources were severely depleted.

When Jacquinot and de Boynes reached Shanghai, they found another
country struggling to deal with and survive a chaotic political and military

situation. Defeated by Japan in the Sino-Japanese War of 1894–95, China had attempted to reform an archaic and tottering political and social order, but without success, further increasing its vulnerability to outside aggression. Powerful Chinese anti-foreign, especially anti-missionary, sentiments found violent expression in events such as the Boxer Rebellion, but failed to save the failing dynasty. A new republic, led in its formation by Sun Yat-sen (1866–1925), laid the framework for the new China established in 1912. This political revolution was a promising beginning, but failed to stave off further social disruption, warfare, and turmoil, all of which Jacquinot witnessed with pain and misgivings. Under these circumstances, the French Jesuits' talents and services were sorely needed.

JACQUINOT AND TEILHARD DE CHARDIN

Another French Jesuit serving in China for many of the same years as Jacquinot was the famous paleontologist and theologian Pierre Teilhard de Chardin (1881–1955). The differences and similarities between the lives of these two Jesuits are interesting. Although they followed very separate paths, each made significant contributions along the way. Teilhard lived and worked in China, mainly in Tianjin and Beijing, on and off for twenty years.[22] He made at least five geological research expeditions, which included work in Mongolia, Manchuria, and areas of eastern China. He wrote his most famous book, *The Phenomenon of Man*, in Beijing in 1940. In addition to his work as a respected scientist, Teilhard's writings on evolution, bringing into prominence a faith-science dialogue, got him in trouble mainly with the Vatican Curia.[23] Against the fundamental differences in their career choices, there is one clear similarity between their performance of their duties. Both were pioneers in their fields, and both stretched the accepted boundaries of their callings, sometimes exceeding the norms and often bringing uneasiness to their Jesuit superiors.

It is uncertain whether Jacquinot and Teilhard ever met in China. It is likely that they were acquainted, in that both studied theology at Hastings, England, during an overlapping time period. In any case, Jacquinot spent his time mainly in Shanghai, except when he visited the southern provinces during his flood and refugee relief work. Teilhard, on the other hand, worked in north China, visiting Shanghai during World War II in November and December of 1942, after Jacquinot had returned to France. On one visit, while lodging at Shanghai's Aurora University, Teilhard received a full account of Jacquinot's humanitarian refugee work, especially involving the key 1937 period, from the university's rector, Georges Germain.[24] Father Germain gave Teilhard a detailed report on the remarkable success of the Jacquinot Zone. The contrast between the two lives of these French Jesuits becomes easily apparent. While Teilhard would make his mark through his work in philosophy and theology, as well as his scientific contributions as an accomplished paleontologist, Jacquinot's work took a different direction and meaning. He would contribute to bringing relief to the Chinese suffering from poverty, floods, and war. His talents as a negotiator would bring warring parties together to find a common ground for compromise and a workable solution to very difficult situations. His organizational skills in relief work earned respect and support even from critics of his many humanitarian endeavors. In short, he was less a philosopher or man of ideas than a man of skilled action dedicated to improving the lives of those around him, in his case, the Chinese.

CHAPTER TWO

Arrival in China

Man was created to praise, reverence, and serve God,
and by this means, attain salvation; the other things
on the face of the earth were created for man's sake, to
aid him in the prosecution of the end for which he was
created. It follows that man must make use of them in
so far as they help him to attain his end or rid himself
of them insofar as they hinder him from attaining it.
    —Saint Ignatius Loyola

Shortly after Father Jacquinot arrived in Shanghai, he was assigned to language school in Zikawei (Siccawei), the Jesuit complex in the southwest portion of the city. This established and respected Jesuit compound included a meteorological observatory, founded in 1871, that provided essential information for shipping along the east coast,[1] a twin-spired cathedral, training workshops, an orphanage, a library, a printing press, and schools for young Chinese. It was a requirement that all young Jesuits arriving at their new posts become proficient in the local languages. At least one year of intensive study of the written language and both Mandarin Chinese and the Shanghai dialects were necessary for Jacquinot's work. His knowledge of Latin and Greek would not help with these new language requirements, but the discipline and language sense needed to master those difficult classical languages must have been of some practical use to him in the process.

The first and tradition-setting early Jesuit in China was Matteo Ricci (1552–1615), whose work paved the way and set the precedents for all of the Jesuit missionary activities that followed. Ricci joined the Society of Jesus in 1571. In Rome, he studied under celebrated scholars such as the Jesuit mathematician Christopher Clavius, friend of Kepler and Galileo, and the Jesuit theologian Roberto Bellarmino.[2] His humanistic and scholarly background played a key role in his acceptance among the scholar official class in China. Had he gone to China without this training, it is questionable whether he would have been successful in establishing the flourishing Jesuit mission in China.

Ricci's first goal was to study the Chinese language intensively. He considered this essential to effective missionary work, thus setting the precedent for later Jesuits, including Jacquinot. His aim was to reach a good understanding of the Chinese classics, the mainsprings of Chinese society. In dealing directly with the classics, Ricci was able to bypass the interpretations of the predominant Neo-Confucianists, claiming that the ancients were more purely inspired. The classical texts had not yet been corrupted by the pernicious influences of Buddhism. At the same time, this approach afforded a new basis and means to root his ideas in the revered wisdom of the ancient sages. Ricci dazzled the Chinese literati with his knowledge of the Chinese language. He mastered the Confucian classics and made the Four Books the basis of his ministry. Bending the Confucian classical texts to serve his own purposes aided psychologically in introducing Christian teachings to elite scholarly circles in China. It also explains his readiness to reinterpret in order to advance the cause of Christianity. Ricci rationalized that after Christianity was sufficiently understood and established in China, the undesirable principles previously tolerated, such as the Chinese exclusive emphasis on man and his human relationships, might be enriched with Christian ideas and teachings and eventually perfected.[3] Ricci was convinced that any approach other than this initial toleration and accommodation would render the Christian message unacceptable to the Chinese mind.

Matteo Ricci can be rightly called the Father of the Catholic mission in China, even though Francis Xavier and Alexandre Valignani were concerned there before him. He initiated policies and established precedents that were carried on after his death in 1615. In following his example, Jesuits in China during the seventeenth and eighteenth centuries turned themselves into mathematicians, geographers, astronomers, engineers, doctors, painters, and musicians, all professions of potential value to the Chinese.[4] The Académie des sciences extolled the advantage of France of having scientific data furnished by the Jesuits concerning travel routes to China and the geographies of the countries visited. And the French king, Louis XIV, was eager to share in the commercial advantages that the Portuguese had already long enjoyed in the lucrative Far Eastern trade. As a leading French scholar, Virgile Pinot, points out: "During this period, if trade already followed the flag, it followed the mission even more so."[5] The Jesuits' combination of religious commitment and training in Western mathematics and science is well expressed in a letter from Father Jean de Fontaney, professor of mathematics at the college of Louis-le-

Matteo Ricci (1552–1615). Courtesy of the Shanghai
Municipal Library.

Grand, to Father La Chaise, Jesuit confessor to Louis XIV: "I consider myself
a thousand times happier in carrying our sciences to the ends of the earth,
where I hope to win some souls for God, and find some occasions to suffer for
His love and the glory of His saintly Name, than to continue teaching them
[the sciences] in Paris at our best colleges."[6]

The Kangxi Emperor, whose reign lasted from 1661 to 1722, greatly valued
the services of the French Jesuits in particular. Their personal instruction to
him and his male heirs in mathematics, geometry, philosophy, music, and art,
and their intensive study of the Chinese classics, history, geography, and chro-
nology made them exceptional foreigners at his court.[7] The emperor viewed

the European Renaissance sciences and arts, especially the former, as valuable for strengthening Manchu rule. The Jesuits translated scientific, even medical texts, into Manchu and Chinese and compiled dictionaries to support these efforts. In 1689, they contributed their talents as skilled linguist intermediaries in the negotiation of the Treaty of Nerchinsk between Russia and China.[8] Written in Latin, the finished treaty was very favorable to the Chinese, and the emperor publicly acknowledged the important role that two Jesuits had played in this agreement. Shortly after, Kangxi issued the Edict of 1692, which established the Catholic religion as a legal faith within the Chinese Empire, giving it a definite status alongside Taoism, Buddhism, and Confucianism.[9]

During the following year, 1693, Kangxi became seriously ill with malaria, and he was on the brink of death when French Jesuits presented the court with quinine, which had been discovered by Jesuits in Peru, to treat him. After testing its effects on others, the foreign medicine was deemed safe for treating the emperor, who showed signs of recovery. To reward the French Jesuits, Kangxi gave them buildings near his palace in the Imperial City as a residence and approved land and funding for their construction of a church. Under the direction of an Italian architect, Brother Gio Gherardini, a large cathedral of Western ecclesiastical design was constructed and completed with a marble plaque above its entrance inscribed: "The Temple of the Lord of Heaven, built by order of the Emperor."[10] Christianity had reached its peak of influence in China.

Through their cartography, the Jesuits shaped what was essentially the European image of the Chinese Empire. The Kangxi Emperor, in 1701, ordered six French Jesuits to assemble and begin planning a map of China. They parceled out the Chinese provinces and worked tirelessly on the projects until 1717, when all the charts and descriptions were brought together and maps were compiled in thirty-two folios. Then, in 1721 or 1722, an atlas covering China, Manchuria, Mongolia, and Tibet was published; this eighteenth-century cartographical masterpiece, which was revised and edited by the great French cartographer Jean-Baptiste Bourguignon d'Anville in 1735, served to inform Europe about China.[11]

At the turn of the eighteenth century, the Catholic Church in China appeared to be flourishing. And yet, a bitter controversy, known as the Chinese Rites controversy, had been raging within the Church and gradually caught the attention of leading circles in both Europe and China. Briefly stated, the disputed issues concerned the Chinese conception of God, *tian,* and *shangdi,* and of the immortality of the soul, and whether they were comparable to Christian conceptions. The Jesuits said they were equivalents of the Christian

concepts of Heaven and Jehovah. Those opposed saw the Chinese as material-
istic and atheistic, explaining that the Chinese concept of heaven emphasized
the dominant role of the *taiqi*, or primal cause, which is purely a material
concept, with no room for the spiritual. Moreover, the Chinese concept of
shangdi asserts mainly that it is posterior and inferior to *taiqi*.[12]

A second key issue was allowing Chinese converts to perform the rites to
Confucius and their ancestors. In reply to a memorial asking him to explain
the Chinese ceremonies in honor of Confucius and the ancestors, Kangxi said
that they were simply civil ceremonies, without religious significance. A century earlier, Matteo Ricci would have found this position very compatible, but
Franciscans, Dominicans, and papal legates sent to China saw in these rituals a
form of idolatry and pagan worship—in effect, calling into question the basic
religious and social practices of Chinese empire.

The debates raged on, with papal legates sent to China to learn firsthand
the arguments and differences among the orders. When asked for his position
in the Rites Controversy, Kangxi's response was: "Henceforth, whoever does
not follow the customs of Li Ma-tou [Li Madou, i.e., Matteo Ricci] shall posi-
tively not be permitted to live in China but must be expelled."[13]

Obviously, this did not bode well for the future of the Christian mission in
China. In March 1715, Pope Clement XI, hoping to terminate the ecclesiastical
struggles in both China and Europe, issued the formal and solemn apostolic
constitution *Ex illa die*, sanctioning what was appropriate terminology and
condemning the Chinese rites.[14] Emperor Kangxi was enraged by an assembly
of cardinals and theologians in Rome deciding whether Chinese rites could be
practiced in his empire. The dispute dragged on until, in 1720, another legate,
George Ambrose de Mezzabarba, patriarch of Alexandria, arrived in China
with papal orders to enforce the apostolic constitution and end the disputes.
Annoyed by what he saw as interference in his empire's affairs, Kangxi com-
pared these Catholic legates to Buddhist and Taoist priests, with their faulty
interpretations and despised writings.[15]

In 1721, reviewing the arguments presented by Mezzabarba, Kangxi ex-
claimed that he had never seen a document that contained so much non-
sense. He ruled that Westerners would henceforth not be allowed to preach
in China. The next year, 1722, Kangxi died, and his successor, Yong Zheng,
adopted a harsh position regarding the divided and quarrelsome Christians in
China. From the Catholic standpoint, the long legal controversy over Chinese
rites and ceremonies was finally brought to conclusion by the papal bull *Ex
quo singulari*, issued by Benedict XIV in 1742. It was the last apostolic bull
and restated the papal admonitions, clarifying the Holy See's firm position for

Christians in China. Subsequently, successive emperors initiated a long period of Christian persecutions in China. Jesuit fortunes diminished further in 1773, when the Society of Jesus was suppressed in Catholic Europe and its colonies, and nearly dissolved, followed by the cataclysms of the French Revolution and Napoleonic Wars.

THE EARLY YEARS

When Jacquinot arrived in China in 1913, the country was a place very different from when Ricci and the early French Jesuits had worked there. The Qing Dynasty, under inept and decaying rule, was threatened with dismemberment by the European powers, which were determined to force China open to their lucrative commercial ambitions. According to the terms of the 1842 Treaty of Nanking, at the conclusion of the Opium War, Shanghai became one of five treaty ports where foreigners were granted very favorable terms of extraterritorial rights. This meant that foreign treaty participants operated under Western legal systems in their dealings in China and were exempt from Chinese law. Equally important, this treaty gave legal sanction to Christian missions in the new ports. Further protection of foreign interests came from gunboats patrolling the Yangzi River and from superior foreign power as it came to be expressed in finance, commerce, invention, and military strength, all of which would further diminish Chinese sovereignty. In 1860, France, in a treaty settlement, demanded the return of properties acquired during past centuries by the Church, which were to be placed under French protection. Westerners demanded and won both the right to proselytize in China and protection in the form of toleration of Christian converts. Members of the restored Society of Jesus began to return to China.[16]

Shanghai was really three cities in one. Most of the business and foreign residential districts were located in the International Settlement and the adjoining French Concession. Both fronted on the Bund, or bank of the Huangpu River. Entirely surrounding these two municipalities was Greater Shanghai. To the north of the two foreign concessions, but still inside the boundaries of Greater Shanghai, was Zhabei. To the south was Nanshi (Nantao), the old Chinese city, and its surrounding area.

China's resistance to foreign economic, political, and cultural incursions sparked numerous attacks on missions and Chinese converts. With the proliferation of Christian missions, the aim was to limit foreign power in China to the extent possible and protect China's heritage from foreign contamination. The protests, sometimes spontaneous and other times deliberate, often had "official" support from the Empress Dowager, as was the case with the ill-fated Boxer Uprising of 1899–1900, which included the slaughter of forty-four Catholic missionaries and mass killings of Christians. Still, the China missions grew substantially during the early decades of the twentieth century. In 1901, there were 1,075 foreign Roman Catholic priests in China; in 1920, there were from 2,500 to 3,000 foreign priests and nuns. Estimates of the numbers of Catholic communicants are 721,000 in 1901 and reached two million by 1920.[17]

Following the precedents established by his French Jesuit predecessors, Father Jacquinot immediately enrolled in full-time Chinese language training at the Jesuit school in Zikawei in southwest Shanghai. There would be no need for extensive study or exegesis of classical Chinese texts, however. Shortly after his arrival, beginning in 1917, China became engrossed in a protest movement aimed at overturning any evidence of orthodoxy, Eastern or Western. The civil service examination system, rooted in the classical traditions, which had for centuries defined the path to power and influence in China, ended in 1905. Chinese intellectuals believed that China was on the brink of disaster and required a thorough transformation of the traditional culture to survive. These ensuing attacks on Confucianism broadened out to include the condemnation of all religions and particularly Christianity. The May Fourth Movement of 1919 helped evoke the upsurge in anti-Christian fervor of 1920–22 to go along with its primary objectives of national unity for China, national sovereignty, and equality with the West. Young intellectuals scorned the Christian religion as unscientific, outdated, and, in practice, detrimental to Chinese sovereignty and their attempts to build a strong nation. Many Chinese of this period described the Christian missionary movement in China as being merely the willing handmaiden of Western imperialism.[18]

Ricci's strategy of honoring Confucian traditions, and the commitment of the early French Jesuits to immersing themselves in the study of Chinese history and the classics in order to find a common ground for the possible integration of Christian and Confucian concepts, was no longer relevant. Father Jacquinot clearly faced a very different set of circumstances and conditions. There was no longer the option of winning over the emperor, because the imperial dynastic system had come to an end in 1911, and China was in the process of establishing a new republican system of government. The ensuing dismantlement of the ancient imperial system and tradition would leave a social and political vacuum, which competing forces and individuals would contend to fill. In 1924, the leading figure in the new China was Sun Yat-sen, who, to address his country's needs, proclaimed an eclectic and progressive revolutionary program of three stages: first, military dictatorship, then a period of political tutelage, and finally constitutional democracy. What actually occurred, however, was a lengthy period of military rivalry between the Guomindang under Generalissimo Chiang Kai-shek; a number of provincial warlords, each with a substantial army and some with foreign backing; and the Chinese Communist Party (CCP), founded in Shanghai in 1921.

Under these different circumstances, Father Jacquinot was faced with the question of what new approaches might be taken to promote his missionary work in ways that would influence and win over the Chinese to the Catholic faith. Which of his talents might he apply to building a strong community in China? How would he deal with the many nationalities that populated Shanghai, each with its own national interests?

The Hongkou Parish

After completing his language training, Father Jacquinot assumed the Chinese name Father Rao Jiaju 绕家驹 and became the parish priest for 7,000 Chinese Christians in Hongkou (Hongkew). This was an area situated in the northeastern portion of the International Settlement and heavily populated by Japanese. He served as vicar of the Church of the Sacred Heart of Hongkou for twenty years, from 1914 to 1934, ministering to Chinese and also to the large Portuguese population, which had been in Shanghai for generations. His signature appears on numerous Macanese baptismal certificates of the period.[19] In addition to his performing the expected priestly functions, Father Jacquinot offered English-language instruction to the local Portuguese, taught English, and offered spiritual guidance to the brothers at the Marist Brothers School in Hongkou. His popularity and competence were such that he became president of the Catholic Circle in Hongkou and was appointed president of the Shanghai General Hospital in 1917 and director of the Apostolate of Prayer in 1918. For his many services to the community, the Chinese government bestowed an award called the Golden Ear [of Corn] (l'Épi d'or) on him in 1924.[20]

Jacquinot's English-language skills and knowledge were again put to work during his appointment as professor of English language and literature at the highly respected Jesuit-run Université l'Aurore (Aurora University), located in the French Concession.[21] He served at the university from 1913 to 1921, sometimes reaching beyond his recognized competence in English to teach the sciences. One of his ventures in the chemistry laboratory resulted in a real disaster. He had intended to help provide a more festive atmosphere, which he felt would please his students, by showing them how to make fireworks in the

Shanghai's one-armed priest. Courtesy of Malcolm Roshost.

laboratory, to be used to enhance the much anticipated annual student procession for the celebration of the Sainte Vierge (i.e., Saint Mary) of the College of Zikawei. Unfortunately, the mixture he produced somehow overheated in the mortar, causing a powerful explosion, which tore off his right arm halfway up to the elbow. The extent of his injury required amputation of most of his arm that same evening. There was also great concern about the condition of his eyes, which had been burned by gases from the explosion. Fortunately, this injury proved to be only temporary, and his eyes were saved. Some of the students were also hurt, but because of their distance from the explosion, their injuries were only minor, and after a brief visit to the hospital, they were sent home. Of course, Father Jacquinot would have to learn to manage all of his daily right-handed activities, including eating and writing, with only his left arm intact.[22] From this time on, he was often referred to as the one-armed priest of Shanghai.

Father Jacquinot seems to have made a strong impression on those who met him in China, as he had in France. He is described as tall, fine-featured, and very manly in appearance, with a physique well developed by his involvement in various sports. His students recalled his positive outlook and easy smile. His peers noted his complete self-assurance, hearty laugh, and charismatic presence, all of which complemented his aristocratic bearing. He was often seen on buses or going about his duties wearing a long black cassock, decorated with a Red Cross pin, and a French beret. In his free time, his favored diversion was writing poetry, usually with themes closely related to his circumstances and experiences. The following is a poem he might have written to celebrate the lives of his Chinese students, many of whom were struggling with poverty, disease, and the chaos of a Peking government in disarray:

> *To Many Years!*
> At the edge of a clearing
> An oak tree drops an acorn
> In the thick grass and the heather.
> It sprouted, grew, and became tall.
> Often the harsh winter winds
> Chased the white snows through its branches
> And covered it with frost.
> But so many young, alive with hope,
> Have grown up under its shade.
> Dear God, after the dark storm
> Give it a long and gentle evening![23]

SAVING THE CHILDREN

The 1920s in Shanghai were replete with local turmoil involving large-scale protests against the foreign presence in China, both the official presence, especially in the foreign concessions, and the missionary movement. The Catholic orders were among Shanghai's largest landowners, with office buildings, apartment houses, and elaborate homes. Their members were not averse to being represented at the tables of local stockholders' meetings. Their power, wealth, and close association with the Western powers made them targets of protest movements. In addition, the reported successes of the Bolshevik Revolution gave added momentum to student expression of universal resistance against foreign oppression through foreign imperialism. The foreign concessions in Shanghai, with their protections through extraterritoriality, became prime targets even though their existence often benefited Chinese seeking sanctuary in their midst. The abuse of rapacious warlord militarism and its frequent connection to the imperialist powers was still another cause for demonstrations. The demonstrators viewed the foreign missionary presence as merely a cultural version of imperialism bent on subverting China's indigenous mores and society.

The momentous May 30 incident of 1925 greatly inflamed these passions and expanded their expression to many parts of the country.[24] Overall, the incident centered on the intolerable working conditions and harsh treatment of Chinese employed in foreign-owned factories. A series of strikes broke out in a Japanese-owned textile mill, and in responding, Japanese supervisors fired on the demonstrators, wounding several Chinese workers and killing one.

A furious outburst of local resistance erupted on May 30, mainly by student demonstrators, and led to the British-run Shanghai Municipal Police opening fire, killing eleven and wounding many more. The immediate effect was to focus Chinese attention on the injustices done China by the treaty system and extraterritoriality and on the obvious foreign feeling that Chinese lives and sovereignty were expendable. It altered relations between Chinese and foreigners, with many Chinese converts becoming increasingly critical of the West.[25] Anti-Christian and anti-Western sentiments remained as important undercurrents in the Chinese community at least until Chiang Kai-shek made public his support of Christianity in 1930. In the meantime, Chinese Communist and other leftist organizers found ample opportunities to influence the emerging revolutionary sentiment, which spread beyond Shanghai.

In the wake of the burgeoning revolutionary movement in Shanghai, Father Jacquinot found himself caught up in some of its most violent aspects. Rather than involving patriotic students, the new violence included well-armed military forces, some with Soviet Comintern support. In the face of so much violence and division, Chiang Kai-shek launched the famous Northern Expedition with the lofty purpose of unifying China.[26] It began in Canton and came to involve communist, militarist, and nationalist armies. These disparate elements, in the course of the fighting, became embroiled in a mutual struggle to become the paramount force in establishing a new Chinese government.

When the Expedition reached Shanghai, its presence set off a furious struggle between leftists and communists, many of them members of the Shanghai

General Labor Union, and the moderate and rightist elements in the city. The Shanghai Municipal Council on March 21 issued a proclamation declaring a state of emergency and putting the city under marshal law. Foreign troops disembarked from ships in the harbor and took up positions guarding points of entry to the concessions. The British Concessions at Hankou [Hankow] and Jiujiang [Kiukiang] had been overrun in January 1927, suggesting that local authorities could not or would not protect the foreign enclaves. On March 24, at Nanjing (Nanking), two French Jesuits were murdered and British, American, Italians, and Japanese residents were assaulted. Shanghai was divided into defense zones to accommodate the arrival of American, British, French, and Japanese troops called in to restore safety and order. The Shanghai Volunteer Corps and foreign police received the assignment to protect the prosperous Central District.[27]

Chiang, who had enjoyed remarkable success in leading the campaign northward, used his influence and took the opportunity to strike out against the leftists and communists, his erstwhile expeditionary supporters. On April 12, 1927, he launched a sweeping purge, which devastated their unions, and organizations, sent their leaders underground, and claimed the lives of several thousand leftists in Shanghai. A virtual massacre took place in Zhabei (Chapei), involving the buildings of the Huzhou Guild and Commercial Press, believed to be a headquarters of communists and leftist labor leaders.[28]

The fighting in Shanghai centered on the Chinese-administered parts of the city, especially in industrial Zhabei, where radical union strength was at its greatest. Father Jacquinot had gotten word that the Holy Family Convent on the North Honan Road extension was under siege, with many of the surrounding buildings on fire. The structure was completely surrounded and isolated in the firefight. Alarming accounts reached him that some of the opposing forces were receiving the aid of White Russian soldiers in the employ of the warlord Zhang Zongchang, manning a colorfully camouflaged armored train called the "Great Wall," which bombarded this dense urban area with its massive firepower.[29] Hastily, he set about trying to persuade the warring parties to allow him safe passage to the convent.

On March 23, 1927, the British consul general, Sir Sidney Barton, the British military commander-in-chief, Colonel Lord Gort, the chief of intelligence of the British Special Defense Force, and Father Jacquinot set out to evacuate the nuns and their charges. Jacquinot's presence was essential, not only because he knew the whereabouts of the convent, but because he also had the language skills to deal with any encounters en route. Gort was in full uniform, but unarmed, when the party arrived at the border between the International Settlement and Chinese Zhabei, where they were met by two Cantonese officers, who asked the purpose of their journey inside the Chinese area. Jacquinot explained the plight of the Catholic group at the convent and the party's wish to come to their aid and escort them back into the settlement. The two officers gave them safe conduct, and they proceeded through the debris and smoldering ruins toward the convent.[30]

The group's second encounter was less fortunate. About halfway between the Settlement border and the convent, they met with a detachment of Cantonese troops, who were less willing to accept their avowal that they were on a goodwill mission. One of the Cantonese, who happened to speak some English, began to interrogate Barton and Gort and ordered the two men searched. He also considered that the two would make valuable hostages for some possible future purpose of the Cantonese. After considerable time and discussion, however, Barton finally succeeded in convincing this leader of his identity. Barton's status apparently did give pause to the Cantonese, probably more than his lecture on the protections afforded by the hated extraterritoriality provisions. The official party was turned back and ordered to return safely to the International Settlement. Jacquinot alone had permission to proceed to the convent.

The Holy Family Convent was located near the North Railway Station, a prime military target, placing it in the middle of a pitched street battle that was taking place. The surrounding houses, which had formed a kind of barrier for the convent compound, had burned to the ground, making the convent an easy target. When Jacquinot arrived in the neighborhood, all around were cannon barrages, bullets flying everywhere, a dangerous broken gas main, and multiple fires burning in the neighborhood. During a brief jostling with one of the fighters attempting to turn him back, he suffered slight bayonet wounds to his hip and hand. Still in the zone of fire as he hurried on, he also received a slight injury to his forehead from an exploding shell just before entering the convent.[31]

The convent housed 400 nuns and various charges. In addition, refugees from the surrounding districts had taken refuge from the street warfare in the courtyard of the convent compound. Among those inside were 150 Chinese children, some huddled with their parents behind the convent walls. Many of the Chinese children in the convent had been orphaned in the fighting. In addition, the mother superior introduced some 53 foreign children from the local school for poor children located in Zhabei. All of the children were in a state of terror and thus very difficult to console. Some welcome help came from the 78 boarders who lived on the premises or who had sought refuge in the convent. Their attempts to entertain the children with stories and mime had good results for a while. Still, the numbers continued to grow and soon included some 600 Chinese and 500 Eurasians who had found themselves caught in the midst of the street fighting. Even more difficult to look after were the 37 babies, who needed fresh milk daily. The mother superior marveled at the courage of a Chinese milkman who braved the dangers in the vicinity to make sure deliveries of milk to the convent were regular and uninterrupted. The beleaguered community was also plagued by the lack of fresh water and, for a time, the convent had to operate without any lights. The power had been shut off, and even the use of candles was forbidden, because of the broken gas main. One of the residents did manage to patch up the gas main, however, so that at least candlelight became available.

Early in the morning of March 22, 1927, during a lull in the fighting, Father Jacquinot managed to lead a procession made up of most of the nuns, the children, and the babies out of the Zhabei fighting zone, across the Garden Bridge, into the International Settlement, where he arranged for their transportation to St. Joseph's Orphanage Institution in Nanshi, next to the house of the Little Sisters of Poverty. Children with no homes to go to were lodged at this institution, where they would remain until they could be returned to Zhabei. The tattered frightened refugees filing out in a semblance of order from battle-torn Zhabei must have been quite a dramatic scene.

Jacquinot was not without prior credentials as a rescue worker. He had served the Shanghai Volunteer Corps as its senior chaplain for several years and attended many of its rescue exercises. Moreover, as part of the accolades he received for accomplishing this successful and dangerous rescue of the convent group, he was promoted to the rank of major in the Corps. During the following year, in a public ceremony, Admiral Marcel Basire, commander-in-chief of the French naval forces in the Far East, recognized Jacquinot's leadership and bravery in the convent rescue by awarding him the French Croix de guerre.[32] The Chinese government awarded him "la Plaque d'Or de la Chine" for his heroism.

Because of his well-publicized success in planning and carrying out the rescue of the nuns and children in 1927, Father Jacquinot began to acquire a reputation as a superb organizer and a man of action. Even the military officers of the various powers in Shanghai expressed their admiration for his pluck and courage. He was becoming known to official circles, both Chinese and foreign, as someone who could handle difficult situations. Although well educated,

Father Jacquinot (far right) in uniform as senior chaplain of the Shanghai Volunteer Corps. Courtesy of Greg Leck.

able to speak multiple languages, and an appointment as university professor, Jacquinot's primary commitment remained working in the community in ways that served his parishioners and engaged his talents in alleviating crises. With China, and Shanghai, in almost a constant state of chaos for much of the late 1920s and 1930s, there were plenty of occasions for him to do so.

THE GREAT FLOOD OF 1931

There is nothing unusual in China's history about the Yangzi or Yellow Rivers flooding and wreaking havoc in the countryside, but 1931 and 1932 were especially bad flood years. The flooded area came to include the Yangzi River, Yellow River, Huai River, and the Grand Canal. A report issued by Chiang Kai-shek's new government claimed that 25 million Chinese in an area of 70,000 square miles suffered from this disaster. The report called it "the

Protecting coffins from the flood in 1931. Courtesy of the Shanghai Municipal Library.

greatest flood in Chinese history." Some 140,000 Chinese drowned, and crop losses were listed at 900,000 *mou*.[33]

Babies were left on rooftops and in treetops, apparently in the hope that they might be found and survive. Some 1,000 persons found refuge living on the top of the Nanjing city walls; others made their homes in godowns along the banks of the swollen rivers. In northern Jiangsu Province, 250 miles of dykes on the Grand Canal collapsed. A similar situation existed on the Yangzi River, where a small portion of dykes that still held became home to 80,000 men, women, and children. Because of their inaccessibility in the treacherous floodwaters, many eventually starved to death. As water levels rose, farmers furiously beat large gongs day and night when any began to trickle over the dykes, rousing helpers to come and repair the break.[34] Many had little faith in these efforts, but the only alternative was to flee, and more than 30,000 refugees poured into Shanghai. In south Shanghai, those without family contacts in the city found support from organizations such as the Nanshi Guild and Nanshi charitable organizations.[35] Besides more flooding, the Chinese who survived feared that famine and disease would follow the floods, as had often happened in the past.

Father Jacquinot became involved when he learned that 40 percent of the people in the flooded area had become refugees. On August 14, 1931, he helped establish a National Flood Relief Commission, chaired by T. V. Soong (Song Ziwen), to provide food, shelter, clothing, and protection from disease to the refugees.[36] The commission raised $10 million in cash to provide these necessary services and to help rebuild the broken dykes. Jacquinot, already secretary of the Famine Relief Committee, took on the additional task of investigating the flood relief efforts. He worked closely with the prominent Shanghai leader Yu Xiaqing (Yu Ya-ching), who was in charge of transportation and logistics. In his new position, Jacquinot had charge of the distribution of relief funds and oversaw the machinery of the local relief organizations, accounting for the funds expended by the commission.

Ever resourceful when faced with a refugee challenge, Jacquinot also managed to persuade the authorities to provide additional funds for producing a film of the flood damage and relief work. He wanted the scenes of flood damage and its victims to be captured by film professionals, so he engaged the French film company Pathé to make the film. Left unsaid for the moment were his intentions to use such a film to attract additional funding from the wealthy Chinese and foreign communities in Shanghai and abroad. If there was any money left over from producing the film, he planned to make it available for purchasing and distributing rice and clothing and providing small subsidies to the destitute.[37]

Sir John Hope Simpson, director-general of the International Flood Relief Commission, in reporting on his own flood relief efforts, emphasized that 50 percent of the flood relief funds came from overseas Chinese and 30 percent of the remainder from Chinese in China.[38] Altogether, the commission reported contributions received during the year 1931 totaling $6,875,456. The commission's field operations department servicing the various provinces undertook the distribution of these funds, the amounts being calculated according to the seriousness of the local flood situation.[39] The most pressing and unexpected expense the commission encountered was that of supplying the refugees with wheat shipped from America. The United States had supplied 173,500 tons of wheat and 105,000 tons of flour for flood refugee relief. The wheat was supplied on credit, but the freight expenses had to be met by the commission.

This body's revenues were insufficient to cover the customs tax and distribution costs, so the wheat remained piled up on the Shanghai docks.

Shanghai was not within the flooded area, but refugees from Hubei, Jiangxi, Anhui, and northern Jiangsu provinces fled there in large numbers. The city's Nanshi and Zhabei districts became sites for eleven refugee camps. Visiting Chinese Boy Scouts reported on the deplorable conditions in these camps, where extreme cold and lack of adequate shelter took a daily toll.[40] The official call for donations of funds and clothing met with considerable initial success. A welcome response came from the author Pearl Buck, who wrote the short story "Barren Spring" especially to help raise funds for flood victims.[41] Multiple and successful fund-raising efforts brought gifts from many different donors in Shanghai. Nevertheless, the overriding concern of relief officials had always been that although funds existed in September and even October, there might not be enough to meet the need when the weather turned cold and people began to tire of making pledges.

With so many refugees forced into deplorable living conditions, a pressing concern was the perceived increased left-wing and communist activity in areas where relief work was still not fully or effectively operational. To help combat this trend, Jacquinot urged placing more refugees in relief work and rehabilitation projects so as to engage them in productive activity and make them less susceptible to communist influence. This situation was especially urgent in the areas around Wuhan, where 300,000 refugees were crowded into camps and suffered greatly from the cold. The construction of mat-shed housing on high ground further exposed these refugees to the elements, but it had hitherto been the only dry ground available. Officials also feared that leftists might use the camps to spread propaganda and agitate among the destitute refugee hoards and so began making plans to relocate the refugees. There were reports that in Jiangxi province, communist activists were actively engaged in reconstructing roads and dykes and helping with relief efforts there. In Hubei province, the Hankou Chamber of Commerce focused its attention on transferring refugees away from the city. According to their strategy, officials promised relief in the form of wheat rations to those who agreed to leave, with additional wheat to be available to them at their new destination. Unfortunately, the number of incoming new refugees more than made up for those willing to accept the offer.

Chapter Three

Shanghai in Torment

Without a declaration of war and without warning
or justification of any kind, civilians, including vast
numbers of women and children, are being ruthlessly
murdered with bombs from the sky.
—President Franklin D. Roosevelt, October 1937

The 1930s were a decade of disruption, violence, and warfare in Shanghai. This troubled period followed a brief respite of relative calm after the formation of the Nationalist government under Chiang Kai-shek's leadership in 1928. The first crisis followed on developments in North China. In September 1931, the Japanese army successfully attacked Chinese troops and subsequently occupied all of Manchuria, setting up a puppet regime, Manzhouguo (Manchukuo), in early 1932. These events confirmed the worst Chinese fears about Japanese imperialist ambitions in China, which included economic and military domination, and aroused a strong sense of patriotism among the Shanghai Chinese. In Shanghai, anti-Japanese sentiment mounted, partly aroused by Chinese newspapers that carried violently anti-Japanese articles and editorials. Students held angry anti-Japanese demonstrations, and other Chinese groups formed anti-Japanese organizations such as the broad-based Anti-Japanese National Salvation Society.[1] Boycotts, and sometimes outright confiscations of Japanese goods and services, were considered to be especially threatening to Japanese interests. Under these pressures, several Japanese businesses were compelled to close down, and Japanese trade and industry suffered severe damage. When the anti-Japanese response as expressed through the national salvation groups rose to a painful level, the Japanese became convinced that firm action, backed by military force, was necessary. Local Japanese had come to doubt that their diplomats took the threat of force and volatile Chinese nationalism seriously enough. They began to see the Japanese Navy as a more reliable and responsive ally.[2]

The Japanese attack Shanghai in 1932. *Oriental Affairs*
(Oct. 1937).

Taking advantage of a local incident in a factory where Japanese were injured and one killed, the local Japanese naval commander confronted Mayor
Wu Tiecheng, head of the city government of Greater Shanghai, with a set
of strict demands, with the implication that armed force would be used if
they were not met. The Japanese representative on the Shanghai Municipal
Council, K. Fukishima, agreed to give the British military authorities under
Brigadier Fleming twenty-four hours' notice prior to any action contemplated
by the Japanese Defense Forces. That information was given on the morning
of January 28, 1932. The Shanghai Municipal Council immediately declared
a state of emergency in the International Settlement.[3] This action apparently
had unforeseen consequences, because the Japanese were later able to claim
that they were responding in defense of the International Settlement.

   The Nationalist government in Nanjing, still faced with threats from the
communists and provincial militarists, chose at first to follow a conservative
course in response to the Japanese demands. The government tried to enlist the
help of the League of Nations believing that under the existing circumstances,
negotiations, international pressure, and possible sanctions were the only way
out of the situation. It pinned its hopes on the belief that the foreign powers
would come to China's aid and see the Japanese threat as a common enemy.
The League did issue a resolution urging the withdrawal of Japanese troops
from Manchuria, but beyond that, nothing of substance followed.[4] Once the
deadline included in the set of demands passed, Japanese naval forces attacked
the elite forces of the Chinese 19th Route Army in Zhabei, stationed near

Refugees seek protection from the fighting. Courtesy of
the Shanghai Municipal Library.

the North Railroad Station. Japanese naval commanders had little respect for
Chinese fighting prowess and believed that the Japanese Navy finally had an
opportunity to win accolades like those that had been going to the Japanese
Army in North China.[5] In a bluster of confidence, they estimated that the job
could be finished in a day or so. And in the process, they would have taught
the Chinese a lesson.

What the Japanese failed to measure was the degree of Chinese resolve. A
surge of national spirit fueled the public to an unprecedented degree in the
face of superior Japanese air and naval power. "If we don't fight here in Shanghai, the Japanese will be like fierce tigers and swallow up our country in a few
years," General Cai Tingkai (Ts'ai T'ing-k'ai), the commander of the Chinese
19th Army, explained to a correspondent who interviewed him.[6] The Chinese

forces put up an unexpectedly fierce resistance, smashing attack after attack over the next thirty days. Organizations such as the Shanghai Green Gang and the Refugee Aid Society helped by providing intelligence on Japanese activities. Thousands were killed and wounded, neighborhoods were leveled, and the famed Oriental Library of precious rare books and early manuscripts, housed in the building of the Commercial Press, China's largest publishing house, was completely destroyed.

The Japanese, initially outnumbered by three to one, relied upon firebombing, tanks, and artillery to make up the difference. Their land forces had the support of the Japanese Third Fleet, which lay in the Huangpu River, including the aircraft carrier *Notoro*, from which the bombing runs were made. The Zhabei area was bombed by aircraft and set afire, but still the Chinese forces held.

Finally, in February, in response to frequent and urgent requests, Tokyo reinforced its troops in Shanghai with 18,000 soldiers. Under heavy pressure from the aroused public and Shanghai leaders of the Guomindang, Chiang Kai-shek eventually responded by deploying the First Army Group, including two of his best National Guard divisions. Another Japanese ultimatum followed, supported by more Army reinforcements rushed to the battlefront. A major Japanese offensive ensued, which broke the Chinese line. Faced with well-armed Japanese forces, now in greater numbers, the Chinese military position became untenable, and Chiang Kai-shek ordered a retreat. By March 3, the fighting had mostly ceased.[7] As many as 10,000 to 20,000 civilians lost their lives during these few months of battle, unsupported by any declaration of war, known as "the Shanghai Incident."

Civilian casualties probably were higher than the military ones. Indiscriminate bombing by Japanese pilots rained down death and terror on urban residents. Many had never experienced a bombing raid before and had no idea of how to cope. Of course, there were no bomb shelters, since this phenomenon was a new kind of urban warfare. Civilians usually simply fled the immediate battlefield area with their families and most precious possessions and huddled in alleys or buildings that looked as though they might offer some protection, but that were often just minutes away from being consumed by fire or bombing.

For Father Jacquinot, the desperate situation in Zhabei must have brought back memories of the rescue of the nuns and children in 1927, but this time the threat was even greater and more terrifying, because the Chinese in Shanghai now faced a modern army. Jacquinot approached both the British consul general, J. F. Brenan, and the U.S. consul general, Edwin S. Cunningham, to ask that they work together with him to organize a rescue mission. Those to be rescued included Chinese and foreign noncombatants who had been trapped between the lines of fire, and also wounded Chinese and Japanese soldiers. In the meantime, the crisis was the topic of several meetings of the Shanghai Municipal Council (SMC). One proposal recommended establishing a neutral zone in the Chinese-administered northern areas of Zhabei and Hongkou, to be policed by forces other than Chinese or Japanese troops. The Japanese member of the council declined support for this idea, saying that he would only trust the defense of the numerous resident Japanese to Japanese forces. Chinese on the council countered that Japan was actively using that area as a base for subversive activities in the adjacent Chinese territories.[8] The British and American authorities, interested mainly in preserving order, raised this protest with the Japanese in the form of a "friendly remonstrance" and were told firmly that if it were lawful for the Americans to maintain U.S. Marines permanently in Shanghai in accordance with the Defense Plan of October 1931, they could scarcely protest when the Japanese landed bluejackets in self-defense.[9]

This argument seemed to receive some support from the Shanghai Municipal Council, whose secretary-general pointed out that the SMC was not responsible for the Japanese being assigned to the Defense Sector, which bordered the Chinese territory. Rather, it had made sense to give them that area, because it was where the Japanese resided in greatest numbers. It was also the Japanese responsibility to protect their own nationals.[10]

The foreign settlements in Shanghai did not base their legitimacy or decisions to use force on any specific treaty provision. Their basis for supporting any forceful action was to provide protection for their nationals in Shanghai, at times when the Chinese authorities would not or could not provide adequate protection. As for the nervous foreign enclaves bordering the battlefields, the American secretary-general of the SMC calmly reassured his foreign colleagues on October 27 that the sections of the International Settlement south of Suzhou Creek and east of the railroad track would not be affected by the change in the local war situation.[11]

The British and American participants worried about the number of Chinese refugees entering the International Settlement and counseled not offering food or much support to them, because doing so would only attract more refugees. Refugees from Zhabei were trying to enter the International Settlement by water, but the Shanghai Volunteer Corps and Municipal Police blocked off all entry points from the creek. This caused Suzhou Creek to become filled with boats of refugees with nowhere to go. Others crawled along the beams of

burned bridges spanning the creek. The council responded with the suggestion that a refugee camp be established at Minghong, outside the settlement
territory. At first, this camp was to house all refugees, but then the plans were
altered to house only Chinese ratepayers from the affected areas. Finally, even
this idea was withdrawn, and the proposed funding of $50,000 was used in-
stead to pay the heavy expenses incurred during the International Settlement's
state of emergency.[12] The SMC decided that in the future, it would not spend
public money on the evacuation or maintenance of refugees, leaving those
duties instead to charitable and volunteer organizations.[13] Concerned about
the spread of disease during the refugee influx, the council gladly received the
commissioner of public health's report that 20,000 refugees had been vaccinated against smallpox. The Chinese Department of Public Health reported
that it had administered 12,430 vaccinations.[14]

Several newspaper accounts document the work of the Red Swastika Society, the Canton Residents' Association, the Ningbo Residents' Association,
the Chinese YMCA, and the Shanghai Citizens' Relief Commission in pick-
ing up these responsibilities. The latter body's Refugee Relief Division spent
$100,000 on repatriating refugees or housing them in camps.[15] It also spon-
sored a substantial medical program to vaccinate refugees. A reported 30,000
refugees from the war zones left Shanghai on eight steamers bound for Ningbo
and other parts of Zhejiang Province. In mid February, that number increased
to 100,000, with the Ningbo Residents' Association hiring additional boats
to transport the refugees.[16] The Cantonese Residents' Association took on responsibility for 2,500 refugees from the Hongkou district of Shanghai, in addition to running four camps for 4,000 war refugees. After registration, refugees
received two meals a day and vaccination against smallpox. This Cantonese
group's shortage of funds meant that efforts increased to repatriate resident
refugees in order to make room for those newly arrived.[17]

Refugee aid also came from Buddhist monks, who opened their temples in
the French Concession as refugee camps. The Shanghai Christian War Relief
Committee collected donations and ran a refugee camp with help from food
kitchens set up by the Chinese YMCA. Meanwhile, the French authorities
marshaled their efforts to construct barricades of barbed wire to control and
minimize the flow of refugees into the Concession.[18]

In addition to the battlefield refugees, there were the thousands who had
arrived in the wake of the heavy flooding in 1931. Zhabei refugees who had
originally come from flooded areas in the Yangzi valley had been forced to
flee again from the fighting. One flood refugee camp on the border of Zha-

bei suffered bombing by the Japanese three times in early February, killing more than fifty people.[19] This particular camp housed 10,399 refugees and 49 staff members. The Shanghai Citizens' Relief Commission took on the task of transporting many refugees in the International Settlement back to their native homes free of charge. Their destinations included the Yangzi port cities, Ningbo, the Canton area, and Hangzhou. By the end of February, Hangzhou had replaced Shanghai as the main destination for refugees.[20]

Another British-American concern was that with Shanghai under the scrutiny of the world press because of the hostilities, which were widely documented and photographed, the protected status of the International Concession might come under further review, especially in the wake of the report on the subject to the Shanghai Municipal Council by Judge Richard Feetham in 1931.[21] The Chinese government had been pressuring the League of Nations to consider rendition of the concessions back to China.[22] There was also the issue of what to do with Chinese soldiers who had been cut off from retreat by the Japanese and wanted to seek refuge in the International Settlement. The SMC chairman, Brigadier General E. B. Macnaughten, ordered that soldiers might be permitted to come into the settlement but must first be disarmed and then temporarily confined to a cage then under construction until shelters for interning them were built.[23]

While all these particular interests were being debated among the authorities, Father Jacquinot was becoming increasingly anxious to rescue those he knew to be still trapped in fighting in Zhabei. Looking for an ally with the right skills, he enlisted the willing support of Major F. Hayley Bell of the Shanghai Volunteer Corps. Bell had been heavily involved in efforts to protect the borders of the foreign settlements and had witnessed the ferocity of the fighting taking place in Zhabei firsthand.

Jacquinot and Bell set out first to meet with both sides to explain the purpose of their proposed rescue mission. The best they could get from the Japanese side during their meeting with Vice Admiral Nomura Kichisaburō, commander of the Japanese Naval Forces, aboard his flagship, *Idzumo*, anchored next to the Japanese consulate, was an agreement for a four-hour truce to begin at 8:00 on the morning of February 11 and last until noon. Additional support came from the British and American consuls, who met with the Chinese and obtained their consent to the four-hour truce. The agreed-upon truce gave the Jacquinot party a window in which to attempt to rescue the 250 civilians, mainly women and children, plus as many injured soldiers from both sides as they could in the fighting area.[24]

Taking along a Chinese interpreter, fourteen French nuns, nine stretcher bearers, and six motor trucks converted into ambulances, the party began its mercy mission.[25] Several members of the Holy Family Institute joined the mission as volunteers. Major Bell, waving a white flag, led the party into the war zone near the railroad station. Chinese soldiers who were not informed of the truce fired some shots, but word quickly went to their commanders about the nature of the mission. The party and its charges succeeded in evacuating the wounded and refugees, often having to coax and prod those too frightened to move. Seeing the extent of their misery and scope of the damages, a request went forward to the Japanese side to extend the truce.[26] An extension would also allow more Chinese outside Zhabei to go in and visit their former homes and perhaps retrieve a few personal items. The Japanese commanders declined to extend the truce, claiming they had reliable reports that many of the departing or entering refugees were young men of military age who were Chinese soldiers disguised as civilians. Any further respite in the Japanese advance was out of the question.

Unfortunately, Major Bell, rather than being rewarded for his brave and successful mission, found upon his return that the commandant of the Shanghai Volunteer Corps had relieved him of his duties, claiming that Bell had failed to inform him of the rescue mission. Major Bell relished his position in the Corps and decided to petition the SMC for an enquiry into the circumstances and his actions. He supplied various documents justifying what he had done. This placed the council in a difficult position, because there had been considerable press coverage of the rescue mission. Public praise and commendation of Bell filled the media. Not wanting the matter to escalate, the council resolved to keep him in the Corps, "if he would withdraw his application for an enquiry." The outcome was in Major Bell's favor, because in the minutes of this council meeting, he abruptly began to be identified as Lt. Colonel F. Hayley Bell.[27]

Father Jacquinot, like Major Bell, felt frustrated with the lack of action on the part of the settlement authorities and took matters into his own hands to rescue those in danger. Jacquinot's willingness to do so, even insistence, is reminiscent of the way he had sought out similar action during the 1927 rescue mission in Zhabei. The chemistry experiment that had cost him his right arm was another instance of his unorthodox behavior. These proclivities, unusual in the general Jesuit community, gave Jacquinot's superiors some uneasiness, although he had a reputation for being an excellent organizer, a budding diplomat, and an able doer, qualities desperately needed on several occasions to deal with refugee crises during the decade. His talents emerged in ways that probably surprised even him. But then his peers described him as one not likely to advertise his abilities or accomplishments. Anyone observing his actions, however, would have noticed that he was a tireless achiever who gave little consideration to his own well-being and even his personal health when it came to meeting a crisis situation. The rector of Aurora University, Father Georges Germain, spoke of Jacquinot "[b]eing reckoned with the orthodox and yet feeling for the heterodox."[28] Not withstanding any reservations that might have existed regarding his motivations or methods, however, the Jacquinot-Bell mission resulted in the rescue of more than 2,000 civilians, mostly women and children.[29]

With the expiration of the truce, the fighting resumed, and both sides brought in more troops. The refugee camps in the International Settlement housed 2,311 refugees, managed with the help of 60 volunteers. The number of refugees arriving increased at a rate of about 2,000 daily. The YMCA and Chinese YMCA facilities opened their doors to the refugees. Three hundred found refuge in a temple in the French Concession.[30] By the end of February, Japanese military reinforcements of land and naval units brought the total of Japanese forces in the Shanghai battle to about 20,000. With the devastation described as the worst in Shanghai history and fear of imminent attacks on Nanshi like those that had occurred in Zhabei, and threats even to the famous Bund, the time had come to work out a truce.[31]

The conflict ended with the signing of a peace agreement on May 5 by Japanese and Chinese representatives, in the presence of British, American, French, and Italian envoys, described as "Representatives of the friendly Powers assisting in the negotiations in accordance with the Resolution of the Assembly of the League of Nations of March 4, 1932."[32] The explanation was given that during the fighting, the Chinese Army's flank had become exposed to Japanese forces, making its position untenable and causing the Chinese to retreat even beyond the line insisted upon in one of the earlier Japanese ultimatums. The Peace Agreement that followed stipulated that the Chinese remain in their present position and the Japanese forces withdraw into the International Settlement, thus creating a twenty-kilometer (12.4 miles) demilitarized zone in between them in the former area of the fighting. Only Chinese police forces would be permitted to function within this evacuated and restricted territory. In addition, any time the Chinese troops wanted to transverse Shanghai, the permission of the Joint Commission, acting in consultation with Japanese consul was required. The "friendly participating powers," acting as this Joint Commission, were to certify the mutual withdrawal of military forces and continue to assure that both parties were observing the agreement.

This Shanghai armistice agreement did not deal with the issue of Chinese troops still serving south of Suzhou Creek. In addition, a proposal accepted by the League Council to convene a conference to clarify that Japan had no political or territorial designs in Shanghai, and that China was fully committed to the safety and integrity of the foreign settlements was considered by the foreign powers to be untimely. Resolving these sensitive matters must have seemed to the committee too ambitious, time-consuming, and difficult to take on. There had been so many heated and stressful rounds of negotiations, requiring a resort to obfuscation and shading to gain agreement. But with this continued lack of clarity regarding these key issues, the still precarious situation in Shanghai was allowed to drift.[33] It was only a matter of time.

The completion of a formal truce aroused significant public opposition from those so impressed by the sturdy performance of the Chinese military, particularly the 19th Route Army. But it was in keeping with Chiang Kai-shek's policy of avoiding serious and prolonged warfare with the superior Japanese forces. No one could question the fact that the Chinese military forces had made a credible stand against the Japanese, but further engagement did not hold promise. The one crucial development that followed the Shanghai Incident was the greatly enhanced intensity of public anti-Japanese feeling. The widespread expression of these sentiments and the organizations built around them would soon come into play and fuel the Sino-Japanese conflict starting in August 1937.

A new phase in Father Jacquinot's service in Shanghai opened with the restoration of peace and calm. In 1934, he left his parish in Hongkou and became vicar of a new parish of St. Pierre and the grand new church constructed on the grounds of Aurora University in the French Concession. This relocation also put him in closer proximity to his teaching position at Aurora University, where he resumed his position as professor of English. For at least a decade, Father Jacquinot made almost daily visits to the Shanghai Central Hospital to visit parishioners and friends there. He served on the board of governors until 1934, when he was elected president of the board of administrators.[34] He also made frequent visits to the Hospital of Saint Marie, which was the hospital of the Catholic Mission. These services were in addition to his preaching in English at Saint Joseph's Church, teaching catechism classes, and acting as senior chaplain to the Shanghai Volunteer Corps in the French Concession. He capped off his new duties in 1937 by becoming spiritual advisor to the European College of the Sacred Heart, the women's division of Aurora University.

Two of his positions, as president of the Famine Relief Committee and a newly appointed member of the International Committee for the Social

Welfare of Shanghai, made him a key person to help deal with China's new disaster, another major flooding of the Yangzi River in 1936. During the night of September 11–12, the great dyke to the north of the city of Hankou (Hankow), 100 kilometers in length, broke under the force of waters of the swollen and flooding Yellow River. In its wake came another period of widespread desolation, suffering, and famine. Just as he had done in 1932, Jacquinot organized relief and support in the form of donations, food, and clothing drives. He toured the region and worked with the local authorities in dispensing money, medical relief, food, and other necessities. He often had to exhort and reprimand lax officials in the interests of the flood refugees.[35] His reputation among Chinese officials as a fair, honest, and effective organizer received still another boost from his performance in providing relief services during the 1936 floods.

Jacquinot realized that the rising tensions between the Chinese and Japanese forces might ignite into warfare at any time. He recalled the intense suffering inflicted upon Chinese civilians, especially by the new urban warfare, with its aerial bombings. He had been close to the individual tragedies that always happened in these circumstances. The feared second attack by the Japanese on Shanghai would begin on August 13, 1937, but the likelihood of its occurring was obvious long before. The distress that followed was greater than ever before. Some of these dark sentiments and bleak presentments gathered from his experiences are reflected in another of his poems:

Prayer

At night when the breeze murmurs,
And the sobbing wood owl
Whispers low its mysterious pain,
Sorrow floods out from the soul.

Hastening dark specters,
Frighten us endlessly, alas!
And the Future and the Past
Turn darkly around in my dream.

The Future frightens us most.
It is not, it was not, maybe it will be
No more than a tear,
An emotion with no more than a pale dream.

God, please renew our hope!
The Future is Yours alone: the shadow
Is spreading more thickly this evening
Make it a little less dark for us.[36]

The 1932 truce aimed at keeping the peace between China and Japan under the watchful eye of the Joint Commission. Just how superficial it was in operation can be seen by the failure of the Joint Commission to meet even once after the truce was signed. Several incidents followed during the succeeding years, but the ongoing decisive factors were the continuing Japanese pressures on North China and the responding anti-Japanese organization of patriotic feelings by the Chinese. The avowed intention of the Japanese Army to separate five northern provinces from China and thus expand its puppet state, Manzhouguo, was widely discussed in the Chinese press. Manzhouguo was already seen as an extension of Japan in China, and with the possible addition of the northern provinces, Japan's imperialist ambitions threatened to consume all of China.

Japanese officials would always claim that the bold actions Japan took were justified by the need to protect Japanese residents or nationals from the anti-Japanese actions and sentiment now widely expressed in Shanghai. If the Chinese (or foreign) authorities would not or could not protect Japanese from negative and harmful actions, the Japanese military was needed to assume that role. In many respects, the foreign settlements were built on just that kind of reasoning. The Mixed Court, the Shanghai Volunteer Corps, and the calling in of foreign troops to meet the perceived threat in 1927 were all actions taken by the foreign powers based largely on the belief that the Chinese, acting alone or operating under a weak government, were not up to the task of protecting foreign rights, lives, and property, or that they chose not to respond.

Given these premises, it seems that war between China and Japan was inevitable, even though when it did happen, it was undeclared. The consequences for mainly the Chinese civilian population, taken hostage by three months of violent combat, were terrible. Traditional Chinese organizations such as guilds, native place associations, and regional bodies played an important role in meeting the desperate needs that arose, and Father Jacquinot's humanitarian endeavors were as notable as before.

Japan's continental policy and China's growing unity through its consensus around anti-Japanese resistance formed the background for an inevitable clash. Events in North China, including Japanese plans for broader autonomy in that region, were the fundamental issues in the impasse in Sino-Japanese relations, the issue that eventually led to war. The Japanese Kwantung and North China Armies engaged in frequent military training operations, often over several days, using live ammunition and in close proximity to Chinese military forces. The Japanese also began strengthening their military facilities in Hebei Province, the location of the former Chinese capital, Peking, a development that greatly alarmed Chinese commanders. A whole series of scattered anti-Japanese activities continued throughout the spring and early summer months, which became so intense that some believed that an anti-Japanese conspiracy existed and was orchestrating these incidents.[37] In the Japanese view, these widespread and damaging anti-Japanese activities were neither inevitable nor demanded by the situation, leaving Japan with no option but to act for the protection of East Asia and its peoples.

The incident that led to war took place on July 7, 1937, when Japanese troops engaged in war games near Marco Polo Bridge (Lugouqiao) in Hebei Province, near Beijing. Japanese units became embroiled in a battle involving Chinese troops of the Twenty-Ninth Army. Attempts to reach a lasting settlement of the incident were made, but the momentum of developing hostility on both sides was so overpowering that renewed fighting constantly flared up, further inciting the will to make war. The Japanese cabinet, by now openly determined to dominate North China, mobilized its military forces to carry out this policy. Eventually, its ambitious plans were to establish a basis in central China for economic development, with Shanghai as the center. A government-controlled company, the Central China Progress Company, located in Greater Shanghai, would administer and control public utilities: telephone service, electric power, water and gas, streetcars, buses, and so on. The whole operation would be supervised by a cabinet-level Department of Economic Relations with China, managed separately from the Foreign Ministry.[38]

China, under Chiang Kai-shek, reached the conclusion that pacification first and then resistance was no longer a viable policy. Both sides resolved to go to fight it out.[39] Known to the Chinese as the Anti-Japanese War or War of Resistance in China, the Asian phase of World War II had begun, four and a half years before Pearl Harbor. It lasted over eight years and by some estimates brought about some twenty million deaths, most of them civilian, as well as immense damage to China's coastal cities.[40]

The incident that brought the war to Shanghai involved the shooting death on the afternoon of August 9, 1937, of a Japanese officer, Lieutenant Oyama Isao, and his naval chauffeur in the Hongjiao or western region of the city. As usual, there were two very different versions of what had led to the incident and the investigation that followed. Unhappy with the outcome and handling of the incident, the Japanese landed forces to reinforce their Naval Landing Party on August 11. Additional ships, munitions, troops, and supplies arrived the same day. Immediately, the conditions of the 1932 truce were brought to bear on the dangerous situation. At a meeting of the Joint Commission, Japanese Consul General Okamoto Suemasa charged that Chinese units of the 87th and 88th Divisions, Nanjing's most elite forces, were gradually filling the North Station and Jiangwan area in direct violation of the 1932 truce. The Chinese mayor, Yu Hongjun (O. K. Yui), rejoined that the Japanese had made the 1932 truce null and void by stationing troops on the Eight Character Bridge near the railway and within the neutral zone area.

On August 13 the Shanghai Municipal Council mobilized the Shanghai Volunteer Corps and British and American units guarding the International Settlement in their respective defense sectors, with the stated purpose of protecting the life and property within the area of council's control. The French consul general, Paul-Emile Naggiar, claimed that he had no record of his country's agreement to serve on the Joint Commission as required by the truce and thus was hesitant to participate.[41] He did initiate a curfew in the Concession, which was duplicated in the Settlement the next day. Sensing the imminence of hostilities, those of the panic-stricken residents of Zhabei and Hongkou who had the means to do so exited these prospective battlegrounds. Some from Nanshi in the southern parts of the city followed. Many of these took up residence in the foreign settlements.

The Nanjing government perhaps hoped that a showdown with the Japanese, employing its best troops and material in Shanghai, rather than in the North, would enlist foreign intervention and support. With the enormous Chinese and foreign interests in the city, such aid might in some form reasonably be expected. If that was part of the planning, it failed to produce intervention by foreign leaders, too preoccupied with conditions at home and in other places to respond.[42] Instead, the attitudes and policies of the great powers displayed a continued unwillingness to challenge Japan on behalf of China.

Chinese public opinion, so well articulated by the Shanghai press, national salvation organizations, and the population in general, combined with the insistence of military generals, must have helped motivate the Nationalist government to treat a local, if serious, issue as a national one. The intensity of feeling and plentiful past incidents were such that the government became willing to entertain the policy of risking Shanghai, and the Chinese and foreign interests there, by resisting the more modern and powerful Japanese Army and Navy.

The first aerial bombing in the battle of Shanghai came on the morning of August 14, when Chinese airplanes, aiming for the Japanese flagship, *Idzumo*, missed it and hit areas of Hongkou, causing numerous casualties and a panic-stricken flight of refugees onto the Garden Bridge and into the Public Gardens and the entire Bund, or waterfront area. An even greater disaster happened later in the afternoon, when Chinese planes dropped a powerful bomb on a traffic circle crowded with refugees, and still another on the Bund end of Nanjing Road, at the location of the Cathay and Peace Hotels. The slaughter was appalling, with at least 1,047 persons killed and 303 injured. At the Nanjing Road location, there were over 200 casualties and at least 145 killed. Most were Chinese, but some Americans and other foreigners were among the victims.

It taxed the efforts and resources of the foreign settlements to cope with these early disasters. Their severity and impact left no doubt that the era of urban warfare, with aerial bombing, street fighting, and waves of terrified refugees was well under way. The ensuing battles were some of the most strongly contested in the Chinese War of Resistance.

The evacuation by ship of British and American women and children began on the morning of August 17, the British to Hong Kong and the Americans destined for Manila. On the next day, Father Jacquinot and others established the International Refugee Committee with headquarters at the Chinese YMCA on the Boulevard de Montigny.[43] This Refugee Committee would serve as a coordinating body for several diverse relief organizations, including the Chinese Red Cross, the Catholic Mission of China, the Chinese Buddhist Associations, the Federation of Chinese Benevolent Organizations, and others. The new body's mission was to deal with the flood of Chinese refugees fleeing mainly from Zhabei and Hongkou, which were under heavy attack by both warring parties. Their key initial task was to set up refugee camps and keep them supplied with all necessary provisions. By August 21, sixty refugee camps were up and operating, housing 50,000 refugees. With crucial support from Chinese native place associations, professional associations, and guilds, arrangements followed to send refugee groups away from Shanghai to safe locations elsewhere. In this regard, Father Jacquinot contacted the Japanese Vice Admiral Hasegawa Kiyoshi and won his permission to send five thousand Chinese refugees a day off to safety at the port city Ningbo, southeast of Shanghai.

By August 20, Pudong became an important target of Japanese aerial bombing, which meant new waves of refugees came seeking safety. On the morning of August 23, Japanese Army troops landed near Wusong, just northeast of Shanghai, under the command of General Matsui Iwane, commander of the Shanghai Expeditionary Force. These reinforcements, totaling more than 50,000 troops, underlined General Matsui's warning that "there can be no peace until China changes her attitude and ceases her provocative attacks."[44]

On August 26, Japanese aircraft machine-gunned the car of the British ambassador, Sir Hugh M. Knatchbull-Hugessen, traveling from Nanjing to

Chinese refugees fleeing the battles, crossing the Garden Bridge. *Oriental Affairs* (Sept. 1937).

Shanghai, which was flying the Union Jack at the time, and the ambassador suffered a serious spinal wound. Even then, however, the foreign response was more than circumspect. On September 28, the League of Nations Council heard arguments proffered by both the Japanese and Chinese representatives in defense of their positions. Before adjourning, the Assembly's only action was to adopt a resolution condemning the indiscriminate bombing of Chinese towns and villages by Japanese aircraft.

The suffering inflicted upon the Zhabei, Pudong, and Nanshi areas of Shanghai is often noted to have been indescribable. The northern Chinese sectors, Zhabei and parts of Hongkou, were either on fire or reduced to rubble, especially Zhabei, which was an industrial area and place of residence for the Chinese. Many among the massive flow of refugees were weeping and crying for help. Families became separated, and the incessant cries of those seeking family members echoed through narrow streets. Cases of fainting and collapse because of exhaustion and hunger were numerous. Having no safe areas to turn to, the panic-stricken refugees, miserable and destitute, entered the foreign concessions. In addition to taking in and providing services for their own people exiting the bombed-out areas, the authorities in the International Settlement and French Concession had to deal with countless others.

The foreign settlements faced their greatest challenge in coping with the incoming tidal wave of refugees fleeing the Chinese-administered areas bordering the settlements, and from the villages and towns ravaged in the path of the Japanese advances. The latter came from the south after the Japanese landing at Hangzhou Bay on November 5, and from the north after the capture of the Wusong Forts and the city of Wusong.

It was a gigantic task. One Chinese report in September estimated that there were 500,000 refugees in the foreign settlements, an area of only thirteen square miles.[45] Adding to the refugee problem was the growing unemployment in the city caused by the destruction of factories, the protective closing of factories, and numerous strikes at mainly Japanese factories.[46] Figures on the number of refugees in just the International Settlement in September 1937 show the establishment of 103 refugee camps, housing 53,767 refugees. The numbers increased in October to 110 camps, housing 72,070, with an additional 4,190 refugees living in alleyways and on the streets. Thousands slept on bedrolls in the parks or vacant lots and wandered aimlessly in the streets during the day. The numbers peaked in November 1937, with 142 camps accommodating 91,815 refugees and counting 3,645 living in streets and alleys.[47]

The figure for the French Concession in December was 40 camps, housing 25,900.[48] On the grounds of Aurora University alone, there were 2,300 refugees living in mat-shed housing.[49] Jiaotong University provided shelter for another large refugee camp, housing 17,000. The Native Bankers' Guild School on Rue Luzon housed some 4,500 refugees.[50] Of course, these figures, precise though they may seem, are really only good estimates. Reliable official figures for the refugees being assisted by native place organizations and guilds are lacking.

What was happening in Shanghai was, of course, only part of the scale of chaos and distress. One journalist estimated that some 30 million Chinese moved westward from the war zones, making this one of the greatest mass migrations in modern times.[51]

The Shanghai Municipal Council seems to have had a difficult time finding the right response to the refugee crisis. The general drift of its policy was not to get involved in refugee work, but to leave it to the International Red Cross, the other international organizations, and the senior Chinese relief organizations.[52] When the SMC did respond, it was in defense of order and the safety and property of the International Settlement. There was also much concern expressed about the potential rise in crime, looting, and rice riots as a result of the massive influx of destitute people. The possible spread of infectious disease inspired a campaign to inoculate those in the camps against smallpox and cholera.[53]

With the onset of cold weather, and the needs that would likely stimulate, the SMC formed a committee of eight persons in early October to map out what actions to take in the coming winter. The air of detachment from refugee affairs continued, however, as is evidenced by the lament that as late as May 25, 1938, the SMC still lacked an overall refugee policy.[54]

Even so, the council's response, at least initially, was more generous than that of the French Concession, which as soon as the hostilities began, closed its doors to the fleeing refugees. Once the numbers of destitute refugees seeking refuge in the International Settlement overwhelmed the available resources, the Settlement authorities also blocked all points of entry and established a rigid policy of registration certificates to help control the flow of refugees. The council exerted increased pressure on the various relief organizations to speed up the repatriation of Chinese refugees back to their native places.[55]

The Chinese response was to continue with the repatriation work and general relief programs. With so many competing national, international, and local organizations responding to the crisis, there were lively political battles over influence and resources. In October, the Greater Shanghai City Government put the Emergency Refugee Relief Committee in charge of overseeing refugee work that had previously been done by various relief organizations.

This committee was to operate under the city government's Social Affairs Bureau and included representation from all the public relief organizations.[56]

At a press conference, the new Emergency Refugee Relief Committee chairman, Pan Kung-chan, explained that refugee work could not "be tackled successfully by the authorities of the affected cities alone," and that it therefore ultimately had to be placed under the supervision of the national government. The size of the problem in Shanghai, where relief organizations had cared for at least 88,303 refugees and repatriated 64,000, had prompted the government to place national relief work under Pan's committee.[57] While the government's policy for national supervision of refugee affairs was a reasonable goal, at least for a while, it would not solve the matter of group competition. The native place associations, such as those of Canton, Ningbo, and Changzhou, continued their work of raising funds, supplying their camps, and repatriating their countrymen.

When the Chinese troops began their retreat, after a ferocious fight, they crossed over the Garden Bridge from Hongkou and Yangshupu and cut west across the city to the countryside. The damage to the Chinese military in battle was immense. The newly trained Chinese officer corps was decimated by losses in the fighting. Almost one-third of the Chinese forces under Nationalist command had fallen in battle.[58] Industrial losses in Shanghai, according to the Social Affairs Bureau, included 5,255 plants in a state of ruin. With aerial bombing and artillery fire, and only flimsy buildings for cover, many did not survive. An estimated 300,000 Chinese men perished at Shanghai during the campaign.[59] As for the enormous refugee problem that followed the fighting, what was needed was firm and experienced leadership to manage the influx.

Father Jacquinot happened to be uniquely qualified for this huge task by reason of his extensive work and experience in relief and rescue work. He had long considered the problem of how to protect civilians in war, based on his experiences and service during the 1932 incident. He had already seen so much suffering by fleeing civilians trying to survive hunger, poverty, and personal loss. At least as important, on a practical level, were his good relations with the mayor of Shanghai and his long-standing friendships with leaders of the various foreign communities. As will be shown in the next chapter, even his work with the Japanese authorities during the Sino-Japanese conflict in 1932 helped give him a basis of credibility with these powerful interests in Shanghai.

CHAPTER FOUR

The Jacquinot Zone

> Before attempting to probe the secret of its life, let
> us take a good look at it. For from a merely external
> contemplation of it, there is a lesson and a force to be
> drawn from it: the sense of its testimony.
> —Pierre Teilhard de Chardin

By the time the undeclared war broke out between China and Japan in August 1937, Father Jacquinot had built a strong reputation in Shanghai based on trust, his competence, and personal charisma. It was upheld by most, including Chinese and foreign officials and diplomats of all sides, local and foreign businessmen, journalists, and charity officials. If there were any reservations about him, it was again in the spirit of Father Georges Germain, rector of Aurora University, who said: "It is his independence that is a little disquieting. I have been unable to have full confidence in the methods of his mission."[1] His religious colleagues echoed these sentiments about Jacquinot's "original methods," but at the same time, they were willing to recognize his ingenuity, talents, and accomplishments in the service of the Catholic Church in China and the Chinese community.

It was Jacquinot's development and realization of the concept of the international safe zone that was his seminal contribution to refugee work in Shanghai. It became a working example of a successful refugee safe zone for copying elsewhere in China and the world. The Shanghai Safety Zone (*Shanghai anquan qu*) brought security to 250,000–360,000 Chinese during the most chaotic and dangerous period of the undeclared war. It lasted until June 1940, when the situation in the Shanghai area had stabilized to the point where the remaining refugees could return to their original home areas. The question arises of how Jacquinot came up with his ideas for refugee protection. Were there any precedents for his proposals? Of course, the idea of a neutral zone had shaped the context of the 1932 Shanghai Truce Agreement, discussed above. The basic concept of a neutral zone would be considered again by the foreign powers as a basis for yet another truce agreement, meant to end the hostilities in 1937.

The immediate concern was that the Chinese forces would not be able to resist Japanese pressure, making densely populated Nanshi a new and horrific battlefield. In the likely association with the 1932 zone, popular conceptions of this new zone framework initially took on the aura and flavor of a wartime designation. Out of both conviction and diplomatic necessity, Jacquinot offered a simpler view of it, saying:

> This district in Nanshi (Nantao), a place of safety for the civilian populations, is not a "neutral zone," for it is neither neutral nor a zone; it is not rightly called a demilitarized region; it is certainly not arranged for the French interests nor to protect the Church property in Nanshi. . . . It is purely and simply what it is called: a district of safety for the non-combatants. It has been possible because both the Japanese and the Chinese are desirous, for humanitarian reasons, to protect the non-combatants.[2]

THE SAFE DISTRICT OR ZONE AS A CONCEPT

This concept that aimed exclusively at humanitarian goals with no political or even religious overtones did have some background in contemporary European thinking. There is evidence that Father Jacquinot was party to the discussion and debates among European friends and colleagues regarding the protection of civilians in wartime. A central figure in the European debates was the French surgeon-general Georges Saint-Paul (1870–1937), who in 1929 proposed creating zones of safety for civilians and sick and wounded troops during wartime. In 1931, Saint-Paul founded the Association des Lieux de Genève in Paris to promote this, which, starting in 1937, published a bulletin entitled *Lieux de Genève: Zones blanches*.[3] He based his thinking on the chaos and atrocities he had seen and experienced during World War I, a war, after all, in which almost half of all French males between the ages of 20 and 32 in 1914 had lost their lives.[4]

The misery and carnage of World War I had created a receptive audience, and Saint-Paul's ideas received the close attention of the French Chamber of Deputies, which voted in 1935 to support the concept of such *lieux de Genève*. Soon afterward, the French government, wanting to make their existence formal and permanent, approached the League of Nations for action in giving these new ideas international and official backing. The League responded by

Japanese battleships in the Huangpu River. Archives de la Compagnie de Jésus, Québec.

developing preliminary accords in support of these recommendations for pro-tected zones. Still, there were many who doubted the feasibility and likely success of his protection plans. Pacifists and others declared that the plans were not practical and would certainly not be obeyed by any wartime military force.[5]

Saint Paul died in 1937, after requesting that the Association be transferred from Paris to Genèva. Henry George, a Swiss citizen resident in Geneva, took charge of establishing the Geneva organization which bore the same name, the Association Internationale des "Lieux de Genève." Its plans and method-ology obviously were inspired by the ideas and action program developed by Saint-Paul in Paris. The new Geneva organization, in order to facilitate further discussion and prepare an agenda for any future international conference tak-ing up this matter of security, launched an *avant-projet*, or pilot study, to bring together information and experience that might be useful to those working in the fields of international law and the laws of war.[6] Father Jacquinot's recent successes in Shanghai were advanced as the most important and persuasive rel-evant evidence. The activities of the Jacquinot Zone are described as "precious testimony" and conclusive proof of the practicality of these new concepts, especially as they relate to innocent victims of aerial bombing. At the same time, such *lieux de Genève*, as related to Jacquinot's work, are praised for representing a high standard of moral, judicial, and humanitarian behavior to be aspired to by every nation. Feelings ran high to somehow redress the tragedy of World War I by considering new institutions that might avoid such carnage and misery in the future.

Another addition to the Geneva Association's program, as espoused by Henry George, was the protection of historic monuments that are not trans-portable during wartime.[7] So often in the past, public opinion had expressed concern over the fate of the most precious monuments, art works, and build-ings threatened especially by aerial bombing. The Geneva organization main-tained that the beauty and civilizing influence of these items could form the basis for an international entente among peoples for including these precious treasures in a secure zone according to an international plan. People would be able to unite around this high-minded goal. Always central to the discussion was Saint-Paul's conviction that the primary motivation must be humanitar-ian. The Association des Lieux de Genève had no prescribed ideology, Saint-Paul observed. It was "neither Catholic nor Evangelical [i.e., Protestant]; not Jewish any more than Buddhist or Islamic; neither royalist nor republican, neither Soviet nor praetorian [i.e., Fascist]."[8] As we shall see, this was also the program carefully followed, and successfully realized, by Father Jacquinot in Shanghai. And in doing so, the issue of safe zones passed from being just speculation, although with substantial written justification and debate, to be-coming a working reality.

Spain was where the first attempt at practical implementation of civilian safe zones was made. It happened during the course of the three-year Spanish Civil War, which began in July 1936.[9] Fascist forces under General Francisco Franco's leadership engaged in a bitter struggle against Spanish Republican forces united in a Popular Front. Franco received crucial support from Fascist Germany and Italy, both of which supplied Franco with arms and supplies and benefited from the opportunity to test out their own military equipment un-der real wartime conditions. German ace pilots mercilessly bombed the small rural town of Guernica with tragic results, made famous by Pablo Picasso's painting of that name. The Germans, after the aerial bombing missions, ma-chine-gunned the streets of Guernica, killing and wounding about half of the city's inhabitants. Only later would the Germans admit that the assault on Guernica had been an experiment to test the effects of aerial terror bombing. The bombings of Madrid, Barcelona, and other Spanish cities were among the earliest substantial aerial attacks on civilian populations in history, the Japanese bombing of the Chinese districts of Shanghai in 1932 being the first. Their suffering became a graphic example for the international community of

Japanese soldiers occupying
a bridge. *Oriental Affairs*
(Oct. 1937).

the terrible inhumanity of modern warfare, suggesting the tragic hopelessness
of unarmed refugees matched against the power of modern weaponry.

Henry George and his Association made three urgent appeals to the Spanish authorities: to establish safe zones for at least the women and children; for
officers and troops to respect the sanctity of these zones; and for neutral police
supervisors to make sure that the areas were not used for military purposes.[10]
The Swiss chargé d'affaires proposed to his government that it demand that the
two warring parties in Spain agree to set aside a part of Madrid, which was
especially hard hit, to serve as a safe zone for noncombatants, in accordance
with the above three terms. The Swiss government agreed to study the request
and contacted the International Committee of the Red Cross, asking that it
do the same. The Red Cross had been the sponsor of the Geneva Conventions
of 1929 for the protection of sick or wounded military personnel, but these

international provisions did not include consideration of ways to protect the civilian population. The earlier Hague Conventions of 1907 included articles that dealt with the protection of buildings that had no military purpose, but, again, not with civilians. The conclusion reached by the Red Cross after its study of the proposals was that any steps that might be taken would come too late to affect the ongoing civil war between the Fascists and Republicans in Spain. Doubts about the efficacy of safe zones in the midst of war, which had earlier dogged the French proposal and League of Nations accords, continued to influence authorities. So the most to be said for the Spanish example was that events there contributed to the official international discourse regarding the need for zones of refuge.

With the Japanese attack at Marco Polo Bridge near Beijing, a new chapter on aerial warfare was soon to be written. The League of Nations would ineffectually condemn the Japanese actions in China. Since no war had officially been declared, the international community could avoid responsibility for taking practical measures or ameliorative actions. Application of the concept of *lieux de Genève* for the protection of the civilian population in Shanghai would thus become the first testimony and proof of their practical merits.

From the earliest stages of the 1937 war in Shanghai, Japan maintained that Nanshi, which included the old Chinese City and its suburbs south of the French Concession, was being used by the Chinese as a base of military operations. Conversely, the Chinese insisted that the area was only defended by the Peace Preservation Corps police and thus could not be regarded as a military base or objective. The position and status of the area became even more perilous, however, when the beleaguered Chinese military forces, forced to withdraw from Zhabei, retreated across Suzhou Creek toward Nanshi, which was located immediately in their rear. This put the troops in the midst of the huge Chinese population tightly situated in Nanshi. Fearing for the fate of these civilians, the Chinese ambassador to France, Wellington Koo (Ku Weichun), made an urgent appeal to the League of Nations on September 9, pleading for it to take action to help resolve the dangerous confrontation.[11] Koo's alarm was heightened by a statement by the Japanese foreign minister, Hirota Kōki, during an interview on September 2 to the effect that the fighting in Shanghai had been caused by Chinese intrusions into the neutral zone set up under the 1932 truce agreement, and that these actions amounted to a "direct provocation of Japan."[12] Accordingly, Hirota claimed that the foreign ambassadors in the Chinese capital of Nanjing had not supervised the 1932 truce well, as they were charged to do. At this stage, the tenor and substance of Hirota's evaluation made it unlikely that Japan would regard seriously or permit the active intervention of a third party, even the League, in the ongoing Sino-Japanese confrontation. The situation had reached too late a stage and began to resemble the comparable situation just described with the Spanish Civil War.

Locally in Shanghai, the two foreign municipal councils maintained their inability to halt the progress of the war and, instead, focused their energies on the troublesome flood of Chinese refugees. By early September, there were 500,000 Chinese refugees crowded into the International Settlement.[13] To deal with this problem, the Shanghai Municipal Council established a Refugee Survey Committee to advise it on developments and to coordinate information and work with the already existing Committee for Coordination of the Evacuation of Refugees and Refugee Advisory Committee.[14] Because of the chaotic circumstances and fears of widespread destruction of foreign property, almost every official entity in the foreign settlements decided it was necessary to establish a working refugee committee to monitor events. Meanwhile, the panic-stricken Chinese in Nanshi sought refuge in the French Concession, crowding up against its iron gates and seeking to force entry into the protected area. There were at least 250,000 refugees without protection, and the idea of Japanese aerial bombing of this densely populated area, whose inhabitants might well be caught between bombs and burning buildings, was horrifying to all. The widespread fear was that the death and destruction that had already occurred in Zhabei, Pudong, and Hongkou would be repeated in Nanshi and areas south of the city where so many had fled and others still lived.

NEGOTIATING WITH THE WARRING PARTIES

From his parish in the French Concession, Father Jacquinot began to seek a way to avoid this potential disaster and managed to calm the terrified refugees by persuading them to await a promised sanctuary just outside the French Concession. His position as a foreign national aided his neutral status and gave him a secure position from which to act. He invited the French Vice Admiral Le Bizot to accompany him to the Japanese consulate and meet with Admiral Hasegawa Kiyoshi, commander of the Japanese Third Fleet, to discuss the refugee problem. He intended to explain his proposal to set aside an area in Nanshi as a protected refugee area that the Japanese would not bomb or attack. He expected the area to offer the same amount of protection that refugees were able to receive in the privileged foreign settlements. After hearing the details of Jacquinot's plan, the Japanese admiral promised to learn if the authorities were ready to respond to this innovative request. Jacquinot in-

A. S. Jaspar   Major Hans Berents   C. Baboud

G. Findlay Andrew, O.B.E.   W. H. Platt   Father Jacquinot de Besange, S.J.   Brig.-Gen. E. B. Macnaghten, C.M.G., D.S.O.

Members of the Nanshi Supervisory Committee. *The Story of the Jacquinot Zone* (Shanghai, 1939).

sisted that, in the meantime, he would move ahead even without the Japanese response and prepare to create the facilities planned, because the dire circumstances demanded such action.[15]

As vice president of the Shanghai International Committee of the Red Cross and head of its Refugee Committee, Jacquinot started a movement to set aside a portion of Nanshi to serve as a protected safe zone where 250,000 Chinese and other refugees could find a haven from the fighting.[16] It would become a Shanghai Safe Zone, or *Shanghai anquanqu*. A new committee called the Nanshi Supervisory Committee, headed by Jacquinot, became the responsible body for implementing his idea. It was multinational in character—the members included three French, two English, one Norwegian, and one American—and represented Shanghai's foreign elite well.[17] The caliber of representation on this refugee committee ensured that Jacquinot would have strong backing when he approached the Chinese and Japanese authorities and, of course, the foreign powers as well. In this regard, both the Chinese and the Japanese had often demonstrated their high regard for status and connec-

Father Jacquinot meeting with
the Japanese consul. Archives
de la Compagnie de Jésus,
Québec.

tion to foreign prestige in their social and professional dealings. To Jacquinot's
added advantage, of course, was the usually unspoken desire on the part of foreign community leaders that a way be found to accommodate these refugees
in some place other than their own privileged and admittedly overcrowded
foreign concessions.

The task at hand was to persuade the Japanese civilian and military authorities that bringing order to the refugee situation and limiting damage to civilian populations and areas of the city would clearly be in Japan's interests. With
this goal in mind, Father Jacquinot began a series of intense secret negotiations
with the Chinese and Japanese authorities that lasted day and night over a
period of three days. He first approached the mayor of Greater Shanghai, Yu
Hongjun. His work with the Chinese mayor produced a letter from Jacquinot,
co-signed by the mayor, marking out the area in Nanshi that would become a
refuge and be free from attack by Japanese forces. It specified that the area was

to be bounded on its eastern, northern, and western sides by Min Kuo Road, just south of the French Concession, and on the southern side by Fong Bang Road.[18] Jacquinot was then able to report the existence of this "agreement" to the Japanese consul general, Okamoto Suemasa. With the Chinese position somewhat clarified, Okamoto agreed to consult with the local Japanese Army and Navy authorities and cabled to Tokyo concerning the contents of these discussions with Jacquinot, noting the proposal to mark out a protected area to accommodate the refugees. A significant personal asset in all of these negotiations was that, as Chinese sources assert, Jacquinot spoke "good" Mandarin Chinese and also the local Shanghai dialect. In addition, they credit him with fluency in Japanese, along with English and, of course, his native French.[19] This would be invaluable in the crisis.

After these consultations, Okamoto praised Jacquinot "for your noble and worthy efforts to save the civilian population in the Chinese city from the deplorable consequences of warfare."[20] He confirmed that Japan was more than willing to minimize damages to noncombatant Chinese and agreed to the following three points: the area in question would be restricted to the enclosure adjacent to the French Concession; the Chinese authorities must assure that no Chinese soldier would enter this zone; and that in the event that Nanshi were captured by Japanese forces, the area in question would automatically come under Japanese jurisdiction, and so long as its occupants behaved to the satisfaction of the Japanese authorities, they would be treated kindly. As early as November 3, the Japanese press carried confirmation that Japan supported the Jacquinot plan and that the Japanese authorities were awaiting Mayor Yu's signature of agreement.[21] Jacquinot would have preferred to have all of Nanshi included in the Safety Zone, not just the northern portion, but given Tokyo's recent military successes, he decided not to ask for too much. Affirming his appreciation and support for Jacquinot's equitable stance and cooperation, Okamoto said, "he [Father Jacquinot] understands our position."[22] The Japanese consul general then informed the local Japanese Army and Navy commanders that he was satisfied with the discussions Jacquinot had had with the Chinese authorities, both civilian and military, saying that these amounted to assurances that Chinese military forces would not enter the Safety Zone area.[23]

When first confronted with the Japanese terms, Mayor Yu Hongjun objected to some points, but after further discussion and prodding from Jacquinot, he at least agreed not to insist upon the Chinese use of two unspecified "military structures" located within the proposed zone. Mayor Yu also confirmed by letter dated November 5, 1937, that "our policemen in the zone will

Mayor Yu Hongjun and
his wife. Courtesy of
Malcolm Rosholt.

be open to the inspection and investigation of the International Committee
at any time for the purpose of ascertaining that the terms of the arrangement
are being complied with."[24] Aware of the acute sensitivities inherent in the
situation, Jacquinot chose not to show the Chinese side one of the letters he
had received from Okamoto. This letter, dated November 5, reported that the
Japanese military and naval authorities were convinced that hostilities in the
neighborhood of the new zone would also affect the zone, and "further that it
is our intention to take over the district after Chinese troops have been driven
out from the adjacent area."[25] Instead, Father Jacquinot shared with the Chinese a letter from Okamoto to Jacquinot, also dated November 5, in which
the Japanese position appeared softer, as is shown by the use of more general
language:

> I now have the pleasure of confirming that the Japanese Military and Navy,
> strongly moved by humanitarian considerations and in cognizance of the guar-

antee offered by the Chairman of the International Red Cross Refugee Committee [Jacquinot], as well as the assurance that any violation of the status of the said district, which will be guarded by special policeman, will be reported at once, have agreed that they will not attack the said district so long as it remains . . . an area exclusively for the civilian population and entirely free from any military operations or armed hostile acts as is guaranteed.[26]

The Japanese stated that when the International Committee reported to the Japanese side that it was supervising the new zone, and confirmation had been received that the Chinese were carrying out their pledges to the International Committee, the overall "understanding" would go into effect. On November 9, Okamoto received word from Jacquinot that the committee had inspected the area and confirmed that the understanding with the Chinese had been carried out. He provided assurances that the committee would carry out its prescribed duties in accord with the understanding. The Jacquinot Zone opened formally at 5:00 p.m. on November 9, 1937, with its boundaries marked by Red Cross flags.[27] To make it official, the Nanshi Supervisory Committee issued a decree stating that it had reserved the area for noncombatants, having satisfied itself that all pledges given had been duly observed, and declared the area open for residence under the conditions of the understanding. There was one slight omission, however, in that Japanese documents indicate that they had never received written confirmation from the Chinese side, as was intended.[28]

It should be noted that the Japanese authorities were not unfamiliar with the concept of safe zones and the arguments offered for their inclusion during periods of armed conflict. The Japanese Red Cross had hosted a conference of the International Red Cross in Tokyo in 1934, often referred to as "Project Tokyo," during which a resolution provided by the Belgian government was adopted to form a diplomatic conference to study the existing rules of warfare and the creation of safe zones, especially with regard to neutral countries dealing with floods of civilian refugees.[29] Such a diplomatic conference followed in Geneva in 1936 and gave some initial consideration to the use of zones for civilian protection. The Tokyo conference, the "XV Conference," was presided over by Prince Tokugawa Iyesato, president of the Japanese Red Cross. As a follow-on, Japanese pride of sponsorship of this prestigious international body inspired the leaders of the Japanese Red Cross Society to write its own history, highlighting various memorabilia from the 1934 conference. The project included establishing a museum to better showcase the souvenirs. In any case, what matters here is that Japan remained party to the several meetings

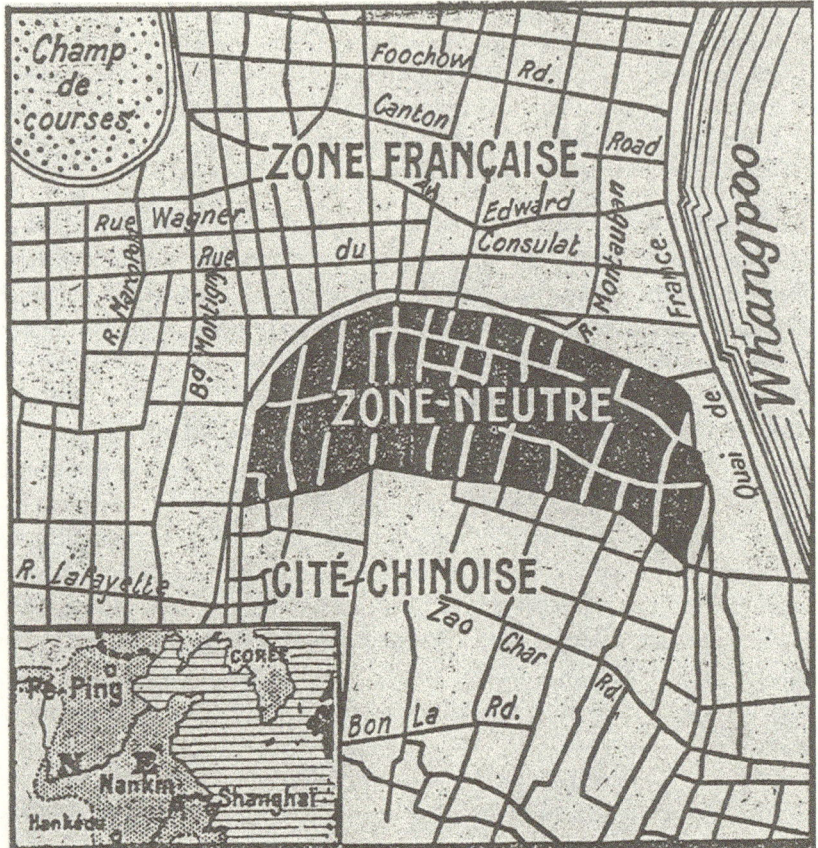

The Jacquinot Zone shaded in on the French map. *France: Dimanche* (September 21, 1946).

and the conference that followed these early attempts to look at the implications of modern warfare, even though Japan was not a signatory to the Geneva Conventions of 1929 and exited the League of Nations in 1938.

The key to Jacquinot's "diplomatic" negotiations with both sides was his ability to work out the language of the arrangements so that the end result, published in the press of the various countries and communities, presented the situation as having the support of both the Japanese military and civilian authorities as well as their Chinese counterparts. Rather than pressing for a formal agreement, Jacquinot focused his attention on reaching a somewhat less conclusive but more palatable "understanding." His strategy involved having both the Japanese and Chinese authorities come to accept the existence of a protected area in Nanshi, the Jacquinot Zone, but without using terminology indicating that an "agreement" had been reached between the two warring sides.[30] The Japanese "acknowledged" the existence of the protected zone, as did the Chinese. A Chinese spokesman emphasized that "the consummation of the plan does not involve any agreement between the Chinese and Japanese authorities . . . the important point is that any understanding is with the International Committee and not with the Japanese. This is also true for the Japanese side."[31] This put the agreement into the hands of a "benevolent group" and not a rival third power. By his astute tactics and terminology, Jacquinot was able to bring the two sides together in a way that enabled their acceptance and, most important, permitted the realization of his plan for a safe area of refuge for Chinese refugees in Shanghai.

THE SAFE ZONE AS REALITY

The Jacquinot Zone, as it came to be known, had its southern border formed by Fang Bang Road, completely crossing the old Chinese city; Min Guo Road, the former site of the old city wall, formed the northern boundary. French Concession boundaries formed the eastern and western borders of the zone. Barbed wire delimited the Fang Bang boundary, but elsewhere there were no barriers.[32] The International Committee issued a second decree repeating that two accords had been reached: one between the International Red Cross Committee and the Chinese authorities, and one with the Japanese authorities. It explained that the efforts that had led to the signing of two separate accords were motivated only by the humanitarian desires of the three parties.[33] "The area was to be kept free from the presence of armed forces, military establishments and acts of armed hostile activity."[34] It was to operate under Chinese civil administration, and Chinese police patrolling the zone were not permitted to carry any arms other than service revolvers and batons needed for the usual police business. The Chinese side considered the policing of the Zone to be a matter of sovereignty and insisted that it be the responsibility of the Chinese. Chinese sources claim that China's historic experiences with the imperial foreign powers in Shanghai regarding issues of territorial expansion made the Chinese authorities determined to ascertain clearly that establishing the Jacquinot Zone was not part of a French plan to extend the area of the French Concession southward. Furthermore, the Chinese also made sure that no other agreement was signed and that the Zone would go out of existence when the war ended.[35]

Surrounded by war, the Jacquinot Zone struggles to survive. *The Story of the Jacquinot Zone* (Shanghai, 1939).

The mayor of Shanghai gave a pledge in writing to free the area from military structures and operations, and Jacquinot's Refugee Supervisory Committee undertook to see that all pledges made were observed. As additional protection, Jacquinot added the condition that if any violent outbreak occurred in the area, making this kind of supervision unworkable, the committee was to inform both the Chinese and Japanese authorities, after which the committee would be absolved of its pledges of maintaining security and all guarantees of safety would be withdrawn. As an acknowledgment to the Chinese side, the committee also made clear that setting up this zone was not to be interpreted in any way as affecting the sovereign rights of the Chinese government, as demonstrated by the 200 Chinese police who would maintain the security of the zone.[36]

A steady stream of refugees that had previously sought shelter and safety in the International Settlement wound through the French Concession to the

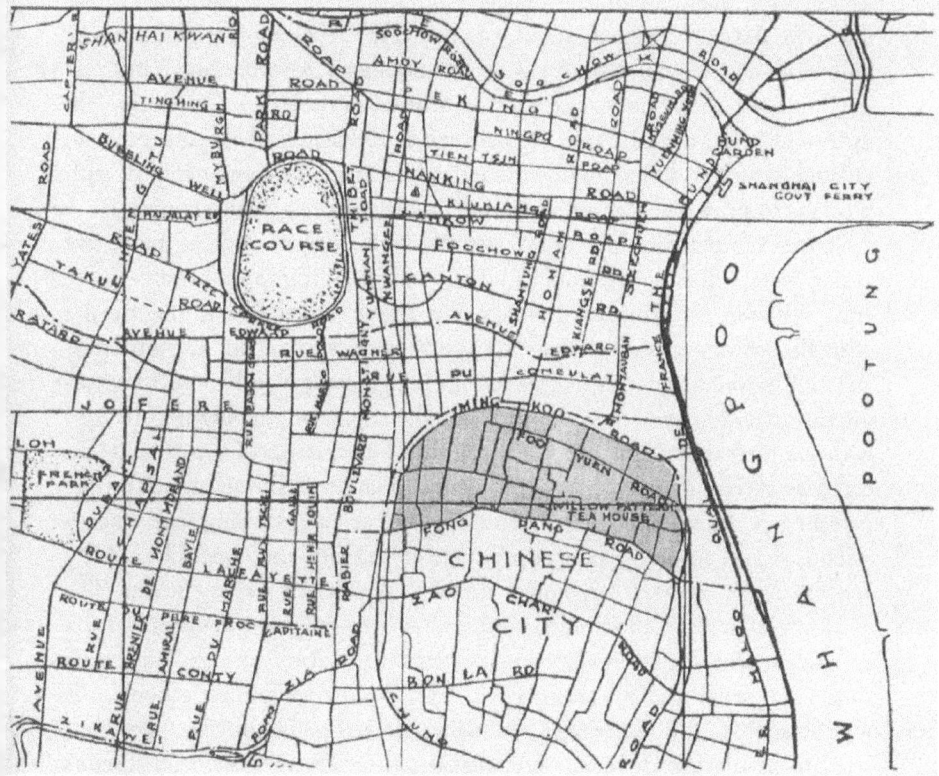

The tiny Jacquinot Zone within the city. *North China Daily News.*

new Safety Zone. Initially, in order to ensure necessary order in the Zone, the Refugee Committee added an additional level of security by engaging a small body of stateless White Russians with military training to support the Chinese police. Refugee status was familiar to these Russian police officers, who had themselves become refugees after the Bolshevik Revolution, fleeing to the open port of Shanghai. Many were former members of the White Army and Navy forces, including even some officers, so their skills were in demand in Shanghai. An inspector from the French police force worked discreetly with these Russian police. Besides keeping order within the huge refugee population, police also had to take into account the widespread existence of bandits and opium and gambling dens operating in the Zone, as they did elsewhere in Shanghai. Passes permitting entrance to the Zone were strictly limited to only those with legitimate business within the area, such as Red Cross workers, doctors, and members of the Refugee Committee, who also needed to have their own passes.[37] These passes, signed by Mayor Yu Hongjun, identified the individual and served as the basis for a preliminary registry containing personal information about the refugee population in the Zone. Oddly enough, the overall effect of the Zone's separate existence was that the area became an isolated island (*gudao*) alongside the isolated island of foreign Shanghai, with precious security like that offered in the privileged foreign concessions.

Jacquinot's presentations to the Japanese civilian authorities, as impressive as they were, still had to restrain and deal with the most important party to the crisis situation, the Japanese military. The International Committee faced a crisis almost immediately after the Nanshi Safety Zone opened. Just three days later, on November 11, fighting broke out in the larger Nanshi area, threatening the safety of the new Zone as well. In the course of ongoing negotiations with the International Committee about the future status of the Zone, General Matsui Iwane directed Japanese troops to launch a furious attack on the Nanshi area. Intense Japanese air bombing and artillery shelling took a heavy toll on life and property in the unprotected area around the Zone. The old city was full of old wooden structures, crowded together on narrow streets. The ensuing onslaught of bombings produced at least thirty deadly fires and destruction that ravaged large portions of Nanshi and also Pootung (Pudong).[38] One large fire lasted for twenty-two days, destroying homes, schools, the railway station, and factories in the Nanshi area. Thousands of refugees suffered from a lack of food or water that lasted for several days.[39] St. Joseph's Convent, run by the Little Sisters of the Poor, burned to the ground. In the midst of this chaos, terrified Zone refugees pushed up against the entrance to the French Concession hoping for protection. The gates opened for only five minutes, during which a huge swell of refugees pushed into the Concession. Immediately, the gates were closed again, barring any more refugees from gaining entrance. People inside the Concession in sympathy with the refugees' plight tossed food and water over the gate to the milling crowds below, who caught most of it in wide baskets and upside-down open umbrellas. Nearby, a large fire threatened to engulf the Zone, aided by wind from the south.[40] Some wooden structures did catch fire, but fortunately, these blazes were small enough to be quickly extinguished or contained. The question prominent in everyone's mind was, who would save the refugees now from the Japanese onslaught?[41]

Japanese batteries near western Xujiahui and St. John's University fired their howitzers located in the Jessfield Park area across the territory of the International Settlement, the French Concession, and the Jacquinot Safety

Refugees press against the closed gates of the French Concession. *The Story of the Jacquinot Zone* (Shanghai, 1939).

Zone, a distance of four miles, at their Chinese targets. Nanshi, the section of the Chinese city, south of the Zone, became the new major battleground, making refugees in the adjacent Zone again feel unsafe, even though both during the shelling and the frequent heavy aerial bombing, the Japanese spared the Zone serious damage and many casualties. Jacquinot remained in the Zone throughout all the attacks, overseeing things from his office base in the Catholic Cathedral. Clearly, he faced an enormous challenge in persuading the Japanese military to abide by his plan. In his entreaties to them, he repeatedly stressed the importance of having local foreign and Chinese support in maintaining order among the burgeoning civilian refugee population. He also pointed out the damaging press reporting that would surely accompany any new and extreme behavior by the Japanese military in heavily foreign and media precocious Shanghai.

Chinese troops, numbering about 5,000 and unequipped to handle the Japanese assault, attempted to escape the Japanese attack on Nanshi by fleeing into the French Concession. The French authorities agreed to take them in, but only after they surrendered their arms. Once inside the Concession, the French stripped them of their arms and placed the soldiers in a temporary holding area until secure housing could be readied for their internment. The next day, General Matsui, commander of the Central Japanese Area Army, occupied Nanshi, excluding the Jacquinot Zone. He told the foreign press that as "virtual master" of Shanghai, he felt free to take "any steps" dictated by military necessities, in the International Settlement as well as in the Chinese territories.[42] As early as November 1, he had declared that within ten days, there would be no Chinese soldiers remaining in the Shanghai region, which was to be encircled, and all communication with Nanjing cut.[43]

General Matsui called together the Japanese ambassador, Kawagoe, and the Japanese Navy commander, Admiral Hasegawa, for a meeting at military headquarters to discuss the Shanghai situation. Disagreement arose over two of the four points raised during the discussions. Matsui intended the Japanese military to occupy the Chinese banks, customs, and telegraph offices inside the International Settlement in order to weaken their economic influence and damage the Chinese economy. Furthermore, he proposed changing the British Defense Sector so that the left bank of Suzhou Creek would be given over to the Japanese forces and allow for the better movement and safety of Japanese military supplies on the creek. The ambassador and admiral countered with worries about the likely British response to these proposals and their possible negative effect on Japanese international relations. Matsui characterized their responses as "passive attitudes" and accused the two of not having the will to destroy the financial and administrative base of Shanghai and bring about the surrender of the Nanjing government. Instead, he complained, "they talk only about international relations."[44]

Japanese reports claim that during the three-day period of intense conflict in Nanshi, the Chinese administrative agencies, particularly the police, fled the Jacquinot Zone. Even Father Jacquinot found himself in serious danger when, on the way to deal with water supply problems in the Zone, the two policemen accompanying him were shot dead. The bullet meant for Jacquinot tore a hole in the hem of his cassock. In the meantime, nine carloads of police officers exited the Zone, the last one on November 13.[45]

This lack of security within the Zone required an urgent meeting between the Refugee Committee and the Japanese military to examine the new security situation. The outcome of the review was that the Japanese military would send a small number of military police to help supervise security in the zone.[46] Their orders were to patrol the Zone twice a day. The refugees hid inside their homes during their rounds. No doubt this Japanese policing was a bitter pill to swallow, but the security situation had to be addressed.

Certainly, the French also had a strong interest in bringing the situation in Nanshi under control. The French Waterworks, essential to a broad segment of Shanghai's population, and the docks on the French Bund, which received desperately needed supplies from abroad, were in danger of being destroyed. French officials were also feeling strong pressure from the Japanese regarding anti-Japanese activities in areas under their control or influence. General Matsui had downplayed earlier press reports that he had far-reaching plans for the foreign concessions, but made it clear that abstention from occupation did not imply indifference to what was taking place within the two settlements. On his instructions, Major General K. Harada informed both the French consul and SMC secretary-general that suppression of all forms of anti-Japanese activities must occur in the settlements to a degree satisfactory to the Japanese Army. Otherwise, it would be imperative to take the necessary action as required from a military perspective.[47]

At a meeting with the French naval commander, Vice Admiral Jules Le Bigot, and the French consul general, M. Baudez, General Matsui heard of their appreciation for his patronage of the Jacquinot Zone, which had brought some order to the general refugee crisis. Taking his turn, Matsui then requested French cooperation in permitting the Japanese military to pass through part of the French Concession near the Huangpu River embankment in order to allow for better communication between Japanese troops in Hongkou and those engaged in Nanshi. After all, the International Settlement authorities had already allowed the Japanese military to stage a victory parade through their concession territory. Matsui also asked the French authorities to terminate the fiscal operations of Chinese banks that were benefiting by their protected location within the Concession. The French argued in response that permitting armed military personnel to pass through the French Concession would be difficult to accept in light of French interests and existing treaty arrangements. And as for the banks, they were private, outside of French jurisdiction. Matsui rejoined that in that case, the Japanese would be forced to consider taking certain actions regarding French forces in Nanshi. Writing later that day in his diary, Matsui wrote: "In this way, I threatened them."[48] French troops subsequently took up protective positions in the Xujiahui village and at Jiaotong University, where there was a large refugee camp.[49] The Xujiahui Zone, under the leadership of the American Jesuit Father James Kearney, provided for more than 11,000 refugees. Housing was provided for 4,000 at St. Ignatius College. Fortunately for the French, Matsui would soon turn his attention to the Nanjing campaign.

By late November, the Jacquinot Zone housed 250,000 refugees, most having crowded in from other parts of Nanshi.[50] It is estimated that at least 100,000 of them were destitute. In addition to hunger and lack of shelter, at

A truckload of refugees enters the Jacquinot Zone. Archives de la Compagnie de Jésus, Québec.

night, certain areas just outside the Zone still experienced the fighting, so that flames from the burning neighborhoods could be clearly seen and heard by the refugees. To calm their nerves and boost morale, members of the Refugee Committee made a point to visit the Zone daily. Most of the Chinese who had lived in what became the Safety Zone had moved out in anticipation of Japanese attacks on the Chinese areas. Like the refugees fleeing from Zhabei and Hongkou, many of these fleeing from Nanshi had sought sanctuary in the International Settlement or the French Concession. The wave of refugees that came later took over their abandoned houses, filling every available space, living eight to ten together in rooms nine feet square. School buildings and guildhalls were turned into dormitories. The typical refugee daily diet consisted of bread and hard cake, twice a day. The Refugee Committee described the conditions for the most destitute as follows: "They live in the tiny rooms tucked away in the huddle of dark houses, a family together, with their bedding on the floor and virtually nothing else. In the same room is generally a sick man, sometimes two; the air has been unchanged for the past few months."[51]

VIOLENCE CONTINUES

Not everything developed smoothly within the Jacquinot Zone. The comparative security lasted until December 4, when Japanese troops entered the Zone after allegations surfaced that a Japanese soldier had been shot at on the boundary road between the Zone and the Japanese security perimeter along the conquered area of Nanshi. The Japanese response to this incident was to expand the security perimeter to envelop the area around the Jacquinot Zone and to initiate a door-to-door search within the Zone for the sniper. At the same time, a Japanese spokesman challenged the reason for the continued existence of the Jacquinot Zone, saying that most of the hostilities had now moved farther west in preparation for the move on Nanjing.[52] Since the fighting had died down, what was the purpose of the Zone?

During the house-to-house search, on December 16, a grenade was thrown at a Japanese sentry. Fortunately, it was a dud, but this was followed by a Chinese sniper attack on a Japanese sentry that resulted in injury. This time, the Japanese expanded their security perimeter into the Jacquinot Zone and expelled its existing security force.[53]

Jacquinot immediately initiated intense negotiations with Lieutenant Colonel Oka Yoshiro. His success at somehow placating the Japanese officer is demonstrated by the statement he issued following their meeting, in which he was able to deny that any shooting had taken place. Jacquinot also stated that the area still remained under the authority of the Refugee Committee, and that the Japanese troops "continued to live up to their side of the agreement by which the Zone came into existence."[54]

On December 16, Jacquinot continued lengthy negotiations with the Japanese over the future status of the Zone. He explained the remedial work of the various Zone committees and recounted his progress so far in meeting the many refugee needs, emphasizing his ability to keep them orderly and calm, housed and fed. After the talks, he stressed that he was "hopeful" that in spite of the presence of the Japanese troops in the Zone, its status would remain unchanged, and the Refugee Committee could continue its primary functions.[55] On December 19, the announcement came that a full agreement had been reached between Jacquinot and the Japanese authorities, under which the Zone would continue to be administered by the Refugee Committee, with "the Japanese giving full cooperation in policing and assisting in administration."[56] A Japanese spokesman praised Jacquinot for having "risked his life while supervising the carrying out of the agreement reached between the Committee and Japanese authorities."[57] What was left unsaid was that the Japanese, before their departure, had independently established a new security force to take over the policing of the Zone.[58]

Jacquinot was putting a good face on a very bad situation. This was revealed in a message from Nelson T. Johnson, U.S. ambassador to China, to the chief of the Far Eastern Division at the State Department, Stanley Hornbeck. Nelson reported that Jacquinot had made a short trip to the city of Songjiang (Sungkiang), just southwest of Shanghai, and that along the way, he had seen almost no Chinese alive and noted that desperately needed rice crops were untended and rotting in the fields. Furthermore, Jacquinot had told him that Japanese troops had entered the Zone to round up refugees, including women.[59] In his public statements regarding this, Jacquinot explained otherwise, saying only that "Japanese troops took charge of a number of refugees yesterday and removed them to the southern part of Nanshi presumably to be used as laborers."[60] In short, Jacquinot was confronted with managing a series of very difficult situations, some of which required uncomfortable compromises and even sacrifices, but his mission of providing credible security to the Zone refugees in his charge remained intact.

On December 22, a detachment of about 100 police officers from the new Japanese-sponsored Great Way [Da dong] Municipal Government Police Department came into the Zone to perform security duty.[61] With this development and the enlargement of the Japanese security perimeter, fears again flared up among the refugees. These only gradually subsided with new and intense efforts by the Refugee Committee to provide various kinds of refugee assistance to the now 300,000 refugees in the Zone.[62] Still other sources put the number of refugees at 360,000, in an area only one-third the size of the entire Nanshi district. [63] In the midst of the rising widespread fear and anxiety, Mayor Yu expressed the common sentiment of most Chinese in Shanghai: "All we have left of the Municipality of Greater Shanghai is Nanshi, but, even if we lose Nanshi, we still have our people and their spirit of resistance, which will last forever."[64]

Monetary support for the new refugee Zone began to come in from a variety of sources. The Chinese government, through Mayor Yu, gave Jacquinot 50,000 yuan to support his refugee work.[65] Even the Japanese military leadership became involved in the funding, in pursuit of its own agenda. Displaying Japanese gratitude for the order and high degree of organization achieved by Jacquinot and the Refugee Committee within the Zone, the Japanese Commander Matsui provided Jacquinot's committee with 10,000 yen.[66] On No-

NANTAO'S GOOD SAMARITAN

BY SAPAJOU

Father Jacquinot as "good Samaritan." *The Story of the Jacquinot Zone* (Shanghai, 1939).

vember 16, Jacquinot met with Admiral Hasegawa aboard the flagship *Idzumo* to express his appreciation for the Japanese assistance in setting up the Zone, whereupon the admiral praised Jacquinot's "good works" and also contributed 10,000 yen to his continued refugee relief efforts.[67]

PRAISE

Praise for Jacquinot and his refugee work came from several quarters. The Japanese minister of foreign affairs, Hirota Kōki, congratulated Jacquinot, stating:

Thanks to your courageous intervention between the Chinese and Japanese authorities, in complete disregard of the greatest dangers, a refugee zone was established at Nanshi, at the time when our forces dislodged Chinese troops, thus sparing from the worst fate about 100,000 peaceful and innocent Chinese inhabitants. I wish particularly to convey to you the sentiments of admiration and respect of the Japanese nation towards your humanitarian task, which was accomplished in a spirit of complete service and sacrifice. I sincerely wish you good health, and the continuation of your beneficial action. I beg you to accept the expression of my highest respect.[68]

Shortly thereafter, the local Japanese Army organ, *Tairiku shimpo*, awarded Jacquinot its first annual prize for his humanitarian work, along with 1,000 yen in prize money. The prize included also a silver plaque showing two female figures symbolizing "Sino-Japanese friendship."

President Chiang Kai-shek expressed his admiration and praise of Father Jacquinot's work and service with the following comments: "Our brothers . . . having neither a piece of tile to shelter themselves nor a peck of grain . . . were brought through cold and hunger to a state of approaching death . . . they owed their lives to the philanthropic and unceasing valuable efforts of your good self. . . . They numbered more than 200,000."[69] Later, Jacquinot received the Medal of the Order of the Jade from the Chinese government in recognition of his services to the Chinese community and humanitarian endeavors.

The commander in chief of the French Naval Forces, Vice Admiral Le Bigot, who had praised Jacquinot for his long and difficult negotiations with the Japanese, had this to say: "Father Jacquinot has found a formula, which is good not only in Shanghai, not only for Nanking, but for the entire world. In this 'treaty,' there are no losers, the adversaries, and the spectators, China and Japan, the Concessions and Humanity gain all, and all win."[70] The French ambassador to China, Paul-Emile Naggiar, said in a letter to Father Jacquinot:

Those who have encouraged your efforts have seen you striving against the horrors of war with the firm patience and courage to which the Refugee Jacquinot Zone owes its existence. Due to your efforts more than a hundred thousand innocent lives have been saved on the borders of the French Concession . . . an admirable project which is to your credit as a Christian, a Priest, and a Frenchman.[71]

Ambassador Naggiar also played a key role in Jacquinot's receiving the Croix de chevalier de la Légion d'honneur for his Shanghai work, stating that he had accomplished a "most conspicuous task or action enhancing the prestige of France."[72]

Finally, some of the heartiest praise came from the local American and British commanders, who no doubt were very glad of any measures that might lead to a more stable atmosphere in Shanghai on their watch. Admiral H. E. Yarnell, from the U.S. flagship, *Augusta,* said of Father Jacquinot: "Your own efforts in securing a neutral zone where over 200,000 people were fed and housed under your direction mark an achievement that will be known to future generations as one of the greatest cases of relief work in recorded history."[73] The British commander, Major-General A. D. Telfer-Smollett, in his letter to Father Jacquinot, said:

> In November when I visited the Jacquinot Zone in Nanshi . . . I found thousands of refugees . . . being cared for under your guidance. I was profoundly impressed by your wonderful work. You have shown the world what can be done in the way of a safety zone for non-combatants in times of war and I am convinced that in the future, the excellent example you have set will be followed.[74]

There were also social events celebrating Jacquinot's remarkable success. Ambassador Naggiar hosted a luncheon in Jacquinot's honor on January 29 and invited eighteen guests, including the French consul general, M. Baudez; Lt. Colonel L. Peretier; the headmaster of the French Collège municipale, M. Grosbois; and Commandant Fabre. Still another luncheon hosted by Ambassador Naggiar took place at the French Club, with fifty guests. Jacquinot was the guest of honor along with members of the Relief Committee. Dr. W. W. Yen, chairman of the Chinese Red Cross, was an honored guest. In his speech during the festivities, Jacquinot graciously gave credit to the "French authorities" for maintaining order in the Nanshi Zone.[75]

There is no doubt that Jacquinot had made excellent connections within the foreign communities during his long career as parish priest, professor, and spiritual advisor. It is safe to assume that he was trusted as a neutral party, without any political agenda. His involvement in many earlier humanitarian endeavors was so apparent that it became a solid foundation for trust among all the parties to the series of crises. In the Chinese community, his work in flood relief and in rescuing those in danger during earlier emergencies gave him a favorable reputation and convinced them that he could successfully address the formidable tasks to be faced during the 1937 emergency. Certainly, his language skills were crucial to his negotiations during the crisis, enabling him to understand the full extent and content of the discussions and to know both what information to provide and what to hold back.

There is the inevitable question of whether Father Jacquinot might be viewed as a collaborator with the Japanese authorities in Shanghai. Of course, France and Japan were not at war during the time he served in Shanghai, so that the term "collaborator" really does not apply. Jacquinot's neutral status as a foreign national appealed to both the Japanese and the Chinese. The Japanese needed to find competent leaders to help them deal effectively with the uprooted civilian population, and Jacquinot's record of service to refugees in China enhanced his suitability for this role. As far as the Chinese authorities were concerned, they could not but be thankful that the agreements ameliorating the lot of the refugees were made through Jacquinot, and not directly with the hated Japanese. Jacquinot's own primary commitment was to protect the refugees, and more than once, he accommodated Japanese demands in order to achieve this goal. A pragmatist, he believed that there was no other way to get the job done.[76]

With the establishment of the Shanghai Jacquinot Zone, a precedent now existed for the protection of noncombatants in time of war. Jacquinot's ambitious plans did not stop at Shanghai. He was so convinced of the need and utility of his zone concept that he decided to apply this refugee organizational experience wherever he could gain official acceptance. He repeatedly stated his vow to create safety zones in all Chinese cities, "wherever the Japanese invaded."[77] As we have seen, similar efforts were going on in Spain at this time.[78] Jacquinot suggested that his Zone might be a useful example, saying: "I am fully aware of the fact that such an arrangement [the Jacquinot Zone] is original, but would it be vain to express hope that it might, with advantage, be copied elsewhere, for instance in Europe[?]"[79] In the next chapter, we shall see that the Jacquinot model was indeed copied, albeit with uneven success, in other parts of China.

CHAPTER FIVE

The Jacquinot Zone Copied

This is not war but merely an incident; foreign nations
are spellbound by Japan.
—Madame Chiang Kai-shek

Word of Father Jacquinot's success with the Safety Zone in Shanghai spread
quickly to other areas—just ahead of the advancing Japanese armies, it seems.
Nanjing (Nanking) was the next city to seek to adopt Jacquinot's idea, followed by Hankou (Wuhan). Then Canton explored the idea, as did Hangzhou, Zhangzhou, Shenzhen, and Ouchang. Conditions were different in
each of these places, as was the level of understanding of how to set up a safe
zone. These and other factors led to differing outcomes, but there is no question that working with Jacquinot's ideas resulted in saving many lives, and
a measure of protection and relief to countless others. This chapter will attempt to describe the safe zones of other areas. Because of a dearth of material,
and the broad scope of any research effort needed to adequately illuminate
some key features, coverage cannot be equally thorough for all places. Rather,
the intention is to broaden and deepen understanding of Father Jacquinot's
unique contributions to the protection of civilian refugees, which extended
far beyond Shanghai.

THE NANJING SAFETY ZONE UNAPPROVED

Nanjing, China's capital city in 1937, has received voluminous reporting
and scholarly research, particularly focused on what is commonly referred to
as the Nanjing Massacre. Books, articles, tracts, memoirs from those on the
scene, postwar trial records prepared in both China and Japan, conferences,
and conference proceedings, films, and even museums all attempt to illuminate the essence or root causes and meaning of this horrific event.[1] The city
had become a primary target, if not the primary target, when the Japanese

forces launched a new stage of their undeclared war with China, beginning with the attack on Shanghai. The city of Nanjing suffered sixty-five aerial bombing raids beginning as early as August 15 and before October 15, 1937; many more followed in December.[2] A map, discovered as early as July in the jacket of a crashed Japanese pilot, noting strategic bomb sites in the city, convinced some that Nanjing had always been the primary target of the Japanese. Adding to the mix of suspicion and fear were *Asahi shimbun* newsreels showing the landing of Japanese troops at Hangzhou Bay. These troops, under the command of General Matsui, are heard to yell: "On to Nanking," even though their immediate mission and destination was Shanghai.[3] In reports to Washington from Nanjing, U.S. Ambassador Nelson T. Johnson said he was convinced that the Japanese believed that once they took the Chinese capital, they would be able to dictate peace terms to the Chinese government.[4]

With the ominous events in Shanghai, and as the bombing grew heavier with each passing day, wealthy Chinese departed Nanjing for Hankou with their families and valuables. Soon, middle-class professionals joined their ranks, leaving only defenseless poor civilians and the Chinese military. John Rabe, the representative in Nanjing of the German engineering company Siemens AG China, was one who chose to stay behind in the service of the resident Chinese and, especially, his trusted Siemens staff. At fifty-five, he had already served twenty-nine years in China, which meant that it was really home to him. As an international businessman, he was fluent in English and French in addition to his native German. He did not know Chinese and relied instead on conversing with the Chinese in Pidgin English like most of the fabled "Old China Hands." He was described as well liked, a simple man, practical in demeanor and with only a moderate interest in politics. He handled his position in the Nazi Party, as number two man to Legation Councilor Lautenschlager, with some modesty, except when it proved useful later on to impress Japanese soldiers. On one occasion, as the story goes, Rabe, seeing a Japanese soldier about to rape a Chinese woman, roared at him in German, and holding his swastika armband to his face, threw him out the door.[5] He had little real knowledge of what had transpired in Germany since his last brief visit in 1930 and had little opportunity in China to learn about events there. His attitude to and views on the Japanese are said to have been rather negative, making his approach notably different from that of Jacquinot, who, while entirely apolitical, was always willing to work amicably with the Japanese, as long as it benefited his refugee mission. However, Rabe seems to have shared many attributes with Jacquinot, among them congeniality, a sense of humor, humanity, and courage.

Rabe left a diary recording many of his experiences in Nanjing, which has become a valuable primary source on events there. Rabe's November 17, 1937, entry records his observations on the departure of the Chinese government from the capital, using every available means of transport.[6] Three days later, the Chinese government announced officially that it was moving to Chongqing, thus leaving the city without a functioning administrative structure.[7] In addition, the heads of many diplomatic missions and members of their staffs also reported their intentions to move to Hankou. The American ambassador, together with certain members of his staff and all U.S. citizens who wished to leave Nanjing, departed on November 23 for Hankou aboard the USS *Luzon*, the flagship of the Yangzi River flotilla.[8] With the eventual departure of most of the foreign community, as well as the legitimate Chinese government, what remained in their place, at least providing relief and some limited amount of protection for the Chinese community, was a kind of quasi-governmental structure known as the Nanjing International Safety Zone.

The Shanghai Jacquinot Zone was up and running by this time, and word of its success had spread to Nanjing. W. Plummer Mills, the American head of the Presbyterian Mission in China, had been impressed by what he heard of Father Jacquinot's work in Shanghai with the Refugee Supervisory Committee and the Zone, and he recommended to his colleagues in Nanjing that they attempt to establish a similar body there.[9] An International Committee was established by November 19, made up mainly of missionaries, including American doctors from Kulou Hospital, professors from Nanjing University, and prominent local foreign business representatives.[10] At a committee meeting just three days later, Rabe was elected chairman of the new committee and spent the evening drafting a telegram to the Japanese ambassador explaining the committee's existence and its purpose. In language closely resembling that submitted for similar purposes by Jacquinot in Shanghai, the telegram read in part:

> The International Committee will undertake to secure from the Chinese authorities specific guarantees that the proposed "Safety Zone" will be made and kept free from military establishments and offices, including those of communications; from the presence of armed men other than civilian police with pistols; and from the passage of soldiers or military officers in any capacity. The International Committee would inspect and observe the Safety Zone to see that these undertakings are satisfactorily carried out.[11]

In addition, the International Committee asked their mentor, Jacquinot, to contact the Japanese ambassador and request permission to establish a Nanjing Safety Zone, hoping that his influence would be decisive in winning Japanese official support.[12]

The committee next outlined the boundaries of the proposed new Zone, which would include, in its area in the western part of the city, Nanjing University, Ginling Women's Arts and Science College, the U.S. Embassy, Rabe's own home, the German Embassy, the Nanjing International Club, and the Japanese Embassy. It would occupy an area of about two square miles, or 12.5 percent of the city, and include the following specific road boundaries: on the eastern border, Zhong Shan Road, to the west was Xikang Street, and on the south and southeast, Hanchung Road. Red Cross flags were to be used to mark the specified boundaries, as in the Jacquinot Zone in Shanghai.

Although appropriately formal, Rabe's telegram had a less amicable tone than Jacquinot's correspondence with the Japanese authorities. It ended with a strong plea for a "prompt reply." Of course, Rabe and the others were not on familiar terms with the Japanese authorities, certainly not with the Japanese ambassador in Shanghai. And as time wore on, Rabe became quite frustrated with his Japanese contacts and was often impatient and rather sharp in his official dealings with them.

The Japanese authorities responded on November 24, saying that they regarded the proposed zone in Nanjing as entirely different from the one in Shanghai.[13] First, Nanjing was the Chinese capital and, as such, the center of military planning. At the local level, while they were still studying the proposal, the Zone as proposed included Drum Tower Hill, which was mounted with Chinese anti-aircraft guns. They also charged that one of the Zone's borders was Zhong Shan Road, the likely passage of Chinese troops along which could not be tolerated. And most objectionable of all, the existence of a Zone would only hamper the Japanese drive on Nanjing. This was, in effect, equivalent to saying no to the proposal. The Chinese authorities, not surprisingly, strongly supported an International Safety Zone Committee in Nanjing.

Thinking to further bolster his case, Rabe took the unusual step of writing a personal telegraph to Adolf Hitler, sending it through the German Consulate in Shanghai and asking the Führer to intercede with the Japanese government to grant permission for the creation of a neutral zone for noncombatants. This somewhat naïve appeal produced no response from Berlin, and, in a state of anxiety, Rabe sent a second telegram to Tokyo on November 28 looking for a positive reply. Finally, it was left to Jacquinot to inform Rabe and his committee by telegram that the "Japanese authorities have duly noted the request for a safety zone in Nanking, but regret that they cannot grant it."[14] The Japanese added that they would respect the area if it were militarily justifiable. Clearly disappointed, Rabe replied that he would continue to wait for an official response directly from the Japanese authorities to him and the Nanjing International Safety Zone Committee.

Rabe lacked Jacquinot's close proximity and long-standing relationship with local authorities, both Japanese and foreign, military and civilian. He was, after all, a businessman whose main job was representing the Siemens China Company. When he did make contact for the benefit of the committee and refugees, he had to go through a circuitous route that often involved officials of the U.S. Embassy, located aboard the USS *Panay*, anchored in the river, during much of the crisis, who queried Japanese officials in Tokyo or Shanghai by military radio. Even mail deliveries depended on when the next gunboat had a scheduled sailing for Shanghai, and official dispatches were often forwarded by foreign news services. It was a very different community from cosmopolitan Shanghai.

Jacquinot, on the other hand, had frequent personal contacts with Chinese, French, American, British, and Japanese officials, civilian, diplomatic, and military, to assist him in dealing with the refugee and relief crises. As already noted, his credibility as a negotiator during this sensitive period was further enhanced in that inasmuch as he was a priest and not a government official, the Japanese viewed Jacquinot as a "benevolent third party" and not a representative of a rival "third power."[15] With a large foreign press establishment in Shanghai reporting on the war, and the existence of two large foreign concessions with primary concern for the lives and property of their inhabitants, Jacquinot's prospects for success were no doubt greatly enhanced. Nevertheless, the Jacquinot Zone was situated outside the protected "extraterritorial settlements" and surrounded on three sides by the devastated Chinese territory in Nantao, an area still wracked by Japanese aggression. It would not be fair or accurate to say that Jacquinot faced lesser challenges in his work of protecting the Chinese refugee community.

The Japanese authorities were willing to say to the Nanjing International Committee largely what they had said in Shanghai: that as long as the proposed zone did not harbor any Chinese military troops, weapons, or military facilities, it would not be attacked. The Japanese military would endeavor to respect the specified district as long as doing so was consistent with military necessity.[16] With three columns of Japanese troops advancing toward Nanjing and 50,000 Chinese troops pledged to defend the capital city "to the last," this was indeed a tall order for the Nanjing Committee to fill. Chiang Kai-shek had ordered his generals to "defend the established lines at any cost."[17]

On December 1, the mayor of Nanjing, Ma Chaojun, turned over the administrative responsibilities for the Zone to the International Committee and provided it with 450 Chinese policemen to provide security, as well as 2,000 tons of rice, 10,000 bags of flour, and a substantial amount of money.[18] The establishment of more than twenty refugee camps followed, as more and more refugees streamed into the Zone area, which eventually housed more than 200,000 refugees. The International Committee asked the Chinese military to remove all military personnel and fortifications from the Zone, including three trenches already being dug in the southwest portion of the Zone, which was done.[19] To aid in their work, the International Committee welcomed the close cooperation of the newly established Nanjing Chapter of the International Red Cross, seven of whose members also served on the International Committee.

But the situation continued to worsen. On the morning of December 1, the U.S. Embassy staff held a meeting to explain to the remaining American citizens in the city the plans for evacuating them. Rabe was invited to leave with the Americans but chose instead to stay, as did the other members of the International Committee. As one of his German colleagues noted, Rabe did not remain in Nanjing for business reasons, but in order to establish a Nanjing zone of refuge for the 200,000 noncombatants, similar to that created by "Pater Jacquinot" in Shanghai.[20] With the foreign departures, the community was reduced to just twenty-seven, including eighteen Americans, five Germans, one British, one Austrian, and two (White) Russians. For purposes of comparison, the resident foreign population in Shanghai was 33,410 in the International Settlement and 10,377 in the French Concession.[21] The Japanese military considered the fact that there were so few foreigners in Nanjing another reason for a forceful attack.

This same German friend of Rabe's doubted the viability of the Nanjing International Safety Zone, because it lacked, in his view, the authority to prevent either Chinese or Japanese soldiers from entering the Zone. His doubts proved to be well founded. In early December, the Chinese military commander in Nanjing, Tang Shengzhi, ordered the entire outside circumference of the city walls be cleared by fire for the purpose of creating a battle zone outside the city. While this allowed certain temporary advantages for the Chinese forces, it also meant that when the Japanese forces arrived, there was no place for them except inside the city walls. Furthermore, the Japanese advanced toward Nanjing so quickly (11 kilometers a day) that they outran their supply lines, meaning that when they arrived in Nanjing, they would need to forage within the city for basics such as food and water. These factors alone would create and inflame an already dangerous situation in this city lacking a government and an effective military force, and occupying what many considered a strategically indefensible site at a bend in the Yangzi River.

On December 7, President and Madame Chiang Kai-shek left Nanjing by airplane for Nanchang, entrusting the protection of the Chinese capital to General Tang. The German ambassador, Dr. Oskar Trautmann, agreed to act as mediator for Chiang Kai-shek with the Japanese, even though he was not optimistic about Japanese willingness to negotiate. The Japanese military considered the terrain of Nanjing and the defense works constructed by the Chinese as having turned the city into one huge fortress. They claimed it was a contradiction in terms that a safety zone should exist in such an area. After the Shanghai Japanese consul general, Okamoto Suemasa, called for the evacuation of all foreigners from Nanjing, Trautmann warned that those who went to the Safety Zone in Nanking did so at their own risk.[22] The next day, the American Embassy evacuated all the remaining staff to the USS *Panay*, where temporary offices were established.[23]

On December 9, the Japanese began their attack on Nanjing with unceasing aerial and artillery bombardment and armored forces. As ordered, Chinese soldiers met the attackers with courage and stamina. But by evening, after a very bloody day of fighting, it was clear how the battle would go. On the next day, Japanese airplanes dropped tons of leaflets with a message from General Matsui to General Tang demanding that the Chinese surrender by noon the next day or "Nanjing cannot but witness the horrors of war, with the attendant destruction of age-old cultural relics." He stressed that those innocent civilians who complied with this order would be treated with mercy, as would "all non-hostile soldiers."[24]

Minnie Vautrin, an American missionary and dean of studies at Ginling College, witnessed the events that followed in the attempt to avert the looming crisis. General Tang received a proposal from the International Committee for arrangements to be made for a three-day truce during which the Japanese would hold their position while the Chinese forces retreated from the city. Rabe also presented the proposal to the American officials aboard the *Panay*, with the request that they contact the Japanese military to arrange the truce and to inform them of the existence of the "Safety Zone" in Nanjing. In the meantime, General Tang sent a radio message to Chiang Kai-shek in Hankou, asking for his approval of the truce proposal, which Chiang, holding to his original policy of all-out defense and no negotiations, immediately rejected. When no Chinese representative appeared the next day to respond to the Japanese demands for surrender, General Matsui gave the order for an all-out attack on Nanjing. Alarmed and anxious, members of the International Committee went on board the *Panay* and requested still another attempt to arrange a truce with the Japanese. The next day, *Panay* left, sailing upstream on the Yangzi, thus ending any contact through the U.S. diplomats.[25]

THE NANJING MASSACRE

Recognizing that the city was about to fall, General Tang sent a telegram to Chiang Kai-shek, reporting on the perilous situation. The city was now without water or electricity, and night was approaching. Chiang responded with an order to retreat "at an appropriate time." Then, apparently upon further consideration of the reported desperate situation, he sent another telegram ordering Tang to organize a retreat. Tang tried one more time to effect a truce. Two committee members agreed to carry a white flag and proceed to the front to negotiate this time directly with the Japanese military, but it was already too late. After meeting with his officers and issuing the order for the troops to retreat, Tang fled the city that evening. When the news spread of his departure, chaos and a state of panic seized the city. The following describes the scene at this time written by an eyewitness to the events:

> There was panic as they made for the gate to Hsiakwan (Xiaguan) and the river. The road for miles was strewn with equipment they cast away—rifles, ammunition, belts,—everything in the way of army impediments. Trucks and cars jammed the roads, were overturned, caught fire; at the gate, more cars were burned—a terrible holocaust,—and the dead lay feet deep. The gate blocked, terror-mad soldiers scaled the wall and let themselves down on the other side with ropes, puttees and belts tied together, clothing torn to strips. Many fell and were killed. But at the river was perhaps the most appalling scene of all. A fleet of junks was there. It was totally inadequate for the horde that was now in a frenzy to cross to the north side. The overcrowded junks capsized, then sank; thousands drowned.[26]

In the early hours of December 13, Japanese forces entered the city under the command of Lieutenant General Prince Asaka Yasuhito, son-in-law of the late Meiji Emperor, grandfather of the reigning emperor, Hirohito. The troops met with little resistance from Chinese forces, most of whom were fleeing or had already disappeared into the civilian population and International Safe Zone. There was no government or even military leadership in the city to negotiate with, although it is doubtful that any negotiations were intended. The Japanese troops still had a vivid memory of the bloody Shanghai campaign, which had claimed the lives of 9,115 of their comrades, as well as 31,257 wounded.[27] Logistics had been poorly planned, so that the troops had not been well supplied with food and water en route and had even received orders to depend on provisions available locally. This obviously carried the intention that the troops should reward themselves by looting and pillaging, which they did no holds barred. Gangs of roving Japanese soldiers entered shops, homes, and buildings where they looted at will and repeatedly raped the women they encountered, brutally killing any husband or child who might protest. Often they killed the woman as well when they had finished with her, or passed her on to others for repeated rape. John Rabe would report to the War Crimes Trial that no fewer than 20,000 cases of rape occurred during the first month of Japanese occupation of Nanjing. This number may well be conservative in light of the likely reticence of family members to report cases.

The International Committee reported 425 cases of looting, theft, rape, and murder to the Japanese authorities.[28] These were ones about which they knew enough and could provide some details. Any examination of the record reveals that the murderous behavior of the Japanese troops included appalling savagery. Any original reasons for the fighting quickly became obscured by the random violence. One observer equated what he heard and saw to the brutality of Attila and the Huns, with the raping of children and cold-blooded slaughter of civilians. He noted one drunken Japanese soldier who, unable to obtain the women and drink he demanded, shot and killed three Chinese elderly women and wounded several others. Photographs of the atrocities and accounts from traumatized women have been made available in several works and illuminate how humans apparently can harden themselves to barbarism and go through strange mental and physical transformations.[29] Given the failure of their officers to restrain the Japanese troops who were out of control and prevent atrocities, the events in Nanjing became a paroxysm of sadism and anguish.

An immediate problem for Rabe and the others on the International Committee and International Red Cross Committee once the Japanese occupied Nanjing was that so many Chinese soldiers had melted into the civilian population, including in the International Safe Zone. They had discarded their weapons and exchanged their uniforms for regular clothing to disguise their identity. In the days and weeks that followed, many insisted on being taken into the Zone for protection. The Japanese Embassy claimed that as many as 20,000 Chinese soldiers in plain clothes were hiding in Nanjing, many in the Safe Zone.[30] In a letter to the Japanese commander on December 14, Rabe naïvely reported that some trapped soldiers had pleaded to be taken in, and that he had agreed to allow them protection once they were disarmed.[31] Rabe was, of course, relying on the promise made earlier by General Matsui that the Japanese would not punish Chinese troops who did not threaten them or harbor resistance. Rabe and the committee learned quickly that there was no protection for unarmed soldiers in the Zone, and that for others, especially women, there was only a limited amount of safety provided, if any. Japanese soldiers entered the Zone in search of former Chinese soldiers. Their method of identifying soldiers was to gather all the able-bodied males together for inspection. They examined the skin on their foreheads for any telltale marks that might suggest a helmet had once been worn; their shoulders for calluses from carrying heavy equipment; and their hands for calluses from carrying a gun. Those who failed the test were tied together in groups and transported out to the edge of the city, where, after digging a trench, they were machine-gunned and bayoneted in large numbers.[32] The American news correspondent for the *New York Times,* who was an eyewitness to the Japanese taking of Nanjing, later estimated Chinese military casualties at 33,000, a figure that included 20,000 who were executed by the Japanese.[33]

Chinese troops similarly trapped in Shanghai's Nantao were more fortunate owing largely to the different local circumstances. As we have seen, the 4,000 Chinese soldiers who had not been able to retreat with their units and became trapped in Nantao were able to flee into the French Concession for protection, where they were summarily disarmed and interned. The most the Japanese authorities could do about this asylum was to complain loudly to the French police and French consul. And with this possible avenue of refuge available to Chinese soldiers, Father Jacquinot could more easily maintain a very strict policy of denying the soldiers access to the Jacquinot Zone. This meant he was able to avoid the prospects of mass killings of former soldiers that occurred so frequently in Nanjing.

Civilians in Nanjing also trusted the Japanese promises of generosity and kind treatment, at least at first. Dr. Robert Wilson, one of the three American doctors in Nanjing and the only surgeon on the scene to care for the wounded after the Japanese conquered the city, reported:

> This afternoon I put a cast on a lovely little girl of 13. When the Japanese came to the city on the 13th, she and her father and mother were standing at the entrance of their dugout watching them approach. A soldier stepped up, bayoneted the father, shot the mother and slashed open the elbow of the little girl giving her a compound fracture. She has no relatives and was not brought to the hospital for a week. She is already wondering what to do when she has to leave. Both the father and mother were killed.[34]

In sharp contrast, the Jacquinot Zone had no reported civilian casualties or bombings after its establishment and for its three-year duration.

There have been many different estimates of the number of people killed in Nanjing. The count is determined by the quantity and quality of the available data and the vantage point, political leanings, or patriotic feelings of the one making the estimate. Rabe offered the low figure of 50,000–60,000, but this excluded the military fatalities and the many killings beyond his knowledge or viewing. The 1985 Massacre Memorial to the Nanjing victims has the figure 300,000 inscribed on its façade. Nanjing University researchers, working with those from the famous Second Historical Archives in Nanjing, further researched the issue and put the number at 340,000.[35] The postwar Tokyo war crimes trial insisted that the number of civilians and prisoners of war indiscriminately killed during the first six weeks of the Japanese occupation was over 200,000.[36]

In contrast to all of these estimates, Japanese revisionists have argued that the Nanjing Massacre is nothing but a historical fabrication, just as some have denied the existence of the European Holocaust. Others claim that the number killed was very small, with one account putting the figure at just 47 civilians killed by Japanese soldiers.[37] Whatever the "correct" number, and many scholars and researchers seem to accept the figure produced at the Tokyo Trial, there can be no question that the Nanjing Massacre of 1937–38 was a horrific event.[38]

In the circumstances, it is perhaps not surprising that the Nanjing Safe Zone was short-lived. Of course, the Japanese had never approved of its existence from the start. The first step in its demise was the announcement by the Japanese military attaché, Fukuda Tokuyasa, that in the future, all refugee and relief business, including the key responsibility for provisioning the refugees with food, was to be handled through the new Self-Government Committee, or Autonomous Government, established on January 1.[39] Having lost its key function, the International Committee received orders to transfer all of its administrative power, cash, and provisions to this Japanese-controlled new body. Next was the required registration of all civilians with the Japanese military authorities by February 4, 1938, after which time they were to leave the Safe Zone and return to their homes. The final blow came on January 28, when the Japanese military ordered all the refugee camps closed.

Even into March, there was still no respite from the rape and killing by Japanese soldiers. Given these circumstances, and still hoping to exert some influence, the International Committee decided to change its name to the Nanjing Relief Committee. Rabe hoped to make clear that the committee, with no administrative authority, still could play a key role in provisioning, especially if the Japanese military could establish security in the city. The name change occurred on February 18 and was followed by a farewell party for John Rabe who in the meantime had been ordered by his company to return to

Germany. Rabe left Nanjing on February 23 after being honored by Chinese and other foreigners for his courageous service in protection of the Chinese community and his leadership of the International Committee.

With the name change and growing Japanese resentment over its continued existence, the Safety Zone ceased to exist, and most of the twenty-five refugee camps were finally closed.[40] The Ginling camp and five other small camps lasted until May 31, 1938. Capping the Japanese conquest of the Chinese capital, a Japanese puppet government, styled the Reformed Government of the Republic of China, was launched at Nanjing on March 28, 1938, under President Liang Hongzhi, amid a flurry of Japanese and five-colored Chinese flags. All authority and services were now firmly in the hands of the Japanese and their puppet organizations.

After the end of World War II, the International Military Tribunal for the Far East (IMTFE), convened in Tokyo, found General Matsui guilty on the last of the many counts brought against him, count 55. The charge read that as a responsible government official, he and others had "recklessly disregarded their legal duty by virtue of their offices to take adequate steps to secure the observance and prevent breaches of the laws and customs of war."[41] Matsui was subsequently condemned and executed. Another key figure in this story, the Japanese Foreign Minister Hirota Kōki, was found guilty of omission under the same count and likewise condemned and executed. To this day, contemporary Japanese foreign ministers' repeated visits to the cemetery containing the Yasukuni Shrine honoring the 2.6 million Japanese war dead, which includes the remains of the executed war criminals, is an issue that evokes continued tension between China and Japan. The Chinese identify the shrine visits and the favorably revised historical accounts of the 1937 Nanjing events appearing in some Japanese school textbooks as major irritants in their ongoing dealings with Japan.

Of course, many Japanese are aware of the catastrophe that played out in Nanjing. One good example of this thinking is contained in a prominent Japanese biography of Foreign Minister Hirota, which makes the key point that "the moral compass had been lost by the Japanese military, causing the Japanese to go below a humanistic standard. That was the primary cause of what happened at Nanjing."[42] What was the moral compass? To some, it was General Matsui. To others, the circumstances were too complicated to settle on one cause.

THE HANKOU APPROVED SAFE ZONE

Along with Hanyang and Wuchang, Hankou is one of three cities that straddle the middle Yangzi River in what is known today as Wuhan. Together, they make up a major commercial transshipment center on the river. Hankou, the governmental center of the three Wuhan cities, became the new focus of Father Jacquinot's efforts to establish another safe zone for Chinese refugees.[43]

In November 1937, as Nanking was about to fall, most Chinese government offices moved to Hankou and Chongqing, with the exceptions of the Customs, the Post Office, and the Special District Court.[44] The Foreign Affairs Bureau and Ministries of Health and Finance set up their offices in Hankou, while the Ministry of Communications went on to Changsha. Other principal organs of government, the Judicial, Examination, and Control Yuans, began their lengthy move to a more protected and permanent residence at Chongqing in western China. In the interim, Hankou would serve as the Chinese capital until the consolidation of the various government bodies could take place at Chongqing.

In a bewildering array of political developments, the Japanese, as noted above, had set up the new Reformed Government of the Republic of China at Nanjing. This body was in addition to the Chinese Provisional Government established earlier in Peking, led by Wang Kemin. So when these two pro-Japanese regimes are added to Chiang Kai-shek's National Government at Hankou and the key Chinese government agencies that had moved to Chongqing, China's confused political scene in early 1938 included at least four governments. And in the midst of these jerry-rigged political developments, the war continued unabated. The Japanese, while reiterating their intention to conduct no negotiations and have no dealings with Chiang Kai-shek, pushed on to their next military objective, Wuhan, where they expected to overcome all organized Chinese resistance once and for all and reduce China's national government to the state of an insignificant local regime.

The Wuhan cities came under severe attack as early as September, when Japanese airplanes launched a daytime raid aimed at destroying the Hanyang Arsenal. The target remained undamaged, but 700 Chinese lost their lives. More raids followed sporadically, taking an enormous toll on the cities and their facilities, with serious loss of life. The refugee throngs, made up of peasants, workers, merchants, students, and teachers raised the population of Wuhan from 1 million to 1.5 million by late spring 1938.[45] The Japanese military regarded the Wuhan complex of cities as a Chinese military stronghold. The ongoing series of bombings and attacks could not have been unexpected, in that General Matsui had made known his intention, after taking Nanjing, of moving on toward Hankou, and even Chongqing, if necessary, to "overcome Chinese resistance."

Father Jacquinot played a very important and direct personal role in establishing a safety zone in Hankou. Because the Hankou Zone opened almost a year after the Jacquinot Zone in Shanghai, he had the benefit of the considerable experience gained from the operation of the latter, as well as of the safety zones in Nanjing and Hangzhou.[46] His deft hand would be needed, because press reports noted that Japanese military authorities were increasingly resentful of refugee zones established without their approval, and that any zones usually caused difficulties for the Japanese military during tactical operations. As for the situation in Hankou, the Japanese questioned why foreigners wanted to stay in dangerous war zones. Suspicious of a hidden Chinese agenda, they urged the foreign leaders to use their influence with the Chinese national government to stop it from using foreign areas of the city for military purposes and to remove the foreign civilians from the city.[47]

In considering plans for Hankou, the Shanghai Jacquinot Zone was held up for praise, because its establishment had been approved by both the Chinese and Japanese forces and it had proved to be very successful, especially as viewed by the Japanese. Hankou, on the other hand, presented a different set of problems, because of its being viewed by the Japanese as a government center and the main base of resistance to Japan. It was also thought to harbor numerous espionage agents and saboteurs. Like Nanjing, it was regarded as strongly defended and the protection of noncombatants (*hi-sentōin*) under these circumstances necessitated the complete and rapid withdrawal of all Chinese military forces from the city. More specifically, the Japanese regarded the Hankou foreign areas (the French and former foreign concessions) and Zone location, where third country nationals were likely to gather to seek protection for themselves and their property, as places where Chinese might hide and carry out resistance, as happened in the Nanjing Safe Zone. The Shanghai Zone had fortuitously been located outside, if adjacent to, the foreign area. The Japanese view was that creation of a refugee area in Hankou could only be allowed when there was no fear that it would be abused by "resist Japan terror groups."[48]

In spite of these reservations, discussions involving Jacquinot and the Japanese continued unabated. As early as February 1938, the Japanese government informed the U.S. ambassador that a safe zone at Hankou might eventually be established. The Japanese Imperial Forces would respect it so long as strict conditions were thoroughly met.[49] So the thinking as described was, not to completely abandon the idea of creating a refugee area in Hankou, but to allow it only when it was certain that anti-Japanese terrorist groups would not abuse such a zone.[50]

The Episcopal Church and the Roman Catholic Church had substantial interests in the Wuhan area and thus were interested in having Father Jacquinot apply his talents and contacts with the foreign powers and, especially, with Chiang Kai-shek to win cooperation for the establishment of a refugee zone in Wuhan. Christian church organizations would establish eleven refugee shelters in Wuhan.[51] The executive secretary of the National Council: Protestant Episcopal Church in the United States, John W. Wood, contacted Stanley Hornbeck of the State Department with these concerns.[52] In response, a cautious U.S. State Department instructed the American consul general in Shanghai that American officials were to "scrupulously avoid any statements of responsibility for either the Chinese or Japanese regarding the observance by either of assurances given the other in connection with the establishment of refugee zones." On the other hand, these same officials were encouraged to give "informal and unofficial" assistance to the Refugee Committee in Hankou—in other words, to the private offices of Father Jacquinot, head of the Refugee Committee, visiting Hankou.[53]

Even more significant than the lessons of the past to Jacquinot's efforts to establish new refugee zones were the powerful contacts he made during a self-described foreign fund-raising trip between May 2 and August 2, 1938. Leaving Shanghai by ship, his first stop was in Japan, where he was able to arrange for a meeting in Tokyo with Foreign Minister Hirota Kōki.[54] It was an excellent opportunity to explain the successes and obstacles to refugee work in China and to learn about Japanese official policy regarding this ongoing work being pursued during wartime. No doubt Father Jacquinot marshaled all of his powers of persuasion to influence Hirota's thinking about refugee conditions and the utility of safe zones.

After his meetings in Japan, Jacquinot sailed on to the United States and met with Stanley Hornbeck and even President Franklin Roosevelt to request aid for his refugee centers and discuss the situation in China. More will be said about his American travels in the next chapter.

During Jacquinot's absence from Hankou, the French consul general reported that the British wanted to try their hand at negotiating with the Japanese without Jacquinot's assistance, reflecting the petty jealousies that his diplomatic successes evoked locally. Rising quickly to his defense, Bishop J. S. Espelage, in charge of Catholic War Relief, responded: "Seul le Père Jacquinot pourra réussir" ("Only Father Jacquinot will be able to succeed").[55]

Jacquinot returned to Shanghai in August 1938 and presently learned that on September 5, the Japanese government in Tokyo had published assurances that on certain conditions, Japanese forces in China would refrain from attacking a designated area in Hankou. A government spokesman said: "Although we believe that, thanks to Father Jacquinot who is an experienced man, any matter will be handled smoothly [we do have certain conditions]."[56] These conditions became the topic of detailed talks between Jacquinot and the Japanese consul general in Shanghai, Hidaka Shinrokurō, concerning plans for establishing a refugee zone in Hankou. The style of this one-on-one negotiation session was that Father Jacquinot would make a clear statement regarding some planned aspect of the proposed zone, such as location or content, which Hidaka then followed up by either adding to or subtracting from Jacquinot's proposition.[57] These talks continued with still more discussions involving Jacquinot and Okazaki Katsuo[58] and S. Kawahara, representing the Japanese consulate, with W. J. Keswick speaking for the Shanghai Sub-Committee of the Special Hankou Notified Zone Committee, formed by Jacquinot. A memorandum followed containing the minutes of conversations at the September 21st meeting, where arrangements appear to have been finalized. The basic condition for setting up the zone was that there must be "complete and absolute demilitarization by the Chinese government of the area."[59] Demilitarization was understood to mean no Chinese military establishments within the zone and no presence in or in transit through the zone area of uniformed men other than special police recognized by the committee. If this was achieved, "Japanese Imperial Forces will not attack the area provided that it is marked with Red Cross flags and closed and barricaded with barbed wire."[60]

Speaking for the Shanghai International Committee and the Japanese consular authorities, Jacquinot held meetings in Shanghai with British officials and Ambassador Naggiar to discuss the plans for a zone in Hankou. Naggiar expressed his complete devotion to the idea, but cautioned that the French Consulate in Hankou did not have the resources in manpower or matériel to support this mission on a level similar to the French Concession's support of the Jacquinot Zone in Nantao. Even the marking of boundaries for the zone and the police force necessary for its protection would exceed French capabilities in Hankou. Jacquinot and Naggiar agreed that the best way to ensure success at Hankou was to combine the territories and resources of all the former concessions in the effort.[61]

The next round of talks initiated by Father Jacquinot concerning prospects for a Hankou Zone took place in Chongqing with Madame Chiang Kai-shek. On October 10, 1938, Jacquinot responded directly to the many policy concerns raised by his charming but firm host. Again, Jacquinot's negotiating style involved a process of give and take. To Madame Chiang's argument that Hankou would not fall and must be defended at any cost, he countered that its position on two rivers (the Han and the Yangzi) made it indefensible, especially with significant Japanese naval power anchored offshore. Madame Chiang next argued that certain tactical preparations needed to be made, and that having the noncombatants out of the way would only enhance chances of military success. She wanted to continue the policy of evacuating civilians and to take other steps that might uphold and strengthen Chinese morale. On this point, Jacquinot maintained that evacuation was important and would help clear the fighting area of refugees, but some could not be evacuated and would need to be cared for. With a zone committee in charge of the refugees, Chinese morale and treatment would be far superior than if the noncombatants were left to be provided for by the Japanese. A zone committee could also take temporary custody of valuable properties and keep them out of Japanese hands. Finally, Madame Chiang was convinced that the Japanese were anxious for the establishment of a zone, so why grant their wish? Jacquinot responded that, on the contrary, the Japanese authorities viewed a zone as a hindrance to their military operations. The discussions ended with Madame Chiang promising her personal support for a Hankou Safe Zone.[62]

French Consul General Lucien Colin reported that Jacquinot had informed him confidentially that both President and Madame Chiang had declared in favor of a zone. Colin praised Jacquinot's role in these negotiations, saying that he conducted himself with the greatest prudence.[63] Then came the question of funds to support the zone. While still in Chongqing, Jacquinot estimated that at least $700,000 would be needed and requested at least $500,000 from the Chongqing government.[64] Before his departure, Jacquinot heard from Dr. H. H. Kung (Kong Xiangxi) that funds likely would become available after the formal recognition of the zone. This good news must have prompted Jacquinot's enthusiastic comment to the press upon his arrival in Hankou that "Hankou refugees will be well taken care of." That said, he hurried off to meet with the French consul.[65] Jacquinot made this official on October 25, when he announced that a Hankou Refugee Zone had been officially recognized and that the Chinese government was financing it.[66]

The agreed-upon zone included the area bounded on the east by the Yangzi River, on the west by the Peking-Hankou Railroad, on the south by Kiangsun or Kiang Han Road, and on the north, across from the Japanese Concession. It embraced the French Concession, and the former German, Russian, and British Concessions. The zone consisted predominantly of foreign-owned property, the inviolability of which had already been conceded. A new consideration added to the conception of the Hankou Zone was the requirement for a margin, or demilitarized no-man's-land, outside and around the area on the west, north, and east for a distance of approximately one kilometer (.62 mile) from the zone boundary to avoid unforeseen damage and the risks of fighting near the zone.[67] This idea came from the Japanese, based on their experience at Shanghai, where they claimed the Chinese were able to use the foreign areas to launch attacks against Japanese forces and also to cause damage to foreign interests.[68] The main intention was to avoid a refugee zone so situated as to afford refuge for defeated Chinese troops. Certainly, this kind of margin would have been a useful feature in Nanjing.

Another provision was that the entry and occupation of the city were to be controlled by the incoming military police and not by regular troops. In addition, a local police force, acting under the supervision of the Hankou Refugee Committee, was to assist in the daily administration of the zone. Even after the Japanese occupation of Hankou, the Refugee Committee was to continue to function, especially during the transition stage and changeover of administration. This was to assure as orderly and practical a process as possible. Clearly reflecting Jacquinot's personal stamp, it was stated that the "main concern of the Zone Committee are the humanitarian essentials," the protection of third party persons and property, and the avoidance of chaos and disorder.[69]

Jacquinot made a strong bid for a refugee district to be set up in Wuchang, where he noted the existence of many hospitals, schools, and mission properties. In presenting his case, he granted that this area was already strongly fortified, but pledged that every effort would be made to arrange for a demilitarized zone to surround the Wuchang district. He stressed the impossibility of overlooking the importance of the humanitarian aspect of the proposed Wuchang Zone. The Japanese were not swayed by these arguments and refused to approve the establishment of a Wuchang zone because of its extensive military fortifications and the near impossibility of converting it into a demilitarized zone.[70]

On October 25, after the official announcement that Hankou would not be defended, Chinese government leaders began departing the city. Taking their place, the established Hankou Refugee Zone Committee, with Jacquinot as temporary head, assumed control of the Hankou Special Administrative District. At the opening of the zone, Jacquinot reported that the new committee had been officially recognized and, indicating that his efforts in Chongqing had gone well, would be financed by the Chinese government.[71] This committee was to serve as the temporary administrative body until it handed over authority "to the successional authority."[72] At that point, the security of the

refugees would become a matter for the new, presumably Japanese, administration to consider. The estimated number of refugees to be protected by the
new zone committee was given as 40,000.[73]

The Refugee Committee included members from Germany, Italy, France,
America, and Britain.[74] Bishop A. A. Gilman would take over as head of the
committee when Father Jacquinot returned to Shanghai. Jacquinot declared
firmly that the zone had no ulterior political purpose, but only humanitarian
goals for the protection of the Chinese community. Its purpose was to assist
the old, sick or infirm, women with children or parents with large families,
who could not easily face the dangers and difficulties of travel and thus must
remain. It would also take over the functions of city administration from the
departing Chinese officials. Hankou Mayor K. C. Wu pointed out that of the
1.25 million residents in Hankou, 400,000 still remained in the Wuhan cities
and needed protection. Before departing, Mayor Wu said at a press conference: "I will leave behind thousands of poor people, some destitute, who have
been unable to evacuate—but I know that I leave this flock in good hands. . . .
The Japanese domination of China is impossible."[75] He praised the work of
Father Jacquinot, declaring the existence of the Hankou Refugee Zone to be
the result of his dedication.[76]

The American journalist Agnes Smedley was in Hankou at this time, reporting on events there for the *Manchester Guardian*. She was known to be
sympathetic to the Chinese communists and while in Shanghai, had had a
relationship with the famous Soviet/Comintern spy Richard Sorge. During
her stay in Hankou, she joined the Chinese Red Cross Medical Corps and
strongly criticized the International Red Cross in China for withholding donations and medical supplies from her Chinese organization in order to support
and fund only mission hospitals and programs.[77] She described the war as a
godsend to missionary institutions, which she described as locations at which
countless civilians found refuge from the Japanese threat and had Christianity
preached to them. Credible and essential institutions such as the Chinese Red
Cross Medical Corps received no supplies or funds, at least initially, so that
the mission work could have adequate foreign help. Still, Smedley apparently
felt compelled to include in her reporting that this International Red Cross
and Refugee Committee did accomplish the amazing feat of establishing a
"'safety zone' which eventually kept nearly 400,000 Chinese" in Hankou.[78]
Not wanting to grant it too much credit, however, she described the zone's
purpose as not specifically for humanitarian purposes, as claimed; in her opinion, it served as a "reservoir of labor" for foreign factories in Hankou and for
the Japanese war machine.

The Refugee Committee's first essential task was to remove all troops, defense works, arms, and ammunition from the area. It was assisted by offers of cooperation from the foreign powers to help carry out these tasks. A British force of 100, billeted in the British Consulate, prepared to take up patrol duty, and a small party of British sailors constructed the barbed wire barrier along the border with the Chinese city. Italian sailors and U.S. naval personnel, quartered at the Navy YMCA facilities, provided support. The British gunboats HMS *Gnat* and HMS *Tern* anchored off the former German Concession. Foreign volunteers in the Hankou Zone, armed only with batons, mobilized to help patrol the streets after the Japanese forces arrived.

When the Japanese forces approached the city, they were met with a minor flood, caused by the Chinese, who had broken some of the dykes. Japanese engineers quickly constructed a bridge, and the first to cross were armored cars, followed by Japanese infantry. Father Jacquinot and French Consul General Lucien Colin met the Japanese officials and participated in the official ceremonies for the recognition of the Hankou Refugee Zone.[79] Next, Italian marines opened the way for the Japanese forces to enter the Refugee Zone area, assuring their officers that there were no armed troops in the Safety Zone. Father Jacquinot arrived at the entrance to conduct the vanguard of Japanese forces along a route that went through the former German Concession and across territory behind the other former concession areas. En route, a naval captain and Father Jacquinot investigated the road ahead to make certain that it had been cleared for passage by the Japanese soldiers, who, resuming their march, passed through without incident.[80]

Thereafter, the takeover and occupation of Hankou proved to be more orderly by far than what transpired at Nanjing. Of course, there was violence, with explosions that damaged the Japanese Consulate and Naval Headquarters, as well as the main railway station. Most of the damage came from fuses set by retreating Chinese forces meant to destroy military buildings, centers of communication, and public utilities of possible use to the Japanese. Regarding the utilities, Jacquinot made a direct appeal to the Chinese authorities to spare the waterworks, which was essential for the survival of the remaining refugees. Only minor damage to the plant followed, which engineers were able to repair within a few days.[81] Telephone and mail services ended, causing anxiety among the foreign population, who were unable to let their families know how they were.

The Japanese did not bomb the Hankou Zone. Instead, the Japanese forces subjected the retreating Chinese forces southwest of Wuchang and elsewhere to intense bombing raids. Other major targets included the destruction of the former Guomindang Offices and the former headquarters of Chiang Kai-shek. Violence accompanied the Japanese move into the city, some caused by their own forces, some by Chinese. Successive explosions rocked the buildings and smashed windows all around the perimeter of the Hankou Zone, and fires set at different sites in the city and in Wuchang burned for several days. Some Japanese looting of houses and shops did occur, with Chinese laborers often being used to transport the stolen goods. A foreign missionary in Hankou reported one murder and several incidents of rape by the Japanese troops.[82] Still, the French ambassador reported that the necessary transition continued to make progress thanks to the measures taken to assure the best conditions given the difficulties of the situation.[83]

By November 1, the situation in Hankou was reported to be calm. The evacuation of Chinese civilians from the former concession areas to the new Refugee Zone took place rapidly, and foreign property remained intact. The Zone was strictly demilitarized, and the Japanese military, having allowed the temporary continuation of the existing police force to maintain order, assumed policing responsibilities.[84] In accordance with the mutual under-standing, armed Chinese soldiers had always been refused entrance into the Zone, as they were in the successful Shanghai Refugee Zone. The eventual disposition of the Hankou Zone, once the Japanese completed the occupation and the situation stabilized, was that the refugee community within the Zone moved to Wu Shien Miao, located two miles further up the river. Because the Japanese military had not bombed or attacked the Hankou Refugee Zone, it remained the only part of the city that was intact and was therefore most at-tractive and livable for the Japanese occupiers, who took over the area for their housing and administrative needs.

A review of the evidence and circumstances suggests that these improve-ments as to the outcome of the Japanese attack and occupation of Hankou emerged because of three major factors. The Japanese military in China had better command leadership at the battle of Wuhan. The buildup for earlier campaigns had been sudden, and the campaigns not really planned. By the time of the attack on Wuhan, the military command in Tokyo had a better grasp of what it was trying to accomplish in China. The passage of one year helped foster the successful planning and development of the mutual under-standing between the two still warring opponents regarding the fate of the Wuhan cities. Also, Japanese tactics and behavior were moderated by the ex-perience of the Japanese rampage in Nanjing and the ensuing sense of shame. Finally, Father Jacquinot's skillful implementation of the understanding, and his having won the backing and cooperation of Chiang Kai-shek and May-or K. C. Wu, was essential to the relatively successful outcome at Hankou. Speaking with extravagant praise, Consul Colin declared that one man saved Hankou from total destruction, "c'est le Père Jacquinot."

OTHER SAFE ZONES

Other areas concerned or threatened by advancing Japanese armies made an effort to establish "Jacquinot Zones" to protect their Chinese civilian populations, sometimes with very unusual variations. Those mentioned below are not known to have had any direct or extensive involvement by Father Jacquinot, other than his model serving as a guide as to how to go about establishing a local safe area. It is known that a safety zone was being discussed as early as December 5, 1937, for the population in Hangzhou. The French Consulate at Xiamen (Amoy) reported that Spanish Catholic Fathers and Sisters in Zhangzhou had established a "sort of Jacquinot zone" in a village two miles east of Zhangzhou. It was to serve as a place of refuge for themselves and 800 Catholics and any others once the war reached Zhangzhou. Their leaders claimed that the Chinese military had guaranteed that no troops would enter the area and had even contributed $1,000 to support the refugees. Rather than marking the zone boundaries with the usual Red Cross flags, they reportedly used the French flag instead, marking off the area with bamboo fencing. This was their own variation of the Jacquinot theme, but, unfortunately, their efforts failed to win the requested Japanese approval.[85]

The French ambassador also recounted efforts by the Catholic Mission at Ouchang, near Nanjing, to establish a safe zone. The priests marked off boundaries for a safe zone area and won certification from the Chinese that no troops were in the area. The Japanese treated this request as they did in the case of Hankou, by informing Father Jacquinot of their requirements and likely approval if those stipulations were met.[86]

A news service reported that a refugee zone had been created at Shenzhen as the result of an agreement between Ronald Hull of the Hong Kong Relief Society and Nakamura Toyoichi, the Japanese consul general. The expected conditions to be met were that there be no Chinese troops in the zone and no anti-Japanese activities.[87] At the same time, Japanese officials agreed in principle to a refugee zone in Hong Kong.[88]

The city of Canton, which the Chinese government decided to yield without resistance, had suffered intense aerial bombing since as early as September 1937. On October 23, 1938, after an orgy of destruction similar to what had taken place in the Zhabei district of Shanghai, local authorities finally got Japanese permission to set up three safe zones for the protection of noncombatants. British and American officials established the Canton Anglo-American Refugee Committee on November 7, identifying the Trinity School, the

Hackett Memorial Hospital, and the Canton Hospital as central points for refugee protection. The Japanese military agreed to designate these areas as out of bounds for Japanese soldiers, and the Chinese assured consular officials that no Chinese soldiers would venture near the zones. The American officials added Lingnan University, which had been bombed in early June, as a zone for women, children, and aged noncombatants. Monetary support in the amount of $50,000 came from T. V. Song, who promised the local Bishop Hall that another $50,000 would soon follow.[89]

Another request for a safe zone encompassing the Cangqianshan area near the port city of Fuzhou came from American officials in Shanghai, not Father Jacquinot, on June 30, 1939. The official Japanese response, given by Japanese Consul General Miura, had become their standard reply and was reported as follows:

> I have now been informed of the decision of the Japanese authorities which states that although they are unable to recognize formally the proposed temporary safe zone, they are prepared not to make that area the objective of their attack so long as no Chinese armed forces occupy or approach that area in question or else use or take advantage of it for military purposes.[90]

Had the request been made through Father Jacquinot, with his guarantees that the required conditions had been met, the Japanese most likely would have formally recognized the requested safe zone. Their affirmed and reaffirmed trust in Jacquinot's word, plans, and actions had become a key factor in their decision-making.

As shown by the evidence, Jacquinot's zone concept provided an essential blanket of security to thousands of homeless and threatened refugees. In fact, if the 250,000 refugees (a conservative estimate) in the Shanghai Refugee Zone, the 200,000 who managed to survive in the Nanjing Refugee Zone, the more than 40,000 refugees protected in Hankou, and the estimated 30,000 protected in other zones are added together, Jacquinot's scheme can be said to have succored over 500,000 Chinese refugees, most of whom would almost certainly have died but for him.

CHAPTER SIX

Raising Funds Abroad

> For benefits received are a delight to us as long as we
> think we can requite them; when that possibility is far
> exceeded, they are repaid with hatred instead of grati-
> tude.
>
> —Tacitus, *Annals* 4.18

The need for funds to cover the many relief requirements inside the Jacquinot
Zone made it imperative that outside sources of funding be found. There
were many requests from different organizations for financial support from
the Shanghai Municipal Council of the International Settlement, the location
of Shanghai's most prosperous business enterprises. The response was always
that the policy of the council was to refrain from spending "ordinary Municipal budget" funds on poor relief work. At meetings of the council, the chairman and others often warned that if the council became involved in refugee
monetary support, it would raise the danger that the large refugee support
organizations, such as the International Red Cross Committee, YMCA, and
Shanghai International Relief Committee, would transfer responsibility for
these services permanently to the council. The council members concurred
on the need to postpone assuming responsibility for the refugees as long as
possible.[1]

American donors were not deterred from raising relief funds in the United
States. A key member of this early fund-raising effort was former President
Herbert Hoover, who organized a committee of wealthy Americans to gather
donations. Hoover had worked in China as an engineer and had even been
engaged in building defenses and rescue work in Tianjin in 1900 during the
Boxer Rebellion. According to Chinese sources, Hoover's effort was very successful, raising 10 million Chinese dollars. To show how important this sum
was, only 2 million Chinese dollars had been raised from all sources by early
December. Only 50,000 dollars had come from the Chinese National Government. Hoover mentioned that the money would be handled by the Interna-

tional Red Cross Committee and delivered with dispatch to provide relief to China's wartime areas.[2] The Geneva-based International Red Cross Committee reported that in 1938, Japan contributed 10,000 Swiss Francs to the Red Cross, some of which likely reached China in relief funding.[3]

In Shanghai, the authorities in the French Concession started a French Refugee Lottery to raise funds for relief needs. Always innovative and willing to meet a pressing need with often less than traditional methods, Jacquinot helped establish the refugee lottery along with Leon Richard Shinazi, a local businessman, who then supervised its successful operation. After extended debate, the International Settlement voted to allow the French Lottery tickets to be sold in the Settlement, as long as the conditions of the sale and supervision met the Shanghai municipal police and council conditions. A suggestion that the SMC also establish a Municipal Lottery for refugee relief was voted down on the grounds that the council had always followed a policy of not countenancing public gambling in the Settlement. Its members saw no need "to lower the customary standard of behaviour of the Council in such matters."[4] While such an explanation of policy might indeed be questioned, given the number of nightclubs, dog and horse racing tracks, and other amusement centers that flourished in the Settlement, the council always claimed publicly to strive for a display of concern for moral standards in the Settlement.[5]

Instead, the accepted method of fund-raising for refugee relief in the Settlement was by the Voluntary Entertainment Fund. Hotels, restaurants, movie theaters, and other entertainment places collected a certain percentage of their sales for the express purpose of supporting mainly refugee needs. For example, 5 percent of every dollar spent on food and of the cost of room rentals went toward the Fund.[6] For many, it seemed like an unfair and unwelcome tax on customers, but it did provide considerable amounts of funds in this city, which thoroughly enjoyed its lively social scene. Local schoolgirls from the foreign settlements raised money by selling copies of their publication, *The Girl's Delight*. Money also came from charitable concerts, and Chinese schoolgirls canvassed the neighborhoods and streets of the foreign concessions.[7]

Still, the needs were unmet, and Father Jacquinot realized that he would have to call upon his own fund-raising skills developed during earlier relief emergencies for raising money. Since the Jacquinot Zone was located outside both of the two protected settlements, he would have a difficult time making a case for receiving relief funds from either of their governing bodies. Instead, he came up with ambitious plans to meet the needs in the Zone by means of a fund-raising tour of the United States and Canada. His campaign was to start on May 2 and last until his return to Shanghai on August 2, 1938.

Before departing China, Jacquinot visited Hong Kong on March 8 to discuss the perils of the refugee situation, his upcoming travels, and the pressing
need for government funds. He met first with the governor, who had asked
that he call during his stay, and brought him up to date on the situation in
Shanghai. Later, he emphasized to a gathering of prospective wealthy con-
tributors that the Chinese government was fully behind his relief efforts. He
selected some of those in attendance at his presentations on the refugee situation in China to serve on a new steering committee he organized for the
purpose of receiving funds for refugee relief work. For any who might still
question the extent of his high-level support, upon his arrival he had waiting
for him three telegrams from Hankou inviting him to add a visit to the capital to his itinerary. The invitations came from H. H. Kung, president of the
Executive Yuan, T. V. Song, and Chiang Kai-shek himself. A private airplane
was sent to Hong Kong to bring Jacquinot to Hankou, where his three hosts
treated him cordially. They praised his work, but also that of the Catholic
Church in China for generosity of service to all those in misery and in need
of relief. Chiang also agreed to include in their final banquet celebration the
apostolic delegate to China, who had been seeking an opportunity to meet
with high-level Chinese officials. Madame Chiang invited the apostolic delegate to offer a prayer before the banquet began. A highlight of the occasion
was the announcement that the existing law forbidding the teaching of religion in classrooms was now to be rescinded in response to the excellent work
of Father Jacquinot with Chinese refugees, especially regarding the Jacquinot
Zone, and the service of the Catholic Church in China.[8] To show his personal
appreciation, Chiang Kai-shek gave Jacquinot a letter of acknowledgment,
with a signed photograph of Chiang and a personal dedication.[9] These items
would prove to be especially useful during his fund-raising tour of the United
States and Canada.

During their discussions, Jacquinot emphasized the plight of the many
homeless children and praised Madame Chiang for her efforts to "relieve their
suffering." He added that he was praying for a quick resolution to what he
feared might be a long-drawn-out conflict with Japan. His diplomatic appeal
to the government leaders must have made quite an impression, because press
reports indicate that the temporary Hankou National Government pledged
$250,000 (in Chinese dollars) for his relief work, to be transferred by the
Finance Ministry. This brought the total amount of money donated by the
government to $750,000 in cash and $800,000 in bonds.[10]

In recognition of this and other substantial relief accomplishments, French
Ambassador Paul-Emile Naggiar hosted a luncheon on March 28 to honor

Father Jacquinot and members of the Jacquinot Relief Committee. Characteristically, Jacquinot told the fifty invited guests, assembled in the luxurious surroundings of the French Club, that his work could not have been carried out without the support of his colleagues, the aid given by the French authorities, the cooperation of the army chiefs, and the help given by the Red Cross.[11] Dr. W. W. Yen (Yan Huiqing), chairman of the Shanghai International Committee of the Red Cross, was one of the distinguished Chinese guests attending. Jacquinot was a vice-chairman of this body, as were W. H. Plant and J. R. Jones.[12] Celebrations included the announcement that Father Jacquinot had been made a *chevalier* of the Légion d'honneur on February 12 for his establishment of the Nanshi Safety Zone. Many of the guests predicted that his work in Shanghai would earn him a place in history.[13] In a final tribute to Jacquinot, Ambassador Naggiar, in a personal letter, said that the priest had already saved 100,000 lives on the borders of the French Concession and he wanted to wish him well on his "errand of mercy" to raise funds abroad.[14]

The official sponsor of Jacquinot's foreign travel was the Shanghai International Committee of the Red Cross Society of China, under Chairman Yen. His official purpose was to confer with officials of the American Red Cross and the China Famine Relief Corporation, both located in New York City, concerning the plight of refugees in China.[15] Another responsible group to be consulted was the American Advisory Committee for Civilian Relief in China. Its chairman was Arthur Basset, and it included as members prominent Americans familiar with Chinese relief problems. This organization was to handle the distribution in China of contributions raised or received by the American Red Cross and transferred through the facilities of the U.S. State Department and American Consulate General in Shanghai. This advisory committee was necessary because the American Red Cross wanted to avoid the responsibility for conducting the actual relief work in China at this time.[16]

To help promote his mission, Jacquinot brought with him films and abundant literature to demonstrate to audiences the severity of the refugee problem and need for relief. One of the most effective booklets, published by the Chinese American Publishing Co., was *The Story of the "Jacquinot Zone," Shanghai, China*, a handsome volume with an artistic cover, sewn together with silk cord. Inside were several good photographs, documents, and cartoons that gave a comprehensive, upbeat view of the work in Shanghai. Officials of the American Red Cross reported that they had effectively used their copy of this document to provide a basis for discussion "of zones of immunity" at the Sixteenth International Red Cross Conference just held in London.[17] Jacquinot told his hosts that, rather than undertaking a general lecture tour, he preferred to speak before small groups of interested (and presumably wealthy) persons.[18]

The American Red Cross had already been active in China relief, raising money according to its policy of making private appeals for funds and then making Red Cross organizations available to receive contributions throughout the United States. The basis of this policy was that contributions be entirely voluntary. This was the policy that guided Jacquinot's request just to speak before small groups and not pursue a national appeal. To this end, Jacquinot planned to call on Norman Davis, chairman of the American Red Cross, in his New York offices on May 21.[19]

Many concerned with the China emergency did not see this low-key approach as being adequate to raise the amount of money that China desperately needed. Fortunately, their concerns were shared by none other than President Franklin D. Roosevelt, who favored a more aggressive approach. Stunned by the events in Nanjing and the sinking of the gunboat USS *Panay* by Japanese naval aircraft on December 12, 1937, Roosevelt made a national appeal for China relief in a letter to the American Red Cross, dated January 17, 1938, and set a national goal for fund-raising at U.S.$1 million.[20] The initial Red Cross response was that we "do not do [fund-raising] drives."

New support came on January 25, when the press published the President Roosevelt's letter, with encouragement from the State Department. Also, enthusiastic support from church groups and charity organizations was impressive and could not be ignored.[21] In addition, Julian Arnold, the American commercial attaché in Shanghai, visiting the United States, urged the State Department to request the president to instruct the Red Cross that a "drive" was in fact necessary to raise the substantial relief funds needed.[22] Under these circumstances, the Red Cross came under heavy pressure to respond with a more active relief program. With the information now public that the president had already set a specific fund-raising goal, Red Cross leaders worried that if they failed to meet the new goal, it would look bad for the president, the Red Cross, and even the country.[23] It was well known that the British relief programs had been very generous. In any case, this new more aggressive direction was what would guide Jacquinot, accompanied by Arnold, once he arrived in the United States.

His first stop on his fund-raising tour was Japan, where, as mentioned above, he met with Foreign Minister Hirota, presumably not for fund-raising purposes, since no monetary transfers are mentioned, but to discuss the situation in China, the Jacquinot Zone, and perhaps the events in Nanjing and future developments elsewhere in China. His travel to the United States was aboard the *Empress of Canada*, where he found opportunities to give lectures to those on board, providing firsthand information on the refugee situation in China and his work in the Nanshi Zone. These lectures, of course, concluded with a call for donations, during which he took up a collection.[24] His first stop along the way across the Pacific was in Honolulu, where he spoke to a gathering of local businesspeople. The turnout was substantial, as was the generosity of those who attended. His audiences seem to have been genuinely moved and charmed by this one-armed priest making a plea for aid to destitute Chinese refugees under attack in war-torn China.

The French Embassy in Washington had made preparations for Jacquinot's official engagements in Washington, backed by letters of support for the relatively unknown priest from American, French, and Chinese officials. These reached the State Department and White House, paving the way for Jacquinot's high-level visits in Washington. One particularly descriptive letter came from Dr. W. W Yen, Chinese ambassador to the USSR from 1932 to 1937. Ambassador Yen said: "A 'missionary statesman,' Father Jacquinot is an impressive figure, tall and lean in his black priestly garb, on which he wears the badge of the International Red Cross Committee—a red cross in a bold blue circle. His white beard and sensitive, kindly eyes never fail to warm the hearts of the wounded and destitute."[25]

On May 18, 1938, Jacquinot landed in Vancouver, where members of the press greeted him and his photograph appeared in the *Vancouver Sun*. The coverage highlighted his work with the Jacquinot Zone in Shanghai and reported that he would be meeting with President Roosevelt during his upcoming visit to Washington.[26]

Shortly after his arrival in Washington, accompanied by Father Edmund Walsh, S.J., founder of the Georgetown University School of Foreign Service, Jacquinot met with Stanley Hornbeck, chief of the State Department's Division of Far Eastern Affairs, on May 24, 1938. Jacquinot outlined the refugee situation in China with special reference to the Shanghai area. He also related the contents of his discussions with Chinese leaders in Hankou and those with Japanese government officials that occurred just before starting his journey to the United States, stressing that both governments held the view that the conflict in China would last for a considerable period. Jacquinot pointed out that because of the extended conflict, the refugee problem in China was bound to continue and that increased efforts were essential to meet the severe and widespread needs. The problem was one of humanity, he said; it had nothing to do with the conduct of hostilities as such. And he added: "in my opinion, the problem of affording relief to the civilian refugees is the most important humanitarian problem facing the world today."[27]

Jacquinot outlined at length the administration of relief in Shanghai, in-

cluding the work being done in the Nanshi Safety Zone. Hornbeck, apparently well briefed ahead of this meeting, gave a brief survey of the activities of the
various relief organizations in the United States, especially as they related to
work in China, including the efforts of various church groups to raise funds.
The meeting concluded with Hornbeck telling Jacquinot that his work in the
United States in assisting in the raising of funds for civilian refugee work in
China "had our official blessing."[28]

At the request of the French Embassy in China, the French ambassador in
Washington, Comte René Doynel de Saint-Quentin, contacted Secretary of
State Cordell Hull and reported that Jacquinot had expressed a strong interest
in paying his respects to President Roosevelt during his visit to Washington.
The chief of protocol, George T. Summerlin, passed the request to Marvin
H. McIntyre, secretary to the president, with the State Department's strong
recommendation that Roosevelt receive Jacquinot before leaving Washington.
After reviewing Jacquinot's background and major accomplishments in China, Summerlin's recommendation emphasized the potential importance of his
detailed "personal knowledge of conditions in China."[29]

Jacquinot met with the president on May 26. He described his meeting
with Roosevelt during an interview given to the *North China Herald* upon his
return to Shanghai. Two days after his arrival in Washington, he said:

> [T]he White House rang me up and asked me to come over immediately and
> I lost no time in doing so. I found myself waiting with a Senator in the Of-
> fice of the President's Private Secretary. The Senator impressed upon me the
> importance of his mission—something to do with locust prevention work—to
> my amusement. I waited only five minutes and then was ushered into the
> President's private office, ahead of the Senator.[30]

The French ambassador accompanied Jacquinot and introduced the one-
armed priest to the seated president. Speaking of his first impressions of the
president, Jacquinot said; "You have probably heard of the famous Roosevelt
charm? It is not in the slightest an exaggerated description." Roosevelt had
smiled and told him to speak freely. Jacquinot had prepared a presentation,
but he realized that the president was a very busy man, and he had been so
much under Roosevelt's spell, he claimed, "that I clean forgot it all."[31] No
doubt, these were comments meant for the special appetites of the Shanghai
press, and his meeting with the president actually had real substance and im-
port. Besides informing the president about the refugee situation in China, he
likely informed Roosevelt briefly about the content of his recent discussions
about the Chinese military and political situation with Chiang Kai-shek in
Hankou and the Japanese foreign minister in Tokyo. In any case, he achieved

his refugee "mission of mercy" during this most important visit, in that Roosevelt approved the generous amount of U.S.$700,000 for the Chinese relief program, which would be transferred to China through official channels using the American Red Cross as the conduit.[32]

The recent China events had helped focus American attention on China and the Japanese threat. President and Madame Chiang Kai-shek had been proclaimed "Man and Woman of the Year" by Henry Luce's *Time* magazine in January 1938. Roosevelt had publicly expressed his deep regret over the Japanese bombing and sinking of the USS *Panay* and the terrible events at Nanjing. In a speech to Congress, he raised the issue of freezing Japanese assets in the United States. These events and the American reactions made it an opportune time for Jacquinot's visit in support of the war refugees in China.

The American Red Cross was to channel the acquired funds to the International Red Cross Committee in Shanghai. The American Advisory Committee, however, remained the important point of contact for consultations with Madame Chiang regarding the distribution of funds and relief work. In August 1938, the Advisory Committee transferred $50,000 through the American Consulate in Hankou to Madame Chiang to cover the emergency needs of women and children in the capital area.

In a press conference, Madame Chiang reported that the national government had taken over all relief work, noting that authorities in cities could not handle the relief work successfully alone. The work and the financial burdens were too great. The national government, with its appropriate supervisory committees, served as the central point for distributing funds and setting priorities.[33] Madame Chiang made another request for $50,000 from the United States to further meet the needs of women and children. This amount arrived in December, along with her indirect plea for still more funding.[34] In November, Madame Chiang asked that all funds be paid in gold and deposited directly in the Central Bank of China.[35] American refugee relief programs were becoming an important source of her government's funds, and some suspected that the funds might be going to programs other than relief work.

The fund-raising campaign in the United States got under way with Jacquinot handling the "drive" in the eastern and central states and Julian Arnold, the West Coast states. A typical event included some local publicity to start, a lecture on China and the refugee problem, and then the inevitable call for funds and a collection.

Jacquinot began his drive in New York by hosting a major gala, which again showed his resourcefulness in raising funds for his refugee causes. He had the important and able assistance of Colonel Theodore Roosevelt Jr., national chairman of the United Council for Civilian Relief in China.[36] Jacquinot announced, with some characteristic hyperbole, that "no disaster in China's history can compare with the war, flood, disease, and famine in that country today."[37] The New York event, called "A Night in Old China," was held in Chinatown on June 17 and started a nationwide drive to sponsor a series of what were called "bowl of rice" parties. Plans were to hold 2,000 of these parties in 280 cities across the country. Many were to be held on or near the Chinese national holiday on October 10. Each guest was expected to contribute to the relief fund the difference between the cost of a bowl of rice and a regular dinner. The partying was to reach its climax with a dinner dance called "The Bowl of Rice Ball" at the Hotel Pierre in New York on November 9, which would feature debutantes dressed for the occasion in Chinese fashions.

Jacquinot said that just $1 provided food, clothing, shelter, and medical care for one person for a month. Glad to participate in this drive, most Chinese restaurants lining Mott, Pell, and Doyers Streets in New York's Chinatown provided seven-course dinners to ticket holders. A special roped-off area, brightly decorated, housed street vendors, Chinese fortunetellers, and gaily adorned booths. Dinner was followed, out on the street, by dancing, tightrope walkers, Chinese boxing matches, tumbling, and juggling, as well as by American stars of the stage, screen, and radio. China's ambassador to the United States, C. T. Wang, joined the festivities, as did most members of New York's social register. The New York police estimated the crowd that gathered at 85,000.

Seven gates were erected in Chinatown to facilitate the sale of tickets, which cost $6, including dinner. The estimate was that more than 5,000 donors participated at this initial fund-raising party. Colonel Roosevelt promised that "not one cent will be deducted from the proceeds of the 'bowl of rice' parties for administrative expenses."[38] The funds raised would be sent to the American Advisory Committee in Shanghai, which would consult with Madame Chiang in dividing the money among the best-qualified relief agencies in China.[39]

These "bowl of rice" parties raised considerable amounts of money according to a telegram Jacquinot sent back to Shanghai. Approximately $1,000,000 had been raised, and in the last month, 1,600 dinners and balls had been held for the "bowl of rice" campaign to raise money for the refugees. The American Red Cross added an additional $700,000 to the funds collected. Again, refusing to accept any accolades, Jacquinot attributed most of his success to the personal appeals made by President Roosevelt and Norman Davis, president of the American Red Cross and former U.S. ambassador-at-large to Europe.[40]

Father Jacquinot gave an interview from the Jesuit House of St. Ignatius Loyola in New York during which he amplified the message of his visits abroad. In addition to fund-raising, he emphasized the importance of extending the principle of neutral districts in wartime. As he explained:

> This zone [in Shanghai] establishes a formula by which non-combatants can be protected in time of battle, and it has passed the test of experience. This was in an Oriental war, in which no quarter is granted, no prisoners are taken, and the wounded are often finished [off] on the battlefield. If this formula would work under such conditions, there is hope that it might also prove of use in other surroundings.

He also showed copies of all the favorable letters he had received from President Chiang and Foreign Minister Hirota, as well as from neutral observers, praising the Zone's operations. He reported that these and other documents were being sent to Geneva in hopes of receiving a hearing for the plan for civilian safe zones and its possible inclusion in the international laws of war. He ended his interview by asking the Americans to act in enlightened self-interest regarding China's situation. As a final salvo, this time specifically in support of his funding drive, he said that "the Chinese market will go to those nations that help to alleviate suffering in China."[41]

Jacquinot joined Julian Arnold in San Francisco for a final grand drive that included a personal and ingenious touch of his own. With the help of local Jesuits, they canvassed the entire city in search of wealthy or comfortably situated persons to approach for support. Rather than following any traditional pitch for funds, Jacquinot devised a scheme whereby each individual was subjected to a mock "arrest," to be alleviated subsequently by agreeing to pay a "fine," the amount to be determined by an assessment of their personal circumstances. According to Jacquinot, "this was all most illegal, but everyone took it in good part, paying three, five or more dollars quite willingly!"[42] The one-armed priest, already admired for his charm and jaunty appearance, was even more appreciated by those he approached for using this innovative and unusual fund-raising approach.[43] The response of donors in Canada was also very satisfying, with newsmen turning out to get the latest scoop on his fund-raising drive and peppering him with questions on the situation in China. Donations from Canadians responding to the Chinese plight reportedly amounted to $700,000.[44]

The results of all these fund-raising efforts were quite impressive, but so were the needs in China. American Consul General Gauss estimated that to continue the current relief measures in Shanghai alone required that funds be available at the rate of 100,000 Chinese dollars per week. Another estimate put the figure at $15,000 per day.[45] To plan relief measures for all areas, the consensus of those knowledgeable, such as the National Christian Council, was a minimum of 10,000,000 Chinese dollars for 1938.[46] As of November 1938, the Red Cross and American Advisory Committee had raised U.S.$197,794, and the American Advisory Committee and China Famine Relief, U.S.$88,500, for a total of U.S.$286,294. Another accounting that considered the amount of funding that was to reach Madame Chiang showed that of U.S.$103,292 raised between July 1 and December 25, 1938, U.S.$60,000 went directly to Madame Chiang.[47] The American Red Cross reported raising U.S.$320,000 between October 16, 1937, and April 27, 1938, with the largest amount collected in April.[48] It is perhaps impossible to sort out all the exact funding amounts, especially when the currency designations are not always indicated, but it is clear that significant funding reached China as a result of this ambitious program initiated by Father Jacquinot. More "bowl of rice" parties continued to be held after Jacquinot's return to Shanghai. Theodore Roosevelt Jr. organized several around the Chinese national holiday on October 12. Guests were expected to contribute the difference between the cost of a bowl of rice and a regular dinner to the relief fund.

Father Jacquinot left for home from Vancouver aboard the *Empress of Asia* and arrived on July 20 at his next stop, Yokohama, where he received a permit to travel by train to Kobe.[49] Before embarking on this trip, he is reported to have rested at the new Grand Hotel in Yokohama. A mystery ensued, because when his friends and colleagues, including Dr. John Baker and A. S. Jasper, both officials of the Shanghai International Relief Committee, met the ship he was supposed to be on in Shanghai, they found that he was not on board. Apparently, he had neglected to inform anyone of his delay or change of plans. He was expected in Shanghai on July 25. Trying to explain his absence, some of those hoping to welcome him attributed his delay to a possible desire to aid the victims of a serious flood that occurred recently in Kobe.

The *Shanghai Evening Post* reported him "missing" when the ship docked on July 27 without him as a passenger. The ship's officers reported that he had left the ship at Kobe and planned to take another ship to Shanghai, embarking at Nagasaki. Confusion and speculation as to his condition and location became rife, with many fearing that something untoward had happened to him in Japan. One report speculated that he was meeting with Japanese Red Cross workers about plans for the creation of the refugee zone in Hankou. Another reporter speculated that he must have left the ship in Kobe or Yokohama in order to view Japan's flooded areas. Then Father Verdier, head of the Catholic

Mission in Nanjing, received a package from Father Jacquinot, postmarked Nagasaki. It was thought that he might be visiting the Catholic Mission there, even though no message of a planned visit had been sent. The package was opened and found to contain a book that the priest had taken on his trip and a copy of *Reader's Digest*. His friends questioned why he would use Kobe as a return address and why mail to himself in Shanghai a book and magazine? Adding to the mystery, the handwriting of the word "registered" on the package was closely examined and found not to match that of Father Jacquinot. These events aroused considerable anxiety in many circles about his safety in wartime Japan.[50]

The French Embassy made enquiries about Father Jacquinot's whereabouts to police officials and the Japanese Foreign Office, America Bureau, 3rd Section Chief, Mr. Kumabe. The French consul general noted that he had inquired in places where the priest might have some connections in Tokyo and Yokohama, and had also sent cables to Kobe, Seoul, Shanghai, and elsewhere inquiring about Jacquinot. No response to these inquiries had been forthcoming, and the French expressed the hope that the Japanese Imperial Government could locate the priest.

When they found that they could not say where Jacquinot was in Japan, the Japanese authorities placed a ban on any articles about him being published in the press. Their intention was to avoid the spread of wild rumors that might spark public anger and violence. Then the Japanese police, aided by the Kempeitai (military police) and with great secrecy, began a serious search effort. The Japanese Ministry of Foreign Affairs informed the Japanese consul generals in Shanghai and Hongkong by telegram that a search was on for Father Jacquinot.[51]

One of the passengers who had happened to be on board the ship with Jacquinot noted a dinner party at the new Grand Hotel in Yokohama on July 20. The party included Archbishop Dos of Tokyo and Bishop Chambon of Yokohama, to name just the best-known ecclesiastics in attendance, and whom Jacquinot might have been expected to join. His absence further raised fears that criminals might have attacked him for the large quantity of cash he was known to have raised in North America. Of course, that money was being transferred through official channels, but fear and anxiety stimulated many fertile imaginations.[52]

On the early morning of July 29, Jacquinot was found to be staying with an old friend he had known previously in Shanghai and who lived near Kobe in the seaside town of Tarumi. His friend, Fujikawa Kazuo, manager of a commercial establishment called "Mereki," was the East Asian representative of the Auguste Dormier Company of London. The prefecture police, to whom Jacquinot would need to explain his situation and failure to inform his Shanghai friends, reported his discovery. Fujikawa accompanied Jacquinot to the police offices in Kobe and listened while Jacquinot apologized profusely for the inconveniences he had created. He was told that his absence had involved a three-day intensive search, during which every clue had been carefully studied.[53] He explained that he had wanted a rest after his fund-raising tour and long journey from America. After missing his ship at Nagasaki, he had decided to stay on and rest for a few days. He stressed repeatedly that there was no other cause for his delay.

Father Jacquinot set sail aboard the SS *Felix Roussel* on July 29, arriving in Shanghai on August 2. When the press met his ship and inquired about his "mysterious disappearance," Jacquinot reportedly beamed with amusement and said he was shocked by all of the uproar. Adding a touch of levity to a situation that must have been quite embarrassing, Jacquinot told the gathering that after he had contacted the French consul general and Japanese prefect of police, "for the rest of the time [in Japan] I was closely followed around everywhere."[54]

In Shanghai, he learned that during his absence, he had, along with other recipients, been awarded the *Prix Verrière*, a prize of 4,000 francs by the Académie française "for services rendered abroad in the propagation of the French language."[55]

CHAPTER SEVEN

Life in the Jacquinot Zone

Charity does not come by organizations, laws or
discourse, but from one man, in this case, Father
Jacquinot.
—Reverend John Ou. Mr. Ou, a Methodist, was a
jurist and publicist of renown who, inspired by Father
Jacquinot's refugee work, converted to Catholism.[1]

The Jacquinot Zone serviced as many people as a fair-sized city. Its population fluctuated in size, but over the entire course of 1938, it provided relief and
security to more than 300,000 refugees.[2] It did so with a Refugee Committee
that set itself up as the municipal council of a borough chopped out of an
occupied city. Its heavy responsibilities included feeding more than 100,000
refugees every day, and providing public utilities such as water and electricity.
The Zone was self-governing, with its own "town council." Father Jacquinot
was its genial mayor. Its budget divided into four categories: food; clothing;
hospital and medical; and miscellaneous. It had its own police force and created a criminal court that allotted punishments and penalties. In the early
stages, the French police opened a branch office in the Zone to help with
security. The police ran three shifts of four officers each, who while on duty
patrolled the area and offered protection to the Zone. The city temple had
inscribed on it the poignant phrase "Under Protection of Heaven's Mercy,"
placed over the figure of a big Buddha. In other parts of occupied Nanshi, a
new Japanese-appointed government known as the Autonomous Commission
for Nanshi, under Chen Yun as chairman and Ling Chi-tan as vice-chairman,
exercised authority and control starting from January 11, 1939.

Jacquinot's initial experience with establishing and running a refugee camp
came with the first refugee camp, located in the French Concession on the
campus of Aurora University, where he taught classes. It was appropriately
called the Number One Refugee Camp, organized by the Shanghai International Rescue Society, chaired by Jacquinot, who also served on the Chinese
Huayang Volunteers' Rescue Society. Established on August 15, just three days

The building that became Father Jacquinot's headquarters in the Zone. Private photograph.

after the Japanese attack, this camp at times housed some 7,000 Chinese, packed inside seven hastily erected makeshift bamboo-supported tents. To address the dire needs, the camp quickly developed services such as a medical clinic, a refugee registration system, training sessions, a supply section for the distribution of food rations and coal, and a security and mediation section. The Bankers' Recreation Club and Native Bankers' Guild furnished valuable aid funds to the refugee committee. The construction of seven smaller tents for cooking, bathing, and barbering rounded out the services.[3] These were the organizations and concepts that Jacquinot would later transfer to the Nanshi Safety Zone, or Jacquinot Zone, but in a location that did not enjoy the favored protection of the foreign settlements. In September and October of 1937, as he became increasingly involved in the negotiations and organization of the Nanshi Zone, he turned over de facto leadership of the Number One Camp to his assistant, Pan Dacheng, who visited Jacquinot frequently to report on it. In addition, because Jacquinot seldom had time to visit the camp, he sent a younger priest from Aurora University every day for an inspection.[4]

For his humanitarian care and work, Jacquinot reportedly became known as the "Christian Savior" or "Old Do Things" among the Chinese refugees.

In the early phase of the Zone, he promised the refugee community that he would make every effort to hold the Jacquinot Zone open for at least half a year. As it happened, the Zone lasted until June 30, 1940, by which time most of the refugees had been repatriated to their native places, established permanent residence in Nanshi, or no longer needed relief or assistance.[5]

When the Zone first opened, Jacquinot and the Committee made their headquarters in the three-storied Fire Brigade building. Father Jacquinot occupied the third floor, while the ground floor became offices for the staff and room for storage of food donations.[6] The Zone administrative structure had the flavor of democratic principles. Its services and activities were run by the Chinese themselves. The Refugee Committee divided the Zone into nine areas, each one headed by a Chinese official elected by the refugees.[7] This official had under him eleven sections staffed by Chinese. The responsibilities under each area head, section, and staff included work on housing, supplies, food, water, discipline, sanitation, medical, education, activities, repatriation, secretarial work, and registration or inventory work.

Running the sections required training, so the Zone administration offered basic management training to selected men and women who were to serve as section heads. Guards and sanitation squad leaders also received special instruction. This was the system that was to care for the 104 refugee camps housed in public buildings, schools, temples, and churches located in the Jacquinot Zone. Some lucky refugees found places in rooms of the large number of empty houses vacated earlier by Chinese who had fled into the foreign concession areas.

The Zone was thus an enormous project, requiring substantial leadership and a great amount of cooperation from foreign and official bodies, charitable organizations, and the refugees themselves. Most people recognized, however, that gathering these refugees into organized camps was the most effective way of avoiding potential riots and urban chaos. This was the aspect of the Zone that appealed to the Japanese.

A first order of business was to search each refugee applying for entrance to the Zone for contraband such as matches and firearms. The next step was to register the refugees so that they could become part of the official Zone community. The intention was that each refugee be given a badge with his or her name and a serial number on it, and if possible, the place in the Zone where the refugee was to live. This was, of course, to facilitate easy contact with the refugees and provide information to the Zone administration for the purposes of planning food, shelter, and other relief. It also came in handy if it was necessary to locate an individual quickly. The next task was to place refugees in housing and provide them with the donated daily rations. It was soon apparent that the best approach was to group refugees from the same home area together in whatever housing was available. This solved daunting problems of communication, because of the many differences in regional dialects, and helped foster contentment and discipline among the refugees. In each housing facility, whether a temple, church, school building, or makeshift shelter, a responsible person kept a register of residents and reported on any illness or other matters needing further attention from Zone personnel.

The Zone administration tried to centralize the handling of donations for the refugees so that they might be used most efficiently and equably. At least at first, the administrators preferred cash donations, so that they could buy the most essential items needed in the emergency. But the needs in the Zone changed over time. Initially, food was in short supply; later, the quantities of food increased to such an extent that spoilage and storage became the key challenges. The situation regarding relief needs and services remained fluid until the wartime situation in Shanghai stabilized to the point where transportation in and out of the Zone became normal and communications regular.

In the beginning, most of the refugees were laborers from the northern industrial districts of Yangshupu and Zhabei. Some refugees from ports such as Ningbo, Tianjin, and Qingdao also sought refuge temporarily in Shanghai, at least until they could return to their home areas. Later, when the war shifted westward, the new arrivals came mainly from the nearby countryside. At even later stages, refugees fled from the interior regions to Shanghai.

As of December 1937, the International Relief Committee arrived at the following percentages for refugees' occupations: laborers, 47.9; farmers, 13.8; small vendors, 8.0; students, 7.9; merchants, 7.6; unemployed, 14.8.[8] With this heavy mix of workers and peasants, the Zone administration grappled with the establishment of zone priorities and how they might best be successfully met. The Shanghai International Relief Committee played a key administrative and supporting role, under the leadership of Chairman K. Y. Li of the China Maritime Customs. The committee's crucial Relief Committee was co-chaired by Jacquinot and Brigadier B. Morris of the Salvation Army. Hans Berents was their chief assistant.

THE REPATRIATION OF REFUGEES

A constant priority for the Refugee Committee was to reduce the number of refugees in the Zone, which all recognized was dangerously overcrowded. *Tongxianghui,* or native-place associations, played the key role in this work, providing care to refugees from their home areas. The example of the Ningbo association in repatriating refugees who had found refuge in the Zone back to Ningbo has been cited. These societies provided a very useful service by compiling directories of refugees in the Zone from their home areas. Knowing who the refugees were, how many of them there were, and what their needs were made it easier to provide help and relief, according to the specific needs indicated by the inventories.[9] Planning for repatriation and transportation also benefited from the catalogued refugee data.

Food Collection and Distribution

Father Jacquinot succeeded in persuading the French Concession authorities to provide water to the Jacquinot Zone, which the refugees could collect in buckets twice a day. A Chinese relief organization made plans to rebuild an old stove so that it could provide hot water and tea in the Zone, which was to be for sale from 7:30 to 10:00 a.m. and from 2:00 to 5:00 p.m. This service was essential to making life in the Zone livable for all. Eventually, the administration established twenty-four hot water depots to service the 104 refugee camps or houses and 4,000 families.

Jacquinot named Pan Tse-chieh as his secretary to help ensure that the day-to-day operations of the Zone ran smoothly and to report on any difficulties. Western organizations helped take care of the food, which in the beginning was in very short supply. The ration consisted of two steamed buns and two large biscuits for each refugee each day.[10] Chinese guilds also offered food and housing to their members in their guildhalls. A Children's Charitable Organization set up a youth center that was equipped to handle 1,000 children.

With battles raging around the Zone in other parts of Nanshi, the Zone became an isolated island without easy contact or transportation to the settlements. Vehicles to haul supplies were in short supply, and because the French Concession would only open the iron North Gate for very short periods of time to let in supplies, the delivery of food, clothing, and other necessities was very restricted. The International Red Cross managed to cross the borders and provided beans and dried salted vegetables.

The Refugee Committee had to call a halt to the common practice by residents of the French Concession of throwing food for the refugees over the West Gate. Usually what happened was that the young and strong collected the food and then profited by its sale to others who could pay. This defeated efforts to make food available to the weak and to children, some of whom were even injured in the fray. The desired procedure was that any food donations be made to the central collection center. The Refugee Committee did its best to inform the refugees that they could get their food free at the donation center.

As the organization began to function more regularly, each of the nine areas or districts established a rice distribution center. The Temple of Mercy became one of the key distribution centers. The largest was the Rice and Bean Dealers' Guild. There were twenty-four rice distribution centers operating and twenty-four collective cooking facilities in the Zone. Each center distributed rice to the poorest refugees, using a ticket system, which entitled the refugee to five cents' worth, or six ounces of rice daily. For children, the amount was four ounces. The refugee distributors stamped and endorsed each ticket. These centers provided a useful and necessary channel for the delivery of other needed services as well, as they arose. In addition, the ticket system helped to provide an accurate count of the number of refugees in each district. When a resident redeemed his ticket for food, he was counted in the census. Those refugees who could buy rice found the prices very reasonable, but the fuel needed to cook the rice was expensive and thus discouraged the independent purchase of rice. The distribution centers also provided clothing or medicines to refugees when they obtained their daily rice at the local distribution center.[11]

During the cold, damp winter months, a rice bus delivered steaming hot rice, plus cabbage and bits of meat, ladled into strong paper bags, to some of the most difficult areas of the Zone, often to houses where refugees could not leave family members or were ill. The rice was kept hot by being stored in well-padded wooden tubs. Sometimes to speed delivery, the workers literally had to throw the bags of rice from the back of the bus to the waiting outstretched hands. When the Salvation Army workers alighted from the rice bus, they were met with polite, welcoming greetings. Children receiving the hot rice bags hugged them to their cold bodies for warmth, often the only warmth of the day. The Salvation Army played a key role in ministering to the refugees, especially in the foreign settlements.

Jacquinot often led tours of the Zone for journalists, local officials, and interested parties. Doing so also resulted in gaining some useful publicity for the Zone once the tour ended. There was also pride in showing the many accomplishments of the Zone in caring for the refugees. The journalist Edna Lee Booker and her husband visited the Zone to interview Jacquinot, accompanied by amateur photographers who planned to make a documentary film about the Zone for Jacquinot to show on his American tour. She described the journey into the Zone across the barbed-wire barricades of the French

Jacquinot leading a tour of the Zone. *Oriental Affairs* (Dec. 1937).

Concession and into the Japanese-controlled border area, manned by soldiers with fixed bayonets, who examined their passes. "It costs so little for each individual, but so much for the whole mass," Jacquinot told them in the interview. "[U.S.]$1.00 a month will provide frugal food and medical care for one Chinese. A bit more will supply a farmer with sufficient seeds and native implements to put his small farm into fruition again."[12]

"They should have more, but this is as much as we can give them." Jacquinot remarked to another foreign journalist visiting the Zone, standing beside a boiling cauldron of rice and shaking his head.[13]

Jacquinot was expert at winning the sympathy and support of his visitors. The China delegate on the International Committee of the Red Cross, Dr. L. P. Calame, visited the Zone in November, shortly after it was established. He was obviously very impressed by the Jesuit priest, whom he described having the visage and demeanor of an old soldier or cavalry officer; lacking his right arm, Calame said, "he was a portrait of one from the Second Empire."

Calame also gave the Red Cross an arresting account of the inhabitants and conditions in the Zone. He described the crowded alleyways, full of ragged children and mothers huddled in doorways with their babies, their faces frozen like mummies. In an old temple, they found families living under tables, squeezed together like a nest full of little cats. He heard how families had lost their homes, livelihoods, and even family members, some dead or just disappeared. Sensing that the delegation was becoming overwhelmed by the spreading misery it encountered, Jacquinot had led them back to the main streets. These bleak passageways were still vacant to allow the passage of the monitoring police patrols.

After this and more visits to the Zone, Calame pleaded in his correspondence with the International Committee of the Red Cross to prepare for a new diplomatic conference that would focus on the protection of civilians in wartime, using the Jacquinot Zone as the example to direct their study. Using the terminology "Zones et villes Jacquinot," he provided details on how the Jacquinot Zone had come into being, including the points of negotiation. He urged the International Committee to spearhead a movement and "ring the alarm bell" for civilian protection against the horrors of modern warfare.

THE CLOTHING DISTRIBUTION COMMITTEE

The 1937–38 winter season in Shanghai was especially cold and wet, creating an additional burden for the refugees and those trying to assist them. Some said it was the coldest winter since the Taiping Rebellion of the mid nineteenth century. One can easily imagine the difficulty of providing warm clothing to 200,000 people who had fled their homes with few of their own possessions. The International Red Cross Committee managed to acquire and distribute 1,500 blankets and 5,000 cotton jackets, but this was far from enough.[14]

The head of the Clothing Committee was Mrs. New Wei-sun, a prominent wealthy resident of Shanghai. Jacquinot chose her to head the committee and be responsible for the clothing of refugees in the Zone after he heard of her many accomplishments. Aware of the discomfort of Shanghai winters, with their penetrating dampness and cold, Mrs. New managed to acquire seventy-one bags of donated clothing from Hong Kong, from which she and her friends, Misses G. F. Dyu and Li-Ming Hwang Chen, sorted the wearable items. As the donations increased, she enlisted the help of Nanjing Ginling College alumnae in Shanghai, who washed and sorted the clothing, much of which was soiled, wearing hospital gowns and masks. When it became known that the clothing was being put to good use, Singapore donors followed suit, sending thousands of bags of clothing for use by the refugees.[15] With this admirable record, Mrs. New took over the clothing responsibilities for the Zone. Her colleague, Miss H. L. Chang, a graduate of Ginling College and the University of Wisconsin, took charge of clothing distribution.

Some of the donated clothing bags contained summer garments that were not suitable for the weather in Nanshi. The solution was to sew together two or three garments of the same size to produce one padded garment. Mrs. New noted that sorting, matching, and sewing to produce one warm padded garment ensured that nothing was wasted and usually produced an item quite pleasing in appearance. Bright printed material made attractive coverings for the cotton-padded quilts that were especially desired by the refugees. The American Women's Club helped with the sewing of quilts and the Sisters of the Sacred Heart primary school also pitched in to meet the need. The Chinese Women's Club donated $200 to employ more "sewing women" and to buy cotton padding. Soon the ranks of the clothing operations expanded to two hundred workers. Mrs. New estimated that the number of new and old cotton garments sewed and distributed from December 7, 1937, to January 10, 1938, was 40,000 items in the Jacquinot Zone and 17,000 in the International Settlement.[16] Still, refugees continued to sicken from the cold, and the need for warm clothing remained a priority.

When funds became more plentiful, the Refugee Committee decided that, rather than requesting cash donations, items such as clothing would be sought. Even if the refugees already had adequate clothing, cooking utensils, or other items of some value, the opportunities to sell the extra items or pawn them for extra cash, which they often wanted to do, were very limited. The pawnshops had moved into the French Concession, where business was much better, and the refugees had no easy access to them there, given the border restrictions and closed gates.[17]

SANITATION AND HYGIENE

The Buddhist Red Swastika Society assumed many of the responsibilities for cleaning the Zone's streets and alleyways and took care of collecting dead bodies and burying them. A truck came in each day to remove the dead. The estimate given was that on average, ten refugees died each day, half of them children.[18] Squads organized sanitation work. Cleaning squads cleaned and disinfected sleeping areas, while all the bedding was taken out to be sunned in the open. They also boiled the bedding each month to eliminate bedbugs and

Father Jacquinot with
some of the 80,000
refugee children in the
Zone. French Jesuit
Archives, Vanves, France.

lice. Leaders of sanitation squads or section leaders, many of them women, recruited children to pick up rubbish and kill flies. With 80,000 children in the Zone, it did not take long for visitors to begin to remark on how clean the streets and alleys were in the Zone.[19]

All adults and older children received training in hygiene and sanitation from the Zone administration. The management of sanitation was essential to preserving the health and well-being of Zone residents. Experience showed that twenty wooden buckets served 1,000 refugees, or one for every 50 refugees. These had to be emptied daily and cleaned with disinfectant. The method adopted to handle the Zone's overall waste followed the trench system used by many military organizations. Squads of men with spades and buckets dug the trenches and spread lime to make the trench areas acceptable. What was once a very unhealthful and malodorous region of Shanghai was soon brought under control, helping the Zone remain sanitary and clean.

The Education Committee

Refugee schools were located in various facilities in the zone, in temples, churches, guild houses, schools, and public buildings. Their suitability varied from place to place. In the least accommodating facilities, students might sit on the ground, on rough benches, or on biscuit tins, provided by the committee. One example involved a structure that served as a dormitory by night and as a schoolhouse during the day. Pupils sat on the floor in front of a blackboard and absorbed course work in arithmetic, Chinese language, something called "basic knowledge," and first aid. Because of the lack of qualified teachers, the more advanced students received instruction from teachers and then passed it along to beginners. Many of the teachers were refugees themselves who had been employed in schools demolished by the fighting. These teachers were unpaid and lived and ate with the other refugee residents.

The earliest refugee school for children opened in December 1937 in what today is the Yu Yuan Garden, with more than 100 children. The youngest children concentrated on learning the most basic Chinese characters. The Zone administration divided the refugee children into two groups, those aged 1 to 4 years, of which there were 30,000, and a second category aged 5 to 14, numbering 50,000. This early class in Yu Yuan must have been older children, because they were able to use textbooks provided by the respected Commercial Press publisher.[20] The Chinese Child Welfare Association was active with the older children, especially the homeless. These older children, along with the adults, also learned etiquette, singing, drama, morals, and concepts of citizenship. Group singing of familiar patriotic and folk songs was a favorite activity of all the refugee camp residents, especially after the evening meal.

The Zone administration believed it was essential to keep the refugees busy and productive. Father Jacquinot stressed that the refugees needed to learn practical skills that would enable them to find work when conditions stabilized. This prompted offering classes in handicrafts such as making baskets, grass rope, paper flowers, straw sandals, and shoes, tailoring, and needlework. Chinese merchants, who wanted to operate again in the Zone, established a committee to coordinate production and supplies and elected officers to maintain a degree of order in the Zone so necessary for conducting good business.[21] Children offered some of the best flowers and woven items for sale on the streets of the Zone. Women learned knitting and how to make hairnets and incense coils to deter mosquitoes. Men who were literate organized a wall-newspaper editing board and a newspaper reading room. Some joined athletic teams. Physical drills and games were popular with the able-bodied.

Refugee children learning a craft. *Final Report,* International Relief Committee (c. 1940).

Schools were also one place where the refugees had opportunities to social-ize and even seemed to be relatively happy. Among them were Chinese Com-munist Party youth, who became active in the camps spreading current news and propaganda and scouting for potential recruits.[22] The existence of a cap-tive population of young people afforded many opportunities to sort and select able candidates for Party membership or work. Later on, refugee repatriation programs gave a wider scope to these Party activities. When conditions in the surrounding areas of Shanghai became quieter and refugees were repatriated, those with camp experience and training were better equipped for life in their home areas. Some eventually used skills learned in the camps to support their rise through the ranks in the Chinese Communist Party or Guomindang.[23] According to a recent Chinese account, in the course of repatriation work, Jacquinot managed to make arrangements for eighty-eight young refugees to join the Communist New Fourth Army in 1939.[24]

MEDICAL SERVICES

The cold damp weather and winter winds, along with the crowded conditions, made medical attention a priority. The Chinese Medical Association established two new hospitals in the Zone, one general and the other a maternity hospital. A mobile library truck served maternity needs until the new, well-equipped maternity hospital was set up, with equipment transferred from the hospital in Yangshupu after the war made it impossible to continue there. The Sino-Belgian Boxer Indemnity Commission supported it. The general hospital was located in an abandoned but elaborate former Chinese house and cared mainly for young boys and women. Besides having its own water well (quite a luxury), it had forty beds and all the equipment of a good clinic of the day. Dr. Zhu Shi'en handled most of the medical and administrative responsibilities initially, until the task became too overwhelming.[25] At that point, a branch of the hospital opened in a neighboring building with forty-five beds, which cared for refugee men. Most of the treated refugee cases involved malnutrition, intestinal diseases, and lung ailments.

A children's hospital was in the planning stage, but in the meantime, serious pediatric cases could be sent to the Children's Hospital run by the City Government of Greater Shanghai in the French Concession. Dr. W. S. Fu, a leading child specialist, was the superintendent of this hospital. Within the Zone, treatment and diagnosis of illnesses were free to refugees, and a Zone clinic implemented an aggressive program of mandatory inoculations and vaccinations against cholera, typhoid, and smallpox. To encourage participation and help overcome the fears of some about inoculations, the Zone authorities issued the "incentive" that only those who had been vaccinated could receive the prized ration cards. After this, the busy clinic handled more than 300 cases per day.

Living in the camps gave the refugees their first exposure to Western medicine, and many had suspicions about its worth and healthfulness. Not being used to the new medicines, some questioned whether they worked for non-Westerners. The sick had to be forced to request treatment because of their old superstitions about Western medicines. The lack of Chinese doctors to treat the enormous population only exacerbated the problem. Once the medical teams had operated for a while, and the results became apparent, the refugees crowded in for services, even for minor aches and pains.

Catholic organizations and charities played a seminal role in the medical work of the Zone. They also worked on reuniting families and posting notices regarding missing relatives. Most active in the refugee work were the members of the Franciscan Sisters of the Convent of the Sacred Heart, the Sisters of Saint Vincent de Paul, the Petites Franciscaines de Marie, and the Auxiliatrices du Purgatoire. They devoted themselves to hospital work and also ran a dispensary.[26] The Franciscans had ten passes for the sisters to enter the Zone daily.

Other sisters attended personally to the serious cases of illness, besides furnishing milk for the babies and cod liver oil for the children. They were able and active collaborators with Father Jacquinot in the medical work. The Jesuit priests and the Franciscan sisters provided most of the contact between the medical staffs and the sick. They carried simple medicines such as aspirin, bicarbonate of soda, and iodine with them on their daily rounds. Their role was also to add some levity to the sad situations whenever that was possible. They soon became well known in the alleys and doorways of the Zone. Sometimes, they encountered a case serious enough to be hospitalized but had to improvise because they had no money for the rickshaw fare to the hospital or it had no free beds. There were many challenges that arose in this key field of refugee work, but by June of 1938, a visiting inspection team gave the Zone a clean bill of health, noting that even with the cold and crowding, there had not been any epidemics there.[27]

THE DISCIPLINE COMMITTEE

The Jacquinot Zone had certain rules and programs that were explained to the refugees when they joined the community in the Zone, with the admonition that they had to be followed. With such extreme crowding and sparse resources, it was of course essential that these rules be respected and obeyed. The Zone camps followed a simple but well structured routine that gave a strong sense of order to camp life. The routine was that everyone rose at 6:30 in the morning and had their first lesson in hygiene, which was to wash as thoroughly as possible. Following this, a sanitation squad of about fifty refugees began the daily cleaning of the camp facilities and grounds. All the bedding had to be rolled up and the grounds swept clean. Next came a morning exercise drill and games for the men and children.[28] School-age children divided into classes and received instruction in the Chinese language and other subjects. Some of the best older students made the rounds of different camps to read the news of the day to the many who could not read. In mid-morning, after activities and school instruction, all camp members had the first meal of the day. Refugees with cooking experience did the cooking or, if too few were available, the Zone managers trained selected refugees for this important duty. The next and last meal was served at 5:00 in the afternoon. Before this meal, more instruction and classes occupied the attention of all adults and the older children. These might include illustrated talks, theater events, and special demonstrations relating to issues of camp life.

When refugees broke the rules or failed to live up to these standards, Father Jacquinot had his own unique approaches to discipline and punishment. For example, one reported incident involved several looters arrested in the Zone. To the surprise of many, instead of incarcerating them in the Zone's makeshift jail, Jacquinot had them paraded around the Zone for three days as an example to others, with signs around their necks saying what they had done. After having been thoroughly shamed in public, they were then to be released. He also ordered that they be well fed while in police custody. Another major case brought before Jacquinot involved three burglars who had invaded and robbed homes in the Zone. He sentenced them to being paraded with signs for three days, after which they were ordered to clean up refuse on the streets for three more days.[29] The traditional Chinese weapon of shame seemed to work effectively as a deterrent in this large Chinese community.

Jacquinot played a key role in mediating disputes between quarreling refugees, a situation that came up frequently. Because of the heavy demands for this kind of mediation and rational settlement of disputes, there was some discussion for a while about creating a Zone branch of the 2nd Special District Court, headquartered in the International Settlement. The Discipline Committee worked hard to support the administration's work in this area, but the caseload was never-ending.

Jacquinot took Major General Telfer-Smollett, the commander of the British Defense Forces in Shanghai, on a tour of the Zone. They visited the Temple of Mercy, where many refugees lived, and attended ceremonies in front of the various revered images. Amid the crowds and incense, the British visitor remarked to Jacquinot on the high level of order maintained in this community living in such crowded conditions. The clean and orderly condition of the streets did not suggest a wartime refugee zone. Other visitors remarked on the strength of Jacquinot's personality and his fearlessness in dealing with the Japanese border sentries.

Some refugee leaders, concerned over the free flow of people within the Zone, recommended that gates be set up to better control the movement of people. There was even talk about building a fence between the Zone and

Father Jacquinot with the British commander in chief, Major-General A. D. Telfer-Smollett. Peter Kengelbacher, *Shanghai 1937: Photographs of Karl Kengelbacher* (1998), p. 88.

other areas. Under the proposed gating system, to pass through the proposed gates, refugees would need to show their identity cards.[30] This gating plan, while appealing to the responsible administration, met strong resistance from the residents, who treasured the freedom of movement that existed throughout the Zone. It was one of few luxuries the refugees did enjoy. In contrast to the Jacquinot Zone, the authorities in many of the camps located in the foreign settlements allowed residents to leave the camps at most once a week and to receive visitors only once a week. Some camp rules forbade any exit from the camp except in a documented emergency. In the Jacquinot Zone, where there were also several camps located in different facilities included in its territory, no restrictions existed on movement between these camps or within the Zone.

As the situation began to stabilize beginning in the spring of 1938, Chinese merchants began to return to Nanshi and the Zone. The Nanshi Trade Union procured permits for the free passage of bona fide merchants into the

Zone from the French Concession authorities. Thereafter, visitors to the Zone reported business and even leisure activities recovering. Clocks, old clothes, pots, pans, crafts, and toys were offered for sale, strewn along the sides of roads and alleyways. In rest areas, people shared stories about the caged birds they had brought along for the outing. The Zone began to take on a new sense of life and vitality. When Jacquinot led the new French ambassador, Henri Cosmé, on a tour of the Zone in early 1939, the latter observed that the rest of the old Chinese city in Nanshi was dead except for the Zone, where merchants operated, corner sellers of curios attracted interest, and the overall misery was less evident. He commended Jacquinot for being the architect of this Zone and doing France honor in the process.[31]

In the Jacquinot Zone's maze of tiny winding streets, temples, and markets—even fish markets, although how the fish got there remained a mystery—refugees could live freely in a familiar Chinese cultural setting, unlike their counterparts in the settlement camps. Life undoubtedly remained difficult, the crowding threatened epidemics, and there were limits on what one could do, but at least safety, familiarity, freedom of movement, and the basic necessities of life could be depended on. During an emotional tour of the human and physical devastation so apparent among the refugees in Nanshi, Jacquinot proudly told his French visitor Claude Rivière "that the Japanese have not gained entry here [the Zone] and the only flags that fly over this place are the French flag and the standard of the Red Cross."[32]

CHAPTER EIGHT

Final Days and Legacy

Loke who that is most vertuous alway,
Privee and apert, and most entendeth ay
To do the gentil dedes that he can
And take him for the gretest gentilman.
—Geoffrey Chaucer, *Canterbury Tales:*
The Wif of Bathes Tale

❦

The situation in and around Shanghai had stabilized by 1940 and most of the Zone's refugees had returned to their home areas. In early June, discussions began about abolishing the Jacquinot Zone that had served the refugees so well.[1] With only about 15,000 Chinese remaining in the Nanshi Zone area, the Refugee Committee ceased its expansive refugee and relief services on June 30, 1940. Upon learning of its closing, the Chongqing government expressed interest in retaining the services of its head, Father Jacquinot, or at least having him remain in China, and queried the French authorities as to whether that was possible. The official Chinese request came from Minister of Finance H. H. Kung, who had had frequent and close working relations with the popular priest and considered him a trustworthy ally in handling sensitive matters. Kung soon was informed by the French ambassador, Henri Cosmé, that the Church authorities in Paris had insisted that Jacquinot return to France and gave his health as the reason for their decision.[2] The Jesuit and French authorities further explained that the local situation in Shanghai, with closing of the Zone, no longer supported the continued maintenance of an organization that had responded to exceptional circumstances, now passed.

RETURN TO PARIS

Left unsaid was the Jesuits' concern with the level of political involvement they saw on Jacquinot's part during his recent years in Shanghai.[3] The view from Paris, and to some extent even Shanghai, was that although his refugee mission seemed to require it, Jacquinot had allowed himself to become deeply enmeshed in political and military relationships and activities in Shanghai and even Chongqing. This was a Church attitude that Jacquinot could not ignore. The record has shown frequent evidence of petty jealousies among the foreign diplomats and even clergy in China over Jacquinot's successes in achieving his difficult goals. These local attitudes and criticisms he could overcome or even disregard. But when the Jesuit Order expressed its reservations, short-sighted as perhaps they were, the message had to be respected. His desire to remain in China had to be forgotten. Jacquinot publicly explained that with his own country under attack by German forces, he had made the difficult decision to depart from Shanghai and return to Europe to serve in French relief and protection work.[4] Seen off by a large gathering of admirers, he sailed from Shanghai, where he had spent most of his adult life, on June 16, 1940.[5]

Jacquinot had been in China for twenty-seven years, never once having returned to visit his homeland. So much had transpired during his absence. The Great Depression, especially during the 1930s, had been very damaging to France and had helped precipitate a crisis in French nationalism. The general malaise and dissatisfaction led to the establishment of a socialist government under Premier Léon Blum in 1936. Catholic France began to fear for its government, which they saw as being run by the Left, a Socialist, and a Jew. The comfortable classes lamented the specter of Bolshevism, and a disgruntled labor force resisted but failed to make noticeable gains. The Blum government fell after one year in office, and while the Third Republic managed to survive, in the meantime, Germany continued to rearm.

Hitler's attack on Poland on September 1, 1939, provoked World War II in Europe. France declared war, along with Great Britain, and French troops embedded themselves in a strategy of static positional warfare behind their great "Chinese Wall," the Maginot Line, confident and assured of its successful defense. Their confidence seemed reasonable, at least until the spring, when the German forces made a swift advance into Norway, Denmark, the Netherlands, and Belgium. Then driving through the Ardennes and skirting the "Chinese Wall," they drove into northern France, occupying Paris on June 13, 1940. The French authorities decided that further resistance was useless and agreed to sign an Armistice with Germany on June 13. The outcome of this agreement was that roughly the northern half of France came under German occupation. The Third Republic had control of the remaining southern area, its capital having moved to Vichy. Leading the new collaborationist government were the 85-year-old hero of Verdun, Marshal Henri-Phillipe Pétain, and the politician Pierre Laval.

Hopes for a Paris Safe Zone

Jacquinot returned to France with high intentions of finding ways to use his Shanghai experience and successes to protect Paris and contribute to the war effort, but he met with a mixed reception there. In Shanghai, he had been well known, influential, and respected by all the local authorities. Paris presented him with a very different atmosphere and set of challenges. First, there were the leaders of the various bureaucratic structures of the French Jesuit Order, who were experienced priests, with arguments and opinions of their own. Second, although the many contributions Jacquinot had made in Shanghai during his refugee and relief work were known to his superiors and colleagues in Paris, the high point of his achievement in 1937 and the publicity it had generated worldwide had passed by now. Added to these facts was the Order's ambivalence and even anxiety about Jacquinot's independent ways and perhaps even his successes.

To help himself readjust and fit into the new cosmopolitan French environment, Father Jacquinot approached his supporters at the Lieux de Genève. He was not without some high-level French contacts, which he readily approached. He succeeded in gaining the attention and interest of Pierre Taittinger, soon to become president of the Paris Municipal Council and founder of the famous champagne house that bears his name. Jacquinot had in mind to establish a "Committee of Paris" to study the need for setting up an organization to provide protection for the city and coordinate relief efforts. His suggestion amounted to establishing a "Paris Safe Zone" following to the extent possible the Shanghai model. Taittinger agreed to hear him out and was sufficiently impressed to explore the matter further. He organized a gathering at the Paris City Hall to discuss and consider the proposal.

It was a prestigious reunion, attended by the president of the Lieux de Genève, Dr. Caillet, along with a retinue of his staff; French Vice Prime Minister Pierre Laval; M. Rousselier of the Red Cross; Taittinger with his various assistants; and, of course, Father Jacquinot. Starting off the meeting, Dr. Caillet gave a brief presentation explaining the nature and purpose of his organization and then turned the meeting over to Jacquinot. It was his golden opportunity to explain how the *lieux de Genève* concept had been fully realized in Shanghai. Conditions in Paris, he claimed, were even more favorable for establishing a safe zone than in Shanghai, where the Japanese occupying powers and the Chinese leaders had failed in all efforts to communicate over their differences. He reported how the foreign ambassadors, military leaders, and civilian officials had tried but could not bring the Japanese and Chinese warring parties together, and how he had been able to step in to act as a neutral intermediary. These local Shanghai authorities had given him this key role in handling the crisis of 1937 largely because of his previous contributions in bringing about a good measure of conciliation during serious disputes. After describing the difficult circumstance in Shanghai, with the various foreign settlements in close proximity to the Chinese areas where the fighting raged, Jacquinot then elaborated on the relief operations in the Zone after it was established. Handling the distribution of food and medicine and establishing the Zone's clinics and vaccination program seemed to be of particular interest to his listeners. He stressed repeatedly that the Shanghai case provided a valuable precedent to draw on in creating a similar zone in Paris.[6] Jacquinot concluded with a brief discussion of the Hankou Zone and assured the group that all that had been achieved in Shanghai could be duplicated in Paris. Thanking Jacquinot for his presentation, Taittinger remarked that he had given them more than mere doctrine or philosophy, but an example, an experience, to work with.[7]

Next, Rousselier offered the viewpoint of the Red Cross concerning the *lieux de Genève*. He recounted the findings of the International Committee of the Red Cross at its Sixteenth Conference held in London (1938) where the Jacquinot Zone in Shanghai was first offered as a successful example for planning the protection of civilians from aerial bombardment in wartime. The recommendation of this conference had been to use the war situation in China and the establishment of the Jacquinot Zone as a model for work elsewhere, even down to how to mark the zones with the Red Cross flag, a red cross on a field of blue.[8] The International Committee described Father Jacquinot's diplomatic efforts as being "almost unbelievably successful" in bringing the Chinese and Japanese together to resolve the refugee problem.[9] The Jacquinot Zone, the committee noted, had been organized completely independently of itself, and its success was the reason for the London Conference's adoption of its groundbreaking "Resolution on Safe Zones."

Rousselier ended the meeting with mention of the May 1940 conference held at Vichy to provide the French government with an official response to a memorandum written by Max Huber, president of the International Committee of the Red Cross.[10] Reflecting on Jacquinot's work in Shanghai, Huber asked all member nations to respond in writing to the following four points: the principle of protecting civilians during wartime; the creation of security zones; the value of Red Cross participation; and the extension of protection to Red Cross staff doing work to help civilians.[11] Apparently not completely satisfied with the responses received to the initial request, the International Committee followed up with another request to the member nations to respond, but this time the emphasis fell on the need for more concrete and practical suggestions.[12] The underlying issue that hampered or diluted any practical recommendations and the implementation of programs was the question of who or what would back up any resolutions or initiatives. Still working within the Geneva Convention of 1929, the Red Cross could only make the claim that its new resolutions on civilian protection served the international community as a powerful and public moral force. What was really needed, of course, was to have the resolutions respected and firmly applied.

Laval insisted that the foregoing discussion and goals have a wider scope. He preferred that the matter of protecting civilians in wartime be extended to the whole of France. Taking this broader view, he viewed any program for the protection of Paris merely as a point of departure for further discussion and action throughout the country.[13] Caillet closed the meeting with the observation that public opinion was ripe for the message of their meeting and recommended that the interested powers be asked to adhere to the principles raised. Left unmentioned was the reality of their actual circumstances. Most understood that the Geneva Convention had to be revised to encompass the subject of civilian protection and safe zones in wartime, duly supported by the necessary authority of contractual regulations, clearly stated and agreed upon. Otherwise, the only available alternative or opportunity was to advertise the moral force of their prepared resolutions.

Jacquinot could certainly take heart at the high level of attention his proposals had received. In the weeks and months that followed, he continued to warn that even though the Germans occupied only part of France, the threat of aerial bombing was always present. Everyone recognized that there was a desperate need for provisioning, and the coordination of civilian food and other supplies still continued to fall short. By pointing out shortcomings, he hoped to keep alive his own purpose regarding the need for and utility of safe zones.

His other opportunity to present his program to an influential audience would be at the next meeting of the International Red Cross Committee—the seventeenth—to be held in Stockholm in 1942. The usual pattern was for this body to meet every four years, but that was the schedule in peacetime, and with Europe embroiled in a broadening war, the gathering had to be postponed. Faced with war, destruction, and the overwhelming problems of displaced persons at the war's end, the International Red Cross Committee would not meet again until after the war. Instead, a lot of official effort focused on negotiating with belligerents regarding prisoners of war and civilians caught stranded in another country. This was in addition to responding to the frequent requests from official delegations wanting to visit prisoner of war camps and trade experiences with officials at other national Red Cross headquarters.[14] Requests also poured in from various member delegates, wanting to make an official visit to the Geneva International Red Cross headquarters. Jacquinot thus missed another good occasion at which to win European, if not international, support for the safe zone concept.

DISAPPOINTMENT AND DISILLUSIONMENT

On a personal level, when he returned to France, Father Jacquinot had difficulty adjusting to the new setting. Residing at the Jesuit House on the rue Grenelle in Paris, he was assigned to pastoral duties at the Sainte-Geneviève parish. The routine nature of this position for someone disposed to action rather than words did not bode well. He had left Shanghai and returned to France with his own plan to organize a Paris safe zone and with high expectations of being able to aid his country in wartime. It seemed that his difficulty was in finding service that he believed suited his background, interests, and talent. The question that must have occurred to him more than once was whether this service as a clergyman was suitable work for an organizer of safe zones.[15]

Not long after his return, Jacquinot began to receive criticism from some who became familiar with his ambitious plans, for Paris especially. Jacquinot's comprehensive and bold plan that would reshape planning and thinking about the protection of the French capital was too much for some, even among his colleagues, and they failed to take him seriously. They expressed their frustration and even ridicule, and some began to refer to Jacquinot as being *un peu "Don Quichottesque"* (a little bit like Don Quijote) in taking on tremendous feats.[16] As the discussion has shown, Jacquinot was not a lone voice advocating safe zones for Paris and elsewhere, but he was probably the most passionate and determined. When questioned as to whether he really believed in the feasibility of his goals, he responded affably, with his customary aristocratic bearing, that belief was essential, because without belief, one could not achieve anything. Nevertheless, the derision of his fellow Jesuits must have been very painful to hear and bear.

A discovery I made in the Jesuit Archives in France suggested that Father Jacquinot envisioned making the creation of safe zones, modeled on the Jacquinot Zone, a reciprocal guarantee arrangement between national powers at war. In the files, I found a version of the modern "post-it" that had been attached to a plan explaining his proposal. Unfortunately, the plan itself was not in the file, but it likely described in detail the Jacquinot Zone in Shanghai. On this hand-written, undated note, Jacquinot wrote that at the request of the French Foreign Office, the Swiss and Swedish governments had taken the initiative of proposing to Japan, Great Britain, and the United States that safe zones be created according to the description and details contained in the attached (but absent Jacquinot model) plan. Jacquinot also recommended that a zone be established in Tokyo to take care of the Japanese civilian population. Perhaps he intended a zone for Berlin too. I estimate that this note was probably written in 1943.

In France, where he lacked the familiarity and deep respect engendered during his years in Shanghai, and without the challenges that had so energized him and drawn upon his unusual personal qualities, Jacquinot felt frustration, if not disappointment. He was also deeply influenced by the horrible tragedies of the war and news of Allied defeats that filled the newspapers and airwaves on a daily basis. Added to these news accounts were the suffering of returning soldiers, some badly disfigured and psychologically scarred, and the ongoing travails of the many war refugees. The following poem helps to reveal some of his personal feelings.Its emotion brings to the reader a sense of disillusionment and even despair, but it is lightened by a powerful expression of his continued religious devotion.

In the Evening of Life

Each day of radiant summer
The evening darkens and beckons mourning;
The flower blooms and sheds its petals.
What remains, my God, of having been?
You, my God, are all that remains
And my poor astonished heart
That to You alone I have strongly given
Attesting to my constant love.
From the Spring I've seized the wave,
From my life, I have long filtered the years.
Oh, what profound sadness!
And now only God awaits me.[17]

Renewal: The Vatican's Representative

The devastation of the war, especially in the early phases, interrupted communications and supplies for food and other necessities. A terrorized population fled southward into unoccupied France, their numbers clogging the roads, while overwhelmed officials tried to maintain control. For much of the French population, subsistence was at only a very basic level. Added to these difficulties was the avalanche of refugees fleeing to France ahead of the German armies and arriving in a state of panic, hunger, and exhaustion. Relief facilities became taxed beyond their limits dealing with the tragedies of abandoned children, personal privation, and the flood of the homeless. The relief work required a variety of skills: soliciting donations, acquiring supplies, shipping them, and handling correspondence, to name only the most obvious ones.

The Catholic Church, responding to charitable impulses, began a series of programs to relieve these multiple needs in the spirit of religious conscience. Its proposals reflected a general disposition within the Church and raised the hopes of those wanting to serve. In this favorable atmosphere, Jacquinot's long experience in refugee relief, enthusiasm for constructive social action, and even his demeanor as a courtly man of affairs all stood him in good stead to once again play an important role. So, at last, an opportunity emerged that offered hope of making the best use of his many talents.

Pope Pius XII made known his desire that the Catholic Church play a seminal role in providing relief, spiritual and material, to alleviate the suffering created by the war. The Church should create a charity organization capable of assuring the Vatican's participation in the repatriation of the millions detained in Germany and those displaced during the war. The Protestant Churches had made a very credible effort with their own charity organizations and programs, making it imperative that the Catholic Church mobilize its resources. The Vatican selected Father Jean Rodhain, already successful in past activities as Almoner General of Prisoners and Deported Persons, to direct these efforts. He became the head of a new executive body based in Paris, where many international groups had their headquarters. This executive body was the Central Catholic Committee of Paris, which was to provide leadership to the larger Comité international de l'Aumônerie catholique (C.I.A.C.). The Catholic mission was to group in an organized fashion all Catholic initiatives regarding relief and repatriation work that so far had been handled individually, with special emphasis placed upon adding a spiritual dimension to these activities. This latter official function would separate the Catholic programs from those of the Red Cross. Vatican directives emphasized repeatedly that the Catholic program did not duplicate the critical Red Cross work.

With the establishment of the Paris headquarters, the next step was to select envoys to go abroad and help coordinate relief efforts. According to the constitution developed by Father Rodhain, each envoy appointment had to receive the approval of the appointing country's Vatican delegate. Each envoy's work in the countries visited would be supplemented by the appointment of a national representative, one who seemed able to assure the success of the proposed national programs. Father Jacquinot and Father Peter J. Boisard, superior general of the Society of St. Suplice, were selected to serve as envoys.

Jacquinot's first task in this service was to visit England and Ireland in order to learn about the current status of Catholic charity work in these countries, and to find delegates who could collect the needed local emergency aid and see that it reached Paris for distribution.[18] England, of course, had suffered terribly from the repeated German bombing campaigns, but the Church expectation was that rations, medical supplies, and clothing were still more plentiful there than on the Continent.[19]

When Jacquinot arrived in London in mid-March 1945, the last of the German V-2 missiles were still falling on Britain. He described the extensive damage to streets and buildings and noted that the city was jammed with foreigners from all over. The reception he received was very gracious, with promises to provide substantial aid and support. British Catholics had been quick to organize their own relief body, called the Catholic War Charity Organization. It helped that Cardinal Arthur Hinsley had long acted as an influential figure with the British government speaking for Catholic affairs. The cardinal's influence could be seen in the British government's formal invitation to the different religious organizations to cooperate in charity and relief work, which the German surrender in May 1945 would permit to be carried out.

At his reception at Westminster, Jacquinot obtained agreement from the Catholic War Charity Organization to appoint Father Keegan as its prospective national representative for charity work in service to the Central Catholic Committee in Paris. His official responsibilities involved finding charity relief, including medicines, clothing, and donations; furnishing the means of transporting the relief items; seeing that they reached the redistribution center in Paris; and forwarding donations to the Paris committee. Shortly afterward, the Catholic archbishops of Edinburgh and Glasgow both provided the necessary documentation for the secretariat of the Paris committee, certifying committees and designating the representatives, including Father Keegan, to represent their communities' contributions to Paris.[20] Jacquinot also made an important visit in Wimbledon with the apostolic delegate, who, in addition to providing his advice and encouragement, organized a visit to several German and Italian prisoner of war camps nearby. Jacquinot left the camps with a promise to request his Paris committee to supply the prisoners with more books to read to fill the hours of their long days.

Ireland was the next stop on Jacquinot's itinerary, but he learned to his dismay that the Irish government had made no arrangements to receive his visit. This alarming news sent Jacquinot back to his high-level contacts in London, who immediately, as time was short, interceded with Father Rodhain in Paris on his behalf. A very hospitable reception at Dublin's airport resulted, and meetings were arranged with Irish government officials, the papal nuncio, and the cardinal primate of Ireland. Most helpful of all was an agreement to appoint M. Travers as Ireland's representative of charity to Paris, once his candidacy received the approval of the Assembly of Irish Bishops, scheduled to meet in June 1945. Jacquinot still wanted to return to Paris with something resembling a firm Irish commitment, so he worked out a plan whereby Travers could immediately serve the Paris committee while awaiting the official approval of his nomination.

During Jacquinot's visit to Ireland, he could not ignore certain sensitive issues. The Irish government had wanted the Irish Red Cross to manage all charitable activities involving Irish relief after the war. Even before his visit, the argument had circulated that the Paris Central Catholic Committee might want to play too great a role in Irish relief work. Jacquinot tried to reassure his hosts by stressing that the Paris committee did not intend to become involved in internal questions such as how the relief would be collected, but instead would follow whatever guidance came from the Irish delegate named by the Irish bishops. He especially made this case during his one-hour meeting at Leinster House in Dublin with Prime Minister Éamon de Valera, the prominent Sinn Féin leader, whom Jacquinot described as very intelligent, strong-willed, austere, and "sans détente, toujours très anti-Anglais."[21] Father Jacquinot closed his travel report with the caution that while he had succeeded in his mission to Ireland, it was urgent that the Paris committee follow up and communicate with the archbishop of Dublin "on all matters."

His next official journey took place during the summer of 1945 and involved meeting with the Catholic hierarchy in the United States and Canada. Jacquinot was directed by the apostolic nuncio in France to use his time to promote the organization of charitable relief and deal with the various issues and stages of repatriation of prisoners and deported persons from all nations.[22] He was accompanied on this part of his mission by Father Peter J. Boisard. In the United States, the Paris-based Catholic charities already had the promised support of the apostolic delegate in Washington, and for secular work, the director-general of the famous House of Cartier. The key affiliated charity organizations that Jacquinot would approach for naming permanent delegates to Paris, as well as relief contributions, included the National Catholic Welfare Conferences of America and its sister organization, War Relief Services. Organizing a response from these bodies produced almost immediate and generous results. The newly recommended Paris delegate of these charity organizations assembled and shipped a large quantity of assorted goods for relief of the stricken in Europe. Jacquinot reported on his success during his Canadian visit, noting that he had won agreement from Cardinal Jean-Marie-Rodrigue Villeneuve to convoke a meeting of Canadian bishops to inform them of the work of the Paris-based C.I.A.C. and to discuss possible Canadian participation in its future relief programs.[23]

Jacquinot's travel reports, showing his successful work with the top Catholic hierarchies in England, Ireland, the United States, and Canada, were well received.[24] Not long afterward, in December 1945, he received a major appointment as chief of the Vatican's delegation in Berlin for the aid of refugees and displaced persons. There could be no question that this was the major problem facing postwar Europe at this time. Just previous to the announcement of his new position, Jacquinot, representing the C.I.A.C., went to Geneva to meet with the Catholic hierarchy and to discuss Catholic charity plans with those who would help determine and support this new work.[25] He began to realize that the challenges he would face in his new position in Berlin were enormous. The war had created at least fifteen million refugees, prisoners of war, and deportees, many of them to be helped by his programs. With transportation in disarray, the successful movement of people and supplies was seriously affected. Not surprisingly, there were several other initiatives, official and private, aimed at helping war victims. Pope Pius XII had just directed that Catholic charity be coordinated on an international scale, with special concern for spiritual welfare. Church officials stressed that the Vatican initiative would operate independently of the International Red Cross, whose mission sometimes might seem to overlap with its own. In any case, there was certainly enough need for all involved to play important and necessary roles.

Plenty of advice to Jacquinot on how he might carry out his responsibilities in Berlin came from the hierarchy of the C.I.A.C. in Paris. The secretary-general of the Paris committee passed on to him instructions as to parties he should meet and what he should accomplish during his stopover in Switzerland. As might be expected, he was to ask the Swiss for material aid such as pharmaceuticals, clothing, and foodstuffs. But in addition, he was to request the services of nursing staff and social workers, who were to join him at his mission in Berlin.[26] He was to provide spiritual and material aid to the displaced persons in the Berlin camps and facilities. Those who had lost family members or were looking for lost children or spouses were eligible for the mission's help. Moreover, in accord with the Vatican, Jacquinot was to make contact with German Catholics and their leaders and bring them up to date on the activities of Catholics in other countries.

When Jacquinot arrived in Berlin, his colleagues noted how exhausted he seemed. They described him as looking gaunt, his face heavily lined, and his posture slightly bent. Their pleas for him to preserve his strength and lessen his workload went unheeded. Rather, his friends noted, he continued to expend himself to the fullest.[27] According to Jacquinot, he needed to travel, observe, and then make timely reports to others, all with the purpose of building a good foundation for carrying out his many duties. He traveled to war-torn Breslau (Wrocław) in Poland and recounted the tragic desolation he encountered in the countryside full of ruined villages and pillaged homes. In Breslau city, he took charge of assisting in the exodus of women and children. He despaired of the ancient hatreds between the Poles and the Russian, rekindled by the war, and still enflaming the relief and relocation programs. He described his aching grief at the sight of plundered cemeteries dug up by Russian troops in search of gold teeth and other valuables. Another detailed report discussed the scheduling of travel for German nationals returning from Poland, Czechoslovakia, Hungary, Yugoslavia, Romania, and Austria, in accordance with the directives of the Potsdam Conference. The repatriated were to be sent to UNRRA camps in the American, French, British, and Russian Zones of Berlin for relief and care. The numbers and problems recounted in the report highlight the gargantuan size and difficulty of this task, especially for one worn out by repeated service.[28]

In late August 1946, Jacquinot made his last trip to Paris from Berlin, mainly to accompany a large group of German priests. The journey and its duties severely tested his strength and further eroded his declining health. When he returned to Berlin, extreme fatigue and his lack of appetite became so severe that he was no longer able to say Mass. The only food he wanted to eat was the small red tomatoes he had grown in his private vegetable garden in the rear of his dwelling. His colleagues urged him to see a doctor, but perhaps knowing that he was terminally ill, he always put them off. They reported that he shared any medicines prescribed for him with the small potted plants adorning his bedside table. When the doctor asked if the medicines helped his condition, Father Jacquinot pointed to his yellowing plants and lamented that the medicines had killed them. It obviously did no good to speak to him of doctors, surgeons, or medicines.

On September 6, he accidentally fell and was injured. The damage this did to his weakened condition finally required his hospitalization at the French Military Hospital at Reinickendorf. Doctors, observing his fragile condition, diagnosed advanced leukemia and administered blood transfusions, which seemed to help at least temporarily. A subsequent alarm over his heart condition led his colleagues to suggest again that extreme unction should be administered immediately. Jacquinot said that he had already received it four times during his lifetime, so it was not now necessary. He would tell them when the end was really near. On September 9, when the offer of extreme unction was again raised, Jacquinot instead asked for a bottle of champagne, and when it was offered to him, he swallowed a few teaspoonfuls and asked all those present to toast his health. For many of his closest associates, the mood of celebration seemed a fitting end to his rich conscious life. The next day, he fell into a coma, causing preparations to be made to administer the last sacraments, general absolution, and, finally, extreme unction. He died at 4:40 p.m. that day, September 10, 1946, at the age of sixty-eight.

Cardinal Konrad von Preysing, the archbishop of Berlin and General Marie-Pierre Koenig, commandant of the French Occupation Troops in Germany, began immediate preparations for his funeral service. At the Catholic Church of Frohnau, Cardinal von Preysing presided over the service, which was attended by, among others, the Russian Orthodox bishop of Brussels and Berlin, His Excellency Alexander. Father Lesage, chief of the Vatican missions, performed the funeral Mass, with an American priest and a French military chaplain serving as deacons. M. Clauzel represented the diplomatic corps and Father Nicot represented the family, the Vatican, and the Society of Jesus. Delegations representing the Allies attended, as well as French, American, and British military chaplains, almost all of the Jesuit priests in Berlin, many diocesan priests, diplomats, professors from the University of Berlin, and others. Although he had not served in the French government, his remains were wrapped in the French flag and that of the Vatican. During the funeral procession, Jacquinot's various French and foreign decorations rested on a velvet pillow, carried by his friend Prince Murat, who served in displaced persons organizations. General Gui Yongqing, chief of the Chinese Mission, placed on the coffin a crown of roses with a large white ribbon inscribed with gold Chinese characters. Translated, the message was that Father Jacquinot had served as a missionary in China for thirty years, mostly in Shanghai, and had organized the zone of refuge called the Jacquinot Zone.[29]

In accordance with Jesuit practices and tradition, the solemn occasion did not include eulogies by those attending. Later at the cemetery, General Roger Noiret, adjutant to General Koenig and chief of the French Conseil de contrôle de Berlin, spoke in the name of France, saying that Father Jacquinot would become part of French history and praised his enormous accomplishments in China and the world. On September 20, a memorial service took place at the Paris Eglise des étrangers and was attended by Church officials and the Chinese ambassador.[30]

His Legacy in the Geneva Convention

Father Jacquinot's untimely death denied him the opportunity to experience his greatest tribute, the inclusion of his concept of safe zones in the documentation considered part of the Geneva Convention of 1949. Not only was the concept there, it was identified with his own name, a rare occurrence in such formal documentation. The "Jacquinot Zone" became cited as a successful example of ways to protect civilians in wartime. So, three years after his death, and without his being present to argue for its inclusion at the secular forum in Geneva, the epitome of his life's work was properly recognized.

World War I had been called the "war to end all wars." Yet within a relatively short time, World War II had broken out. When it ended in Europe and in Asia, there was very great hope that with the founding of the United Nations, the world could avoid another world war in the future. The Geneva Convention was a vital part of this hope. One of the primary concerns, even before the war, was the fate of civilians. International attention to the critical matter of civilian protection during wartime was interrupted by the war itself. Still, the message offered repeatedly was that the changes in modern warfare required the development of new regulations. The old categories needed to be extended and new ones added. A new response was needed to deal with aerial warfare and bombing that usually led to great loss of civilian lives. Economic and military objectives had become targets that exposed civilians to danger. There was particular concern for the protection of civilians in occupied areas. Populations had suffered deportations, mass extermination, the taking and killing of hostages, looting, and pillage. Officials needed to reflect on the horrifying events of the past war years and contemplate how World War I had led to another war, even broader and more deadly for civilians. What measures could be taken to ensure that these travesties would never again occur?

Preparing for a New Convention

The assumption normally is that war is fought for the well-being of civilians. And yet the outdated Convention of 1929 protected only the wounded and the sick, as previous wars had demanded. Civilians had for the most part remained outside the war zones in those earlier conflicts. World War II differed in that it had been fought on an unprecedented scale. It would provide a plethora of tragic evidence and examples that needed to be analyzed and addressed in bringing humanitarian principles in line with international law.[31]

Developing new responses was to be a broadly cooperative activity. It required consultation with religious and secular bodies that had charity experience during the war. In addition, the assistance of specialists was needed to draft amendments of existing laws, based on real-life experience. This was all done at the behest of the International Red Cross Committee. Then, after much discussion and circulation of the drafts received by the International Committee, the approved drafts were passed on to the Geneva Diplomatic Conference, the body empowered to give the drafts the force of international law.

The International Red Cross Conference met in Stockholm from August 20 to 31, 1948, and the specialists' drafts, with some amendments offered by the International Committee, were formally adopted. The texts eventually became the sole Working Documents of the Diplomatic Conference of Geneva, out of which came the 1949 Geneva Convention.[32] Sixty-three governments sent representatives; China was a signatory; Japan, Germany, Austria, and Italy were not until 1953–54. The most important convention for the purposes of this study is the fourth, the "Geneva Convention Relative to the Protection of Civilian Persons in Time of War, of August 12, 1949." This is the one that also prohibits torture, mutilation, or cruel treatment, and so on. Within this convention, Articles 14 and 15 are especially relevant in that they cover safety zones mutually agreed upon by parties in conflict. What they state in general terms is further elaborated upon in Annex I: "Draft Agreement Relating to Hospital and Safety Zones and Localities." Briefly summarized, the mutually concluded agreements require that civilians in safety zones take no part in hostilities and perform no work of a military character. (We have seen that this was required of civilians in order for them to have protection in the Shanghai Jacquinot Zone.) Further, the zone must not be attacked, but be protected and respected by the parties to the conflict. (Again, the similarity with the successful Jacquinot Zone is apparent.) The party that establishes the zone must accept the control of a special commission by the power that recognizes the zone. This commission can even reside within the zone and must be supported in its duties of inspection. (This was the condition that came into force once the Japanese occupied the entire Nanshi portion of Shanghai, but still allowed Jacquinot's supervisory committee to continue its work.) If the commission finds evidence contrary to the stipulations in the mutual agreement, it may set a time limit for its remedy, and if this additional time does not resolve the problem, it may declare itself no longer bound by the zone agreement. (This stipulation was included in the original agreement Jacquinot negotiated with the Chinese and Japanese authorities in Shanghai.) These obvious similarities show conclusively that the Jacquinot Zone was the primary example and inspiration for key concepts and findings in the new laws.

While all of this expository discussion is rather general, which is customary for high-level formal documents, the subject did receive extensive elaboration in the commentaries to the 1949 Convention. In a comprehensive discussion of neutral zones, how they can be established, who would benefit, and the recommended content and format of the initial agreements, the Jacquinot Zone is cited by name as a provider of practical experience that led the Diplomatic Conference to adopt Article 15.[33] Also mentioned as early examples for consideration are the Madrid Zone and the zones established in Jerusalem during the conflict in Palestine in 1948. The Madrid Zone was only partially successful, in that the Nationalist and Republican forces never could come to agreement and clashed over its supervision. It did, however, represent an early example of the idea or concept of a zone. The Jerusalem case went through three stages. The first envisioned the entire city as a safe zone. When this scheme broke down, certain buildings in the city were identified as areas protected by the Red Cross as safety zones. Refugees in some of the buildings could only stay in those zones for a few hours and were not entitled to either food or lodging. The zones only sheltered just over one hundred refugees.

Among these examples, certainly the Jacquinot Zone had the most to offer as a precedent. The Jerusalem zones housed far fewer numbers, for shorter periods, and did not have to cope with aerial bombing or even long-range artillery. Ironically, in Shanghai, when consular representatives suggested in 1945 that in the face of the Communist takeover of the city, a safety zone be instituted to safeguard the civilian population, the concept was rejected by the Chinese Nationalist government.[34]

The next time the Jacquinot Zone was singled out as a successful example of wartime protection for use by countries in conflict was in the *Protocol Additional to the Geneva Convention of 12 August 1949* produced in 1977.[35] In this, the Madrid example is omitted. As for the Jerusalem precedent, the King David Hotel, which is included, was only part of a large zone that failed. It became pared down to include only this international hotel. Nevertheless, the hotel did become a zone, and it is mentioned as a useful example. But in fact it was used only occasionally, for a few months, and most often for the purpose of housing the administrative staff of the I.C.R.C.

Epilogue

In 1930s China, the national government had yet to develop centralized, responsive services able to handle large-scale natural and wartime disasters. In the absence of official services, the Catholic charities came to play a major role. The Chinese networks of guilds and native-place societies were effective locally, but when the Japanese invasion overran entire cities and provinces, the Chinese national government had to find new and better ways to respond. The tools of modern warfare blasting away at cities, neighborhoods, and populations brought a new challenge. No longer were the traditional Chinese bodies that responded directly to only their own local people adequate in these circumstances. And yet the government could not set up the desired broad new organizational network quickly, especially in the midst of war. In the interim, Catholic relief services, the work of the International Red Cross, with its China national branch organization, and, in Shanghai, the concerted efforts of both Chinese and Western civic and religious organizations became essential to perform the crucial relief work. Working with these conditions, the Catholic Church, its functioning closely tied to secular power and civic organizations became an important source of information and understanding to the Chinese. It clearly illustrated the importance and utility of having governing organizations imbued with a clear sense of broad social responsibility.

There was another factor at work, at least in the case of relief and social welfare work in Shanghai. This was the role of human agency in the person of Father Jacquinot, whose talents, work, and contributions have been apparent throughout this study. He benefited from his immersion in the Chinese community as a parish priest and garnered the respect and trust of Chinese officials by reason of his flood relief work. The courage and ingenuity he displayed during the first Japanese attack in 1932 impressed both the Chinese and Japanese leaderships. Of course, his most decisive contributions involved setting up refugee safe zones, which won him support and recognition from all sides and communities, including the foreign powers, after the second Japanese attack in 1937.

If there had already been in place a modern welfare system with disaster plans ready to be implemented in the event of an invasion, and bodies to supervise and coordinate the work, would Father Jacquinot have been important, influential, or even needed? Or if such a system had existed, would its functioning bureaucracy, supporting the underpinning of its operations, have allowed him to play such a key role? Is there ever a place for just an individual to exert such influence in dealing with a major crisis? Did not even the Jesuit Order see Jacquinot as having overstepped its organizational boundaries and taken on too visible a role in working out the solutions to the refugee crisis?

Jacquinot clearly understood what was needed to deal with the humanitarian crisis brought on by Japanese invasion and the new phenomenon of urban warfare. The key factor was avoiding any show of support for one side against the other. The goal was twofold: to perform humanitarian work in the interests of civilian, noncombatant populations in a war zone and, at the same time, to convince the belligerents involved that it was in their political interests that this be done. To be successful at this mission required a foundation of trust among the principals, consummate organizational skills, a strong sense of purpose, and a substantial measure of political wisdom and discernment. Possessing most of these qualities, Jacquinot was able to grasp and employ what he knew to be crucial to each involved party and use this knowledge to bring about the necessary common ground for establishing a safe zone.

Jacquinot also recognized that the primary requirement for a successful safe zone was the absence of any military presence in the zone, not just a prohibition against targeting the zone. The complete demilitarization of the safe zone and disarming of its population were both mandatory. When the parties agreed upon a zone location on this basis early in the conflict forming a lasting zone became possible. Thereafter, any discussion of defending the zone or deterring attacks against it became unnecessary, because the arrangement was wholly based on the initial consensus about the zone's nonmilitary nature that already had been reached between the belligerent parties.

Maintaining internal order and discipline in the zone could only be performed by a civilian police force. Even then, it took all of Jacquinot's skills to realize this goal over the long term. A serious burden was that his policies and relief work had to function against the backdrop of a devastating war scenario, with constant tensions testing and stressing the arrangement. He had to respond decisively, but with enough flexibility and finesse to keep negotiations going forward, for the Jacquinot Zone to survive. In the fast-paced situations he frequently faced, he most often did not have the luxury of spending many hours or days examining and discussing various options that might be pursued to deal with a crisis.

In reviewing all these qualities and necessities, one cannot but postulate whether such an approach and a similar kind of individual might be what was needed to aid in the resolution of the many refugee crises of the past decade. A serious drawback has been the reality that existing international organizations have not wanted to respond to the internal conflicts, even to alleviate the civilian turmoil and disastrous suffering. Notably, by contrast, Jacquinot set up the Shanghai Zone without the assistance even of the International Red Cross Committee. It may be, however, that the emergence of such a remarkable individual is not likely today in any circumstances. Jacquinot's work and service may be only an anomaly, or at least not readily duplicated. Still, the engagement of outside powers, even military power, for the sole purpose of humanitarian causes, such as negotiating the setting up of civilian safe zones, would seem to be obligatory, given the severity and intractable nature of many conflict situations. In the recent emergencies, relief work in distributing supplies and aid often dictated a coalition of forces. Working through a coalition also helps to reduce the appearance of a more sinister purpose for outside intervention.

The concept of the safe zone would seem to afford potential solutions in present-day situations. In the new global environment, this approach would require a substantial interplay between human, political, and military participants and, especially, a pairing of skills between diplomats and military commanders. The United Nations Security Council in fact recommended and authorized the use of safety zones to ensure the safety of people in the 1990s.[1] In important respects, such as the role of the military, internal policing, and the essential political ingredients required to establish the zones, these recent areas or zones have not followed the Jacquinot model. A major difference is the Jacquinot Zone's reliance upon politics and negotiation, resulting in consensus early in the crisis, in contrast to the UN's heavy reliance on outside direction and enforcement, even to the point of restricting the host country's sovereignty.

Today, the threat to civilians, refugees, and displaced persons in large-scale civil conflicts is perhaps greater than ever before. In fact, in today's conflicts, irregular armies target civilians deliberately, take hostages, and commit atrocities when their demands are not met, or use civilians as a target of reprisals. Civilians often bear most of the casualties or become refugees, with women and girls exposed to sexual violence and prostitution. Moreover, because of the large numbers of civilians involved, and the degree of emergency in these situations, it would seem necessary for international bodies to play a role, but only when firmly engaged under humanitarian auspices. As guidance in these conflicts, international humanitarian law remains the primary legal reference. Of course, an essential element of the legal framework, and perhaps its most vulnerable point, is the required commitment of the parties to the conflict to abide by the rules.

The role of civil society in establishing schools, clinics, and even small commercial opportunities remains essential and is at least as important as security concerns. In the Jacquinot Zone, the establishment of schools, small businesses, clinics, and food depots gave a sense of normalcy and stability, besides occupying the time and talents of the refugees. Construction of refugee camps and requisitioning and distributing emergency supplies is another important area for coalition focus. Modern tragedies such as the carrying out of genocide and "ethnic cleansing" have become new high-water marks of historic injustice. So often they are practiced in large refugee camps exposed to a heavy military presence and have resulted in death, misery, as well as substantial population movements. The massacres and atrocities against towns and villages always involve families and children and other civilians. Often they have had as their only purpose the potential political gains to be won at the peace table. The existence of these practices illustrates the degree of cynicism involved in this warfare.

The occurrence of such tragedies leads to speculation as to whether further revisions of the terms of warfare are necessary, perhaps through another updating of the Geneva Convention of 1949. The purpose would be to bring the new warfare and the rules for conducting hostilities in line with common international understanding of human rights and humanitarian concerns. It would attempt to clarify, based upon contemporary practice and understanding, the legal basis for certain conflicts, of war practices and customs, and policies. It would represent another effort to bring international law into harmony with humanitarian concerns and provide a new opportunity to present clearly and broadly the meaning and content of the law so that no one can claim ignorance of it.

There is no missing the fact that successful humanitarian endeavors require a high level of political and even historical acumen. Whatever the crisis, it must be carefully and thoroughly analyzed. For those likely to deal with crises, the need is to embrace opportunities to become educated in history, politics, and area studies, the latter including language training. In a nutshell, there needs to be more careful and serious research in the humanitarian field, with an underlying appreciation and respect for social and cultural differences. Some of the challenges to be faced are new in the post–Cold War age, and some of them are timeless.

Many other individuals have engaged in humanitarian pursuits in recent history and accomplished unusual success. The late Iris Chang, in her well-known work on the Nanjing Massacre, referred to the German Nazi John Rabe as "China's Schindler." There is no question that Rabe was a determined rescuer of Chinese during the massacre in Nanjing. Knowledge of his many accomplishments is aided by the fact that his name resonates with the vast number of people familiar with Steven Spielberg's 1993 film *Schindler's List*. In seeking some comparison to Jacquinot's work, and some degree of historical congruence, we might also note the Swedish diplomat Raoul Wallenberg, who is credited with having saved at least 70,000 Hungarian Jews under attack in Budapest during the dark days of the Holocaust in Europe. Like Jacquinot, Wallenberg displayed a rare combination of courage, determination, and imagination. One of his most acclaimed tactics for saving Jewish lives was to establish "safe houses," rather than a safety zone, to conceal Jewish families and individuals in the Hungarian capital. This proved very effective in rescuing Jews from certain death in the Nazi death camps. In their originality and effectiveness, Wallenberg's methods bear some similarity to those employed in China by Jacquinot.

Although one tries to resist playing the numbers game, it seems to be almost a necessity when researching major tragedies in history. And on that basis, the fact of Jacquinot's achievement in having rescued at least 500,000 Chinese from all but certain death during the Japanese invasions goes unmatched.

Reference Matter

Convention (IV) relative to the Protection of Civilian Persons in Time of War. Geneva. 12 August 1949.

Part II: General protection of populations against certain consequences of war

ARTICLE 15—NEUTRALIZED ZONES

[P. 129] GENERAL BACKGROUND

The neutralized zones mentioned in Article 15 are based on the same idea as the hospital and safety zones covered by the previous Article. They too are intended to protect people taking no part in the hostilities or placed *hors de combat*, from the effects of military operations by concentrating them in a given area. It has already been pointed out however, that neutralized zones differ from hospital and safety zones in that they are established in the actual regions where fighting is taking place and are intended to give shelter to both civilian and military wounded and sick, as well as all civilian persons who take no part in hostilities. Furthermore, they are generally set up on a temporary basis to meet the tactical situation at a particular moment, whereas hospital and safety zones tend to be more permanent in character.

The historical outline at the beginning of Article 14 holds good for Article 15 too, since neutralized zones are merely one instance of what are described generally as places of refuge (1). It need only be said that Article 15 is the result of a certain amount of practical experience: it will be remembered that at the instance of the International Committee of the Red Cross a neutralized zone was established in a district in Madrid during the Spanish Civil War; that during the conflict in Palestine in 1948, two, and at one time three, neutralized zones, directed and administered entirely by the International Committee of the Red Cross, were set up in Jerusalem and that, in 1937, during the Sino-Japanese war, a neutralized zone was also established in Shanghai (2). It was called the **Jacquinot Zone**,* in honour of the man who organized it.

The experience gained on these occasions, especially in Jerusalem, let the Diplomatic Conference to adopt this Article, which reproduced, without any change of importance, a draft text submitted by the International Committee of the Red Cross.

* My emphasis added to this excerpt.

Protocol Additional to the Geneva Conventions of 12 August 1949, and relating to the Protection of Victims of International Armed Conflicts (Protocol I), 8 June 1977.

Part IV: Civilian population # Section 1— General protection against effects of hostilities # Chapter V—Localities and zones under special protection

(p. 697) Part IV, Section I, Chapter V—Localities and zones under special protection

2259 It should be noted that the possibility of creating places of refuge, as an option, was already provided for in the Geneva Conventions. Thus Article 23 of the first Convention provides for "hospital zones and localities" for protecting the wounded and sick of the armed forces. In addition, the fourth Convention provides for the establishment of "hospital and safety zones and localities" in order to shelter the civilian sick, children, the elderly etc. Article 15 adds the possibility of establishing "neutralized zones" in regions where fighting is taking place intended to shelter from danger not only the wounded and sick, but also civilians not participating in hostilities. (1)

2260 The Protocol supplements these provisions with the present Chapter, which comprises two articles dealing with non-defended localities and demilitarized zones, respectively. These are not specifically concerned with sheltering particular categories of the population such as those who are especially vulnerable (the wounded and sick, children, etc.)—although there is nothing to prevent these from being allowed in. The intention is rather to place certain localities or zones with their entire population, apart from combatants, outside the theatre of war, as was already the case with the neutralized zones of the fourth Convention (Article 15__).

2261 The reason why the Diplomatic Conference, on the ICRC's initiative, decided to lay down new rules is that the 1949 provisions were not applied in practice as had been the intention. However, the ICRC has achieved various temporary solutions to this effect. In Dacca in 1971, Nicosia in 1974, Saigon and Phnom-Penh in 1975, Nicaragua in 1979 and the Falkland Islands (Maivinas) in 1982. (2)

2262 Experience has shown that it is very difficult for States to prepare places of refuge already in time of peace, and if they do so, they take care to keep it confidential. In truth the only way in which it is possible to establish protected zones or places of refuge is in the "heat of the moment," i.e., when the fighting comes close and the defence of the particular locality or zone is of no military interest or of relatively minor interest in comparison with the civilian losses which (p. 698) might result from a protracted defence. This convinced the ICRC that the creation of a non-defended locality should be possible unilaterally and very rapidly. The Conference followed these proposals to a very large extent, as evidenced by the fact that a declaration of an open city will have effect if it is not immediately contested. This represents an important reaffirmation of an elaboration on customary law. The other achievements of this Chapter are certainly useful, but since they are subject to the agreement of the Parties to the conflict, they have less chance of being put into practice as it is often difficult to conclude agreements once the Parties are actively engaged in hostilities.

NOTES

[(1) p. 697] The "Jacquinot zone"* established in Shanghai in 1937 and the neutralization by the ICRC of a large hotel in Jerusalem in 1948 have been mentioned as examples of such places of refuge. Commentary IV, pp. 121–124 gives a historical background on places of refuge which it was possible to set up on various occasions with limited degrees of success;

[(2) p. 697] Cf. Y. Sandoz, "*Localités et zones sous protection spéciale*," a study presented at the Tenth Round Table of the International Institute of Humanitarian Law, San Remo, 1984, in "*Quatre études du droit international humanitaire*," Geneva, 1985, p. 35; S. S. Junod, "Protection of the Victims of Armed Conflict Falkland—Malvinas Islands . . . ," op. cit., pp. 33–34.

* My emphasis added to this excerpt.

Notes

ABBREVIATIONS USED IN THE NOTES

JA   Archives des Jésuites, Vanves, France,
CWR   *China Weekly Review*
JFMA   Japanese Foreign Ministry Archives
JMFA   Japanese Ministry of Foreign Affairs
NCDN *North China Daily News*
NCH   *North China Herald*
RG   U.S. National Archives and Records Administration Record Group,

CHAPTER ONE

1. *China Press*, Nov. 19, 1937, p. 1; an article in *Xinmin wanbao*, June 18, 2005, estimates more than 300,000 refugees in the Zone.

2. MacKinnon, "Tragedy of Wuhan, 1938," p. 949; Coble, *Chinese Capitalists*, pp. 1–2.

3. Key biographical and related materials for Jacquinot are found in JA in folders included in archival boxes identified with his name. See also Meehan, "Savior of Shanghai" and "Îlot de refuge"; "Le Pére Jacquinot de Besange," in *Compagnie*, no. 8 (Spring 2006), pp. 123–27; *Relations de Chine*, no. 13 (1937–38): 336–42; *Diccionario histórico de la Compañia de Jesús*, 3: 2120–21; *Études*, November 1946, 258–60; *Dictionnaire du monde religieux dans la France contemporaine*, 1: 153–54; *Bulletin de l'Université l'Aurore*, no. 3 (1946): i–iv; *Bibliotheca missionum*, ed. Streit et al., vol. 14: *Chinesische Missionsliteratur, 1910–1950*, pp. 528, 613; *Dictionnaire de biographie française*, vol. 18, p. 352.

4. Jacquinot, *Lettres de Jersey*, 1937–38, p. 105, JA. This source provides information on the life and activities of Jesuits of the Paris Province (see Bibliography).

5. Donnelly, *Principles of Jesuit Education*, p. 20.

6. Thomson, *Democracy in France*, p. 66.

7. Wright, *France in Modern Times*, pp. 232–36.

8. Ibid., p. 257.

9. My understanding of the Jesuit formation programs benefited significantly from the advice and guidance provided by Father John David Meehan, S.J., of Toronto University and John W. Witek, S.J., Georgetown University, and from related biographic holdings in Georgetown University's Woodstock Library.

10. *Diccionario histórico de la Compañia de Jesús*, 3: 2121.

11. Society of Jesus, Catalogus Provinciae Franciae, 1904, Woodstock Library, Georgetown University.

12. *Diccionario histórico de la Compañia de Jesús*, 3: 2120–21.

13. Society of Jesus, Catalogus Provinciae Franciae, 1905–6, 1906–10, Woodstock Library, Georgetown University.

14. For the biographical details in this and the next two paragraphs, see *Diccionario histórico de la Compañia de Jesús*, 3: 2121; Jacquinot, *Lettres de Jersey*, vol. 47. no. 1, p.105, JA.

15. Fernande Monnot, interview, Mar. 14, 2006.

16. *Compagnie*, no. 8, p. 123.

17. Jacquinot, letter to provincial superior, Aug. 3, no year, JA.

18. Ibid., p. 2

19. A document in JA dated Nov. 17, 1937, reports the following makeup of the Catholic mission in Shanghai: 201 Jesuits; 183 auxiliaries; 31 nuns of the Sacred Heart; 86 Franciscans; 95 daughters of Saint-Vincent de Paul; 54 Chinese priests; 68 Marist brothers and 680 Chinese novices.

20. Meehan, "Îlot de refuge," unpublished paper, p. 3.

21. Louis Froc, S.J., letter, May 31, 1914, to his godmother mentioning the death of Jacquinot's mother, JA. Froc was director of the famous Jesuit observatory at Zikawei.

22. Rivière, *En Chine avec Teilhard*.

23. Teilhard's book *The Phenomenon of Man* was denied publication during his lifetime and censured by Church officials. The Vatican Curia, under Pius XII, continued its conservative stance during Teilhard's lifetime. He was not allowed to reside in France. Teilhard's difficulties led to his decision in 1951 to make arrangements to leave the country and take up residence in New York, much to the relief of his Jesuit superiors. He died there on April 10, 1955.

24. Rivière, *En Chine avec Teilhard*, pp. 78–79.

CHAPTER TWO

1. This observatory became the center of a network of stations from Siberia to Manila and from Indochina to Guam, bringing together laboratories for scien-

tific research and forming the Earth's Physics Institute. Run by priest-scientists, they were dedicated to following in the tradition of Father Matteo Ricci—to gain influence by prestige in the sciences. See *The Story of the Siccawei Observatory, Shanghai*, Shanghai: North China Daily News, 1921, pp. 268–77.

2. Cronin, *Wise Man from the West*, p. 26.

3. Rosso, *Apostolic Legations to China*, p. 75; Ricci, *China in the Sixteenth Century*, p. 94. For more information on what happens when a Christian concept of God is introduced into a sophisticated culture, see Gernet, *China and the Christian Impact*.

4. Gernet, *China and the Christian Impact*, p. 20.

5. Pinot, *La Chine et la formation de l'esprit philosophique en France*, p. 27.

6. Compagnie de Jésus, *Lettres édifiantes et curieuses écrites des missions étrangères*, 9: 391.

7. See Marcia Reynders, "Father Joachim Bouvet: His Contributions East and West" (master's thesis, University of Hawaii, 1965).

8. Sebes, *Jesuits and the Treaty of Nerchinsk*, p. 106.

9. Rowbotham, *Missionary and Mandarin*, p. 111.

10. Compagnie de Jésus, *Lettres édifiantes*, 10: 1–17.

11. Interview with Walter Fuchs, Cologne, Germany, 1963.

12. Claude de Visdelou, S.J., a reputed Sinologist, dissented from this view.

13. Rosso, *Apostolic Legations to China*, "Document 5," p. 243.

14. Minamiki, *Chinese Rites Controversy*, pp. 58–60.

15. Ibid., "Mandarins' Diary," p. 364.

16. Hayward, *Christians and China*, pp. 14–15.

17. Lutz, *Chinese Politics and Christian Missions*, p. 2.

18. Yip, *Religion, Nationalism and Chinese Students*, p. 2.

19. Silva, *Todo o nosso passado/All Our Yesterdays*, p. 47.

20. "Le Père Jacquinot de Besange," JA, p. 1.

21. The Université l'Aurore, founded in 1903, had strong departments in medicine, mathematics, physics, chemistry, and law. In 1923, it had 393 students, 45 professors (33 European and 12 Chinese). *Journal de Shanghai*, Apr. 29, 1933.

22. "Le Père Jacquinot de Besange," p. 1; Froc, letter dated May 31, 1914, JA.

23. Poem signed by Father Jacquinot, JA. Translated from the French:

Ad multos annos!

Tout à l'orée d'une clairière
Un chêne laissa cher un gland
Dans l'herbe épaisse et la bruyère;
il germa, poussa, devint grand.
Souvent au travers de ses branches
Les souffles après des hivers

Ont pourchassé les neiges blanches
Et l'ont de frimas tout couvert'
Mais que de jeunes à son ombre
Ont grandi très riches d'espoir.
Dieu Bon après l'ouragan sombre
Faites lui longtemps un doux soir!

24. For discussion of the May 30 incident and its background, see Clifford, *Spoilt Children of Empire*, pp. 97–112. See also Rigby, *May 30 Movement*.

25. Lutz, *Chinese Politics and Christian Missions*, p. 161.

26. For discussion of this period, see Liu, *Military History of Modern China, 1924–1949*, chap. 3.

27. *NCDN*, Mar. 21, 1927.

28. For discussion of Shanghai's 1927 leftist period, see Clifford, *Spoilt Children of Empire*, chap. 13.

29. *NCDN*, Mar. 22–23, 1927.

30. Ibid., Mar. 23, 1927; *China Press*, Mar. 23 and 24, 1927.

31. *Bulletin de l'Université l'Aurore*, 7, no. 3, 1946, pp. ii–iii.

32. The citation signed by Rear Admiral Basire giving the account of Jacquinot's bravery and rescue of the convent inhabitants is cited in ibid., p. iii. See also *Études*, November 1946, p. 258; Clifford, *Spoilt Children of Empire*, p. 218; Consul General C. E. Gauss to State Department, Apr. 21, 1927, U.S. Department of State, General Records, 893.00/8006.

33. Republic of China, *Report of the National Flood Relief Commission, 1931–1932*.

34. *NCDN*, Sept. 14, 1931

35. Ibid., Sept. 15, 1931.

36. Republic of China, *Report of the National Flood Relief Commission, 1931–1932*; *Bulletin de l'Université l'Aurore*, 2d ser., 7, no. 3 (1946): iii.

37. "Le Père Jacquinot de Besange," p. 2, JA.

38. *China Press*, Jan. 27, 1932. John Hope Simpson had been sent to China by the League of Nations to help with flood relief by organizing volunteers and requesting funds and supplies.

39. Ibid., Jan. 9, 24, 1932.

40. *NCDN*, Sept. 3–10, 1931.

41. *China Press*, Jan. 20 and 24, 1932.

CHAPTER THREE

1. *Shanghai shi nianjian* (Shanghai yearbook), 1935, pp. 13–14.

2. Goto-Shibata, *Japan and Britain in Shanghai*, pp. 150–51.

3. Shanghai Municipal Council, "Minutes," vol. 25, pp. 142–43.

4. Sun You-Li, *China and the Origins of the Pacific War*, pp. 21–24. For a detailed discussion of the 1932 war, see Jordan, *China's Trial by Fire*, esp. chap. 3.

5. Coble, *Facing Japan*, pp. 39–55.

6. Finch, *Shanghai and Beyond*, p. 248.

7. The battles were costly for both sides. The Chinese suffered some 4,000 killed and 7,698 wounded, according to Jordan, *China's Trial by Fire*, pp. 187–88. Finch, *Shanghai and Beyond*, pp. 47–48, cites Japanese casualties of 3,091, of whom 769 died; Chinese of about 14,000, of whom 4,086 died.

8. Shanghai Municipal Council, "Minutes," vol. 25, meetings held Feb. 1, 26, and 29, 1932.

9. Viscount Kikujiro Ishii, "History Repeats Itself," pp. 234–235.

10. *NCDN*, Feb. 15, 1932.

11. Council for the Foreign Settlement of Shanghai, *Municipal Gazette*, no. 31, Nov. 1938, p. 353.

12. Shanghai Municipal Council, "Minutes," meeting held Mar. 2, 1932.

13. *NCDN*, Feb. 7, 1932.

14. *China Press*, Feb. 24, 1932.

15. Ibid., Feb. 9, 18, 19, 21, and 27, 1932.

16. Ibid., Feb. 3, 15, 1932. A newly formed Shanghai Citizens' Emergency Committee took charge of helping to distribute food and inspecting living conditions in camps, as well as paying repatriation expenses for refugees being returned to their native places. Members included: B. Y. Woo, Yu Ya-ching, O. S. Lieu, C. C. Woo, Y. F. Kwei, Y. C. Woo, Yang Yin, and F. C. Yen.

17. Ibid., Feb. 28, 1932.

18. *NCDN*, Feb. 1, 1932.

19. *China Press*, Feb. 12, 1932.

20. Ibid., Feb. 21 and 26, 1932.

21. The 1931 *Report of the Honorable Richard Feetham, C.M.G., Judge of the Supreme Court of the Union of South Africa to the Shanghai Municipal Council* was a comprehensive study of the International Settlement, its history, business interests, politics, police administration, and questions affecting its future.

22. Shanghai Municipal Council, "Minutes," meeting held Feb. 17, 1932.

23. Ibid., vol. 25, meeting held Feb. 21, 1932.

24. *NCDN*, Feb. 12, 1932.

25. *NCDN*, Feb. 11, 1932.

26. *NCDN*, Feb. 13, 1932.

27. Shanghai Municipal Council, "Minutes," meeting held June 1, 1932.

28. Georges Germain, *Making of the Mind*, p. 277.

29. *Bulletin de l'Université l'Aurore*, 3d ser., 7, no. 3 (1946): iv.

30. *China Press*, Feb. 5, 1932.

31. *NCDN*, Feb. 5 and 15, 1932.

32. The main points of this agreement are in *Oriental Affairs* 8, no. 3 (Sept. 1937): 123–25. For discussion of the concerns of both sides and the crafting of the truce, see Jordan, *China's Trial by Fire,* chap. 13. See also Coble, *Facing Japan,* pp. 48–55.

33. *Oriental Affairs* 8, no. 3 (Sept. 1937): 124.

34. Unpublished French document,, pp. 2–3, JA; *Études,* Nov. 1946, p. 259. Father Desjacques of the Society of Jesus founded this hospital in 1862.

35. *Compagnie,* no. 8 (1946): 2.

36. In the original French:

Prière

La nuit quand la brise murmure
Et la hulote en gros sanglots
Chuchote bas sa peine obscure,
De l'âme un chagrin coule à flots.

Sombres spectres au vol presse
Nous affolant hélas sans trêve,
Et l'avenir et le Passé
Tournent en ronds noirs dans mon rêve.

L'Avenir surtout nous fait peur
Il n'est pas, il ne fut pas; même
Peut-être il ne sera qu'un pleur,
L'émoi sans plus d'un songe blême.

Dieu, veuilles nous rendre l'espoir!
L'Avenir est à Toi seul: l'ombre
S'épand plus épaisse ce soir,
Fais la pour nous un peu moins sombre.

37. Council for the Foreign Settlement of Shanghai, *Municipal Gazette,* July 1937, notes the release of the seven leaders of the National Salvation Movement who had been arrested in November 23, 1936, and sent to Suzhou for the trial. This was disturbing news for the Japanese, who saw these leaders and their movement as clearly anti-Japanese and very effective.

38. U.S. National Archives and Records Administration, Red Machine, RG 457, box 3, No. 1065, Tokyo to Washington, Apr. 5, 1938.

39. Coble, *Facing Japan,* pp. 373–74.

40. Ch'i, *Nationalist China at War,* pp. 41–43.

41. Nelson T. Johnson and Paul E. Naggiar, Memo of conversation, July 3, 1937, in Nelson T. Johnson Papers, vol. 31, 1937 A-K, Library of Congress.

42. Ibid., pp. 43–45; Hsü, *Japan and Shanghai,* p. 23.

43. Included on the Executive Committee were Norwegian Consul General

N. Aall and Y. K. Chu. Executive Committee: Jacquinot, J. Fredet, Major Hans Berents, J. R. Jones, Wong I-ding, Sung Han-chang, K. Z. Loh, and K. Y. Li. General Affairs: K. Y. Li, K. Z. Loh, K. Y. Ou. Finance Division: Sung Han-chang, J. R. Jones, Loh Pa-hong. Relief Committee: Jacquinot, Ma Siu-san, and Hans Berents; Secretary, K. Y. Ou. *NCH*, Aug. 25, 1937; *Annual Report: International Relief Committee, 1937–1938*, Xujiahui Archives.

44. Cited in *Oriental Affairs*, Sept. 1937, p. 144.

45. *Shen bao*, Sept. 7, 1937, p. 5.

46. Council for the Foreign Settlement of Shanghai, *Municipal Gazette*, vol. 30 (1937). A police report for July 1937 noted nineteen strikes; *Shen bao*, Sept. 14, 1937.

47. Council for the Foreign Settlement of Shanghai, *Municipal Gazette*, vol. 30 (1937).

48. Feng, "Elites locales et solidarités régionales," 78, gives refugee camps and camp residents for the International Settlement and French Concession for August 1937–December 1940.

49. *NCH*, Sept. 22, 1937.

50. International Relief Committee, Annual Report, 1937–1938, Xujiahui Archives.

51. Finch, *Shanghai and Beyond*, p. 362.

52. Shanghai Municipal Council, "Minutes," vol. 24, meeting held Sept. 1937; Feng, "Elites locales et solidarités régionales," p. 84.

53. *China Press*, Oct. 1, 1937.

54. Shanghai Municipal Council, "Minutes," vol. 25, meeting held May 25, 1938. Anti-Japanese activities are not inevitable, nor demanded by the present international or national situation in Asia. Japan is acting only for the protection of East Asia and the Asiatic peoples.

55. *Shen bao*, Aug. 24, 1937.

56. *China Press*, Oct. 2, 1937.

57. Ibid., Oct. 9, 1937.

58. Yeh, ed., *Wartime Shanghai*, p. 3; Eastman, *Seeds of Destruction*, p. 144.

59. Ch'i, *Nationalist China at War*, p. 43.

Chapter Four

1. Father Georges Germain, letter to Provincial, Dec. 27, 1934, JA, quoted in Brossollet, *Les Français de Shanghai*, p. 171.

2. "China at War," *China Weekly Review*, special supplement, Dec. 1937, p. 8.

3. Georges Saint-Paul's initial ideas are contained in *Progrès médical*, Apr. 27, 1929. See also www.icdo.org/ab-history.html (accessed August 17, 2007).

4. Association des Lieux de Genève, *La guerre moderne et la protection des civils*, p. 13.

5. Ibid., p. 14.

6. On the *avant-projet* concerning secure zones, see ibid., chap. 4.

7. Ibid., p. 18.

8. Ibid.: "l'Association n'est ni catholique, ni évangélique, ni isréalite et pas davantage bouddhiste ou mahométane; elle n'est ni royaliste, ni républicaine, ni soviétique ni prétorienne," p. 18.

9. Thomas, *Spanish Civil War*, p. 221.

10. Association des Lieux de Genève, *La guerre moderne et la protection des civils*, p. 22.

11. *NCDN*, Sept. 14, 1937.

12. *Journal de Shanghai*, Sept. 5, 1937. The full text of the Hirota interview is included.

13. *Shen bao*, Sept. 7, 1937.

14. *NCDN*, Sept. 29, 1937; *Journal de Shanghai*, Sept. 29, 1937.

15. *Shen bao*, Sept. 23, 1937.

16. To coordinate relief efforts and cope with the emergency in Shanghai, an International Committee of the Red Cross Society of China, generally called the Shanghai International Red Cross, was formed on Oct. 2, 1937. This body received a charter from the Red Cross Society of China. Headquartered at the Park Hotel, members of its Executive Committee were Dr. W. W. Yen, chairman; Father Jacquinot, L. W. H. Plant, and J. R. Jones, vice chairmen, Dr. J. E. Baker, director, Dr. Y. Y. Tsu and C. W. Petitt, executive secretaries; C. W. Bennett, treasurer, Dr. S. M. Sze, secretary; G. Findlay Andrew, R. Calder-Marshall, J. K. Choy, J. Donne, Feng Ping-nan, J. Hers, Rev. R. D. Rees, Dr. Sao-Ke Alfred Sze and Dr. F. C. Yen, members. *Chinese Recorder*, Dec. 1937, p. 781; *Journal de Shanghai*, Oct. 29, 1937; *China Press*, Nov. 6, 1937; *Shen bao*, Oct. 30, 1937.

17. The members of the Nanshi Supervisory Committee were Father Jaquinot, chairman; G. Findlay Andrews, honorary treasurer; C. Baboud, a member of the French Municipal Council; A. Jaspar, treasurer of Public Works, French Concession; Brig. Gen. E. B. Macnaughton, vice-chairman, Shanghai Municipal Council and British Chamber of Commerce; Major Hans Berents, former president of the Engineering Society of China; and W. H. Plant, president of the American Chamber of Commerce and member of the Shanghai Municipal Council. *Story of the Jacquinot Zone*, p. 23; *Shanghai Directory*, 1938; "La Zone Jacquinot," *Relations de Chine*, Apr. 1938, p. 336.

18. *Story of the Jacquinot Zone*, Annex; Japanese Foreign Ministry Archives (hereafter cited as JFMA), S 1.1.1.0–27, p. 4174; this detailed report on the Jacquinot Zone written in 1937 became part of another work published by the Japanese

Ministry of Foreign Affairs (JMFA), *Shitsumu hōkoku: Tōa kyoku* (hereafter *Shitsumu hōkoku*).

19. See, e.g., Xu, "Qichuang de Shanghai."

20. S. Okamoto, letter to Jacquinot, Nov. 5, 1937, in *Story of the Jacquinot Zone*, Annex. See also intercepted cable #2533, Nov. 8, 1937, to Tokyo from Okamoto regarding conditions to be met, NARA, 947004, D(7–869), trans. Nov. 12, 1937.

21. Intercept of cable #2533, Nov. 8, 1937; *Asahi shimbun*, Nov. 3, 1937. The Japanese referred to the Zone as the Shanghai *anzenku* or Shanghai *anzenchitai*.

22. JFMA, S 1.1.1.0–27; JMFA, *Shitsumu hōkoku*.

23. *Shanghai wenshi ziliao*, no. 51, 1985, p. 174.

24. Letter from O. K. Yui to Father Jacquinot, Nov. 5, 1937, in *Story of the Jacquinot Zone*, Annex.

25. JFMA, S 1.1.1. 0–27; JMFA, *Shitsumu hōkoku;* intercept of cable #2533, Nov. 8, 1937.

26. Ibid., letter from S. Okamoto to Father Jacquinot, Nov. 5, 1937, *Story of the Jacquinot Zone*, Annex.

27. *Shen bao*, Nov. 6–7, 9–10, 1937; the Japanese press confirmed the opening saying that Mayor Yui had formally accepted so the procedure was complete, *Asahi shimbun*, Nov. 9, 1937.

28. Cable intercept, D(7–869), Nov. 8, 1937.

29. *Revue internationale de la Croix-Rouge* 243 (April 1939): 300; Perruchoud, *Les résolutions des conférences internationales de la Croix-Rouge*, p. 299. The International Committee of the Red Cross was established in 1863; by 1919, it included sixty-three national societies, including those in China and Japan.

30. *Dalu bao*, as quoted in *Shen bao*, Nov. 7, 1937.

31. *NCDN*, Nov. 5, 1937.

32. *Story of the Jacquinot Zone*, p. 5.

33. *Journal de Shanghai*, Nov. 10, 1937.

34. Ibid., "Notices Appearing in the Public Press Formally Announcing the Opening of the Safety Area," in *Story of the Jacquinot Zone*, Annex.

35. *Shen bao*, Nov. 6, 1937.

36. *Shen bao*, Nov. 10, 1937.

37. A copy of the pass issued by the government to the committee is in *Story of the Jacquinot Zone*, Annex.

38. *Shen bao*, Nov. 22, 1937; *Shanghai Evening Post & Mercury*, Nov. 13, 1937.

39. He Shengsui, *Lunxian tongshi*, pp. 296–99.

40. Xu, "Qichuang de Shanghai."

41. *Dagong bao*, Nov. 13, 1937.

42. General Matsui Iwane, interview published in the *CWR*, Aug. 13, 1938, p. 364.

43. *Journal de Shanghai,* Nov. 2, 1937.

44. Matsui, *Matsui Iwane taishō senjin nikki,* entry for Nov. 12, 1937, pp. 116–17. An announcement by a Japanese Embassy spokesman on Nov. 21 indicated that similar control was intended in the French Concession, including the Chinese courts. *CWR,* Jan. 1, 1938, p. 181.

45. *Shen bao,* Nov. 14 and 15, 1937.

46. JFMA, S 1.1.1.0–27; JMFA, *Shitsumu hōkoku,* 1937, pp. 212–16.

47. Matsui, *Matsui Iwane taishō senjin nikki,* entry for Nov. 21, pp. 124–25.

48. Ibid., Nov. 26, 1937; for the French description of this meeting, see Archives of the French Ministry of Foreign Affairs, Shanghai, ser. C, box 86, *compte-rendu,* Nov. 26, 1937, pp. 1–3. On Dec. 3, the British permitted the Japanese to hold a victory parade in the International Settlement, provoking considerable Chinese anger and resentment. The French authorities refused to permit the parade to proceed into the Concession.

49. The French sources established a zone arrangement to protect Xujiahui, not by agreement but as a de facto measure. It was handed over to the Japanese in June 1940 with the French saying it "had served its purpose and now can resume normal status." *Oriental Affairs* (July–Dec. 1940), p. 14: 4; *China Press,* Nov. 7, 1937.

50. *NCDN,* Nov. 18 and 20, 1937. A recent account in the *Xinmin wanbao,* June 18, 2005, uses the figure 200,000 refugees in discussing the Zone and its establishment under Jacquinot's leadership. Later, the Zone population surpassed 300,000.

51. *Story of the Jacquinot Zone,* p. 11.

52. *NCDN,* Dec. 12, 1937.

53. JFMA, S 1.1.1.0–27.

54. *CWR,* Dec. 18, 1937, p. 67; *NCDN,* Dec. 13, 1937; *Shen bao,* Dec. 13 and 14, 1937.

55. *NCDN,* Dec. 17, 1937.

56. Ibid., Dec. 19, 1937.

57. *Shanghai Evening Post & Mercury,* Nov. 13, 1937.

58. *Trans-Pacific News Service,* May 25, 1938, sheet B.

59. Nelson T. Johnson Papers, Library of Congress, entry dated Dec. 6, 1937.

60. *NCDN,* Dec. 13, 1937.

61. The Da Dao Municipal Government, the Japanese puppet government and organ of local administration, formed in December 1937. It would be renamed the Shanghai Municipal Administrative Office in April 1938, and placed under the control of the new Reformed Government of the Republic of China, which was set up in Nanjing on March 28, 1938. The new Shanghai Municipal Ad-

ministrative Office was reorganized and renamed the Shanghai City Government under a new mayor, Fu Xiao'an, in November 1938. Shanghai Municipal Council Report, 1938: Budget 1939, p. 117.

62. *NCDN*, Dec. 12, 1937; *Asahi shimbun*, Nov. 17, 1937.

63. Feng, "Elites locales et solidarités régionales," p. 79; Transpacific News Service, May 25, 1938.

64. *CWR*, Dec. 4, 1937, p. 10.

65. *Oriental Affairs*, Dec. 1937, p. 341.

66. "La Zone Jacquinot," (cited n. 17 above), p. 341; *Asahi shimbun*, Nov. 15, 1937.

67. *Asahi shimbun*, Nov. 17, 1937. Similar Japanese Army contributions would occur in Nanjing, notably by the Fujita Unit (2,000 yuan), and Major General Harada Kumakichi (500 yuan); see Brook, *Collaboration*, p. 150.

68. *NCH*, Jan. 15, 1938.

69. Minister of Foreign Affairs Hirota Kōki, letter to Jacquinot, Mar. 9, 1938, trans. with original in *Story of the Jacquinot Zone*, Annex.

70. *NCDN*, Nov. 27, 1937. Jacquinot often exchanged views with Admiral Le Bigot and informed him of the views of various diplomats; *Journal de Shanghai*, Nov. 18, 1937.

71. Ambassador Paul-Emile Naggiar, letter to Jacquinot, Apr. 30, 1938, trans. with original in *Story of the Jacquinot Zone*.

72. *NCH*, Feb. 8, 1939.

73. U.S. Admiral H. E. Yarnell, letter to Jacquinot, Apr. 9, 1938, in *Story of the Jacquinot Zone*.

74. Major-General A. D. Telfer-Smollett, letter to Jacquinot, Apr. 19, 1938, ibid.; *NCH*, Jan 15, 1938.

75. *NCH*, Mar. 30, 1938.

76. For discussions of the dynamics of collaboration, see Brook, *Collaboration*, esp, chap. 1. In his chap. 6, dealing with Shanghai, Brook makes no mention of the Jacquinot Zone, which was a model for the Nanjing International Safe Zone.

77. *Shanghai wenshi ziliao*, no. 51, 1985, p. 174.

78. Efforts at developing a nonintervention plan were reported in *NCDN*, Nov. 7, 1937.

79. "China at War," *CWR*, Dec. 1937, p. 8.

CHAPTER FIVE

1. A few of the key sources on the Nanking Massacre are: Rabe, *Good Man;* Yamamoto, *Nanking: Anatomy of an Atrocity*; Hu, *American Goddess at the Rape of Nanking*; Chang, *Rape of Nanjing*; Brook, ed., *Documents on the Rape of Nanjing*; Hsü, *Documents of the Nanking Safety Zone*; Yin, *Rape of Nanking: An Undeniable*

History in Photographs; Fogel, ed., *Nanjing Massacre*; Li, Sabella, and Liu, *Nanking 1937*; Suni, ed. *Nanjing datusha*; *Nanjing Massacre*. A team of scholars in Nanjing has just recently published a 28-volume set on the Nanjing Massacre.

2. "A Message from Nanking," *Oriental Affairs*, Dec. 1937, p. 270.

3. *Asahi shimbun* newsreel, no. 204.

4. Nelson T. Johnson Papers, box 34, "Reporting of Recent Events in China," p. 17.

5. Rabe, *Good Man*, p. ix.

6. Ibid., p. 22.

7. U.S. Department of State, *Papers Relating to the Foreign Relations of the United States: Japan, 1931–1941*, vol. 2, p. 417.

8. A Reuter's dispatch of September 20 reported the Chinese indignation over the American decision to evacuate Nanjing and the U.S. embargo on the shipment of arms to the Far East, including China.

9. Interview with Agnes Mills, daughter of H. Plummer Mills, April 2005.

10. The following are the committee officers and members: John Rabe, Chairman; American missionaries: Dr. Lewis S. C. Smythe, secretary, Rev. John G. Magee, Dr. M. S. Bates, Rev. H. P. Mills, Dr. C. S. Trimmer, Charles Riggs; American business: J. V. Pickering; British business: Ph. H. Munro-Faure, P. R. Shields, Iver Mackay, J. Lean; Danish business: J. M. Hansen. Hsü, *Documents of the Nanking Safety Zone*, p. 3.

11. Rabe, *Good Man*, p. 28. All committee members signed the telegram.

12. *Shen bao*, Dec. 4, 1937.

13. *Yomiuri shimbun*, Nov. 25, 1937.

14. *China Press*, Dec. 4, 1937; a Chinese account of Jacquinot's Safe Zone mentions how he helped John Rabe establish the Nanjing Safe Zone. See *Minzhu ye fazhi shibao*, Feb. 5, 2006 at www.sina.com.cn (accessed Oct. 4, 2007).

15. *NCDN*, Nov. 4, 1937.

16. Consul General C. E. Gauss to State Department, in U.S. Department of State, *Foreign Relations of the United States: Diplomatic Papers, 1940*, vol. 4, *The Far East*, pp. 757–58; French consul, Peking, to French Embassy, Tokyo, Aug. 24, 1937, in Archives of the Ministry of Foreign Affairs, Nantes, Archives rapatriés du consulat de France à Pékin, ser. A-81, #72

17. Yamamoto, *Nanking: Anatomy of an Atrocity*, p. 45. A discussion of the Shanghai battle and the prelude to Nanjing is contained in chap. 2.

18. Timperley, *What War Means*, p. 24.

19. *Shen bao*, Dec. 5, 1937.

20. Wolf Schenke in Rabe, *Good Man*, p. 30.

21. "The International Settlement at Shanghai," Nelson T. Johnson Papers, box 60.

22. *NCDN*, Dec. 9, 1937.

23. Hu, *American Goddess at the Rape of Nanking*, p. 73.

24. *Oriental Affairs*, Jan. 1938, p. 30.

25. Hu, *American Goddess at the Rape of Nanking*, pp. 73–74; Rabe, *Good Man*, p. 56.

26. Timperley, *What War Means*, pp. 26–27.

27. Yamamoto, *Nanking: Anatomy of an Atrocity*, p. 89.

28. Hsü, *Documents of the Nanking Safety Zone*.

29. One graphic account is Yin, *Rape of Nanking: An Undeniable History in Photographs*.

30. *NCDN*, Dec. 20, 1937.

31. Hsü, *Documents of the Nanking Safety Zone*, pp. 4–5.

32. As related by George Fitch in Chang, *Rape of Nanjing*, pp. 116–17; as related by M. S. Bates in Yamamoto, *Nanking: Anatomy of an Atrocity*, 203–4; Brook, *Documents on the Rape of Nanjing*, pp. 43–44.

33. *New York Times*, Jan 9, 1938.

34. Brook, *Documents on the Rape of Nanjing*, p. 220. The other American doctors were C. S. Trimmer and James McCallum (p. 15).

35. Ibid., p. 14; Fogel, *Nanjing Massacre in History and Historiography*, pp. 46–47.

36. International Military Tribunal for the Far East, *Tokyo War Crimes Trial*, pp. 40, 147–48; Brook, *Documents on the Rape of Nanjing*, p. 261. The IMTFE found Japan guilty of conspiring, planning, and waging aggressive war. All 25 defendants were found guilty. Seven received the death penalty.

37. Ibid., pp. 106–7.

38. For an account of the Japanese campaign and massacre in the Xuzhou region, see Lary, "A Ravaged Place: The Devastation of the Xuzhou Region, 1938," in *Scars of War*, pp. 98–116.

39. Brook, *Documents on the Rape of Nanjing*, p. 74.

40. Ibid., pp. 95–100; 113–16; Hu, *American Goddess at the Rape of Nanjing*, pp. 105–10.

41. Brook, *Documents on the Rape of Nanjing*, pp. 16–17.

42. Hirota Kōki Denki Kankōkai [Committee for the publication of Hirota Kōki's biography], comp., *Hirota Kōki*, p. 315.

43. There were over 1,000 foreigners in Wuhan, including 300 from the USSR, 260 British, 140 Americans, 110 Germans, 100 Indians, 60 French, and various other nationalities. Domei News Service, no. 2 (July 10, 1938).

44. Shanghai Municipal Council, *Report, 1937, and Budget, 1938*, p. 98.

45. Steve MacKinnon, "Refugee Flight at the Outset," in *Scars of War*, p. 124.

46. *NCDN*, Dec. 5, 1937, notes a Safety Zone for Hangzhou city; *Shen bao*,

Dec. 6–7, 1937, reports confidential discussions between the American president of Zhejiang University, Consul General Gauss, and the Japanese authorities regarding a proposed zone, which was to be located alongside West Lake. Discussion in Shanghai of a zone in Hangzhou was heated, with the Japanese spokesman emphasizing that he could not give an official response until he had the Chinese government's response or attitude.

47. *Mainichi shimbun* report carried in *NCDN*, July 20, 1938.

48. Japanese cabinet, various information materials, "Establishment of a Refugee Area in Hankow," JMFA, Tokyo, #00025100, pp. 153–54.

49. French ambassador, Tokyo, telegram to French ambassador, Shanghai, Sept. 6, 1938, Archives of the Ministry of Foreign Affairs, Nantes, Archives rapatriés du consulat de France à Pékin, ser. A, box 81.

50. "Establishment of a Refugee Area in Hankow," JMFA, Tokyo, #00025100, pp. 153–54.

51. MacKinnon, "Refugee Flight at the Outset," in *Scars of War*, p. 129.

52. U.S. Department of State, John Wood, letter to Hornbeck, June 12, 1938, 793.94/13377.

53. U.S. Department of State, telegram to Shanghai, Aug. 4, 1938, 893.48/1609. This American position was shared by the British, French, Germans, Italians, and even the Japanese in Shanghai. Lockhart to U.S. secretary of state, Aug. 3, 1939, 893.48/1610. See also Hornbeck to Wood, June 14, 1938, 793.94/13377.

54. *North China Herald*, Aug. 3, 1938.

55. Colin to Naggiar, #176, Oct. 9, 1938, Archives of the Ministry of Foreign Affairs, Nantes, Archives rapatriés du consulat de France à Pékin, ser. A, box 81.

56. *NCDN*, Oct. 27, 1938; *China Press*, Oct. 26, 1938.

57. "Minutes of Conversation on Hankow Zone," Archives of the Ministry of Foreign Affairs, Nantes, Archives rapatriés du consulat de France à Pékin, ser. A, box 81.

58. Okazaki is identified as Japanese consul general at large in Archives of the Ministry of Foreign Affairs, Nantes, Archives rapatriés du consulat de France à Pékin, ser. A, box 81.

59. "Memorandum on Hankow Zone," ibid.

60. Ibid.

61. Naggiar, telegram to the French Consulate, Hankou, Sept. 3, 1938, Archives of the Ministry of Foreign Affairs, Nantes, Archives rapatriés du consulat de France à Pékin, ser. A, box 81.

62. W. H. Dupree, telegram to W. J. Keswick, Oct. 12, 1938, #926-S. Archives of the Ministry of Foreign Affairs, Nantes, Archives rapatriés du consulat de France à Pékin, ser. A, box 81.

63. Colin, telegram to "V.E." (Bishop Espelage), Oct. 18, 1938, #268. Archives of the Ministry of Foreign Affairs, Nantes, Archives rapatriés du consulat de France à Pékin, ser. A, box 81.

64. Telegram #288, Oct. 22, 1938. Archives of the Ministry of Foreign Affairs, Nantes, Archives rapatriés du consulat de France à Pékin, ser. A, box 81.

65. *NCDN*, Oct. 23, 1938.

66. *China Press*, Oct. 25, 1938.

67. Ibid. An interesting provision was that the committee would attempt to include the Japanese Concession in the Zone, but that if this were unsuccessful, failure would not prejudice the Zone area as described. Okazaki was not troubled by this possibility, but the committee apparently feared the local Chinese response to inclusion of the Japanese Concession.

68. Telegram #243, French ambassador, Tokyo, letter to French ambassador, Shanghai, Sept. 6, 1938. Archives of the Ministry of Foreign Affairs, Nantes, Archives rapatriés du consulat de France à Pékin, ser. A, box 81.

69. Ibid.

70. Ibid. "Minutes of Conversation."

71. *China Post*, Oct. 25, 1938; *Toronto Star*, Oct. 25, 1938.

72. *NCDN*, Oct. 26, 1938; French Consul General Collin, #322, Oct. 25, 1938. Archives of the Ministry of Foreign Affairs, Nantes, Archives rapatriés du consulat de France à Pékin, ser. A, box 81. Collin claimed there were 500,000 refugees in the Zone, and that the Zone had been organized in less than one day.

73. State Department note, Aug. 15, 1938, U.S. Department of State, General Records, 893.48, box 7229.

74. The members of the committee were: Bishop A. A. Gilman, chairman of the American Church Mission; Bishop J. S. Espelage, American, Catholic Mission, Wuchang; Bishop E. J. Galvin, British, St. Columban's Mission, Hanyang; Reverend A. J. Gedye, British, Methodist Missionary Society; Mr. W. H. Dupree, British, Hankou Agent for Jardine, Matheson, and Co.; and Mr. A. E. Marker, British, chairman, British Chamber of Commerce and director, Arnold Trading Co., Hankou; Bishop Masse, Italian, Catholic Mission, Hankou; Mr. E. A. Chaudoin, French, manager, International Savings Society, Hankou; and Mr. G. Tolle, German, manager of Carlowitz & Co., Hankou. Telegram from P. R. Josselyn, U.S. consul general, Hankou, Aug. 1, 1938, U.S. Department of State, General Records, 893.48, box 7229. See also, *NCDN, Oct.* 25, 1938.

75. *NCDN,* Oct. 26, 1938.

76. French Consul General Collin to French Ambassador, Tokyo and Paris, #309–10, Oct. 25, 1938. Archives of the Ministry of Foreign Affairs, Nantes, Archives rapatriés du consulat de France à Pékin, ser. A, box 81.

77. Smedley, *Battle Hymn of China*, p. 216.

78. Ibid., p. 222.

79. French Consul General Collin to Tokyo and Paris, #324, Oct. 26, 1938. Archives of the Ministry of Foreign Affairs, Nantes, Archives rapatriés du consulat de France à Pékin, ser. A, box 81.

80. *NCDN*, Oct. 28, 1938.

81. Ibid.

82. Yamamoto, *Nanking: Anatomy of an Atrocity*, p. 164.

83. Ambassador Naggiar to Paris and Tokyo, Oct. 26, 1938. Archives of the Ministry of Foreign Affairs, Nantes, Archives rapatriés du consulat de France à Pékin, ser. A, box 81.

84. Ambassador Naggiar to Paris and Tokyo, Nov. 1, 1938; telegrams 330, 331, Oct. 27–28, 1938. Archives of the Ministry of Foreign Affairs, Nantes, Archives rapatriés du consulat de France à Pékin, ser. A, box 81.

85. French Consulate at Amoy to Ambassador Naggiar, #47, June 15, 1938. Archives of the Ministry of Foreign Affairs, Nantes, Archives rapatriés du consulat de France à Pékin, ser. A, box 81

86. Ambassador Naggiar to Hankow Consulate, #149, Sept. 5, 1938. Naggiar requested that the consulate inform Bishop Espelage "for his personal information."

87. Domei News Service, no. 2 (Oct. 18, 1938). Archives of the Ministry of Foreign Affairs, Nantes, Archives rapatrés du consulat de France à Shanghai, ser. A, box 86.

88. *NCDN*, Oct. 19, 1938.

89. *NCDN*, Oct. 23, 1938.

90. Miura to U.S. Consul General C. E. Gauss, July 5 and 6, 1939, U.S. Department of State, General Records, 893.48/1789.

Chapter Six

1. Shanghai Municipal Council, Minute Book, vol. 27, pp. 271, 283.

2. *Shen bao*, Dec. 2 and 9, 1937.

3. *Revue internationale de la Croix-Rouge* 21, no. 1 (June 1939).

4. Shanghai Municipal Council, Minute Book, vol. 28, pp. 44–48; Interview with Pauline Witt, daughter of Leon Richard Shinazi, Jan. 2007.

5. The *NCDN* reported that there were 125 gaming establishments in the International Settlement. See *Oriental Affairs*, Mar. 1939, p. 142.

6. "Aides aux refugiés," Apr. 30, 1938. Archives of the Ministry of Foreign Affairs, Nantes, Archives rapatriés du consulat de France à Shanghai, ser. A, box 86.

7. *Shen bao*, Dec. 9, 1937.

8. *Compagnie*, no. 8 (1946): 4; José Arturo, *El siglo de las misiones*, no. 33 (Dec. 1946): 456.

9. Undated manuscript, JA, Vanves, France, p. 4.

10. *NCDN*, Mar. 17, 1938; *China Press*, Mar. 25, 1938. *Chinese Recorder*, Dec. 1937, reports the total cash amount at $800,000, p. 782. These amounts are in Chinese currency.

11. *China Press*, Mar. 29, 1938; *North China Herald*, Mar. 30, 1938.

12. *Chinese Recorder*, Dec. 1937, pp. 781–82.

13. *NCH*, Feb, 1938; Jacquinot, *Lettres de Jersey*, Feb. 15, 1938, JA.

14. "Aides aux refugiés," Apr. 30, 1938, Archives of the Ministry of Foreign Affairs, Nantes, Archives rapatriés du consulat de France à Shanghai, ser. A, box 91.

15. U.S. State Department, 893.48/1495, Apr. 6, 1938; 893.48/1512, Apr. 26, 1938.

16. Hornbeck memorandum, Dec. 19, 1937, U.S. Department of State, General Records, 893.48/1821.

17. Ernest J. Swift, letter to George Summerlin, chief, protocol, Department of State, July 19, 1938, in 811.4611, France/121.

18. Lockhart, Shanghai, telegram to State Department, Apr. 26, 1938, in 811.4611 France/114.

19. Lockhart to State Department, May 13, 1938, U.S. Department of State, General Records, 893.48/1531.

20. Roosevelt memorandum for "The Secretary of State, Admiral Grayson," dated Jan. 11, 1938, 893.48/1407–1/2.

21. Secretary Hull to Ambassador Johnson, Jan. 22, 1938, 893.48/406A; American Red Cross to State Department, Mar. 10, 1938, 893.48/1498.

22. Hornbeck to Secretary of State, May 21, 1938; memo, Apr. 1, 1938, 893.48/1493.

23. Ibid. The Chinese response was also enthusiastic, although setting any limit, even one as high as U.S.$1 million, was regretted.

24. *NCH*, Aug. 3, 1938; *Commonweal*, Aug. 3, 1938, pp. 195–96; U.S. State Department, RG 84, Consul General C. E. Gauss to State Department, Apr. 6, 1938. Jacquinot was to be accompanied by Dr. Alfred Sze, Jr., son of Alfred Sze, secretary of the International Red Cross Committee of Shanghai.

25. Trans-Pacific News Service, May 25, 1938, sheet no. B.

26. *Vancouver Sun*, Aug. 19, 1938; *Toronto Star*, May 19, 1938.

27. Memorandum of conversation, May 24, 1938, U.S. Department of State, General Records, 893.48/567.

28. Ibid.

29. Lockhart to State Department, Apr. 26, 1938, 811.4611 France/114; Comte de Saint-Quentin to Cordell Hull, May 24, 1938, 811.4611 France/116; *Rela-*

tions de Chine, Oct. 1938, p. 512; Summerlin to McIntyre, May 24, 1938, 811.4611 France/116.

30. *NCH,* Aug. 3, 1938, p. 195.

31. Ibid.

32. *CWR,* Mar. 23, 1940.

33. American Advisory Committee, Aug. 12, 1938, RG 74, pt. 125.

34. C. R. Bennet, National City Bank, Aug. 12, 1938, in RG 74, pt. 125; Headquarters of Chiang Kai-shek, Dec. 23, 1938.

35. Johnson, Hankow to Shanghai Consulate, Nov. 12, 1938, RG 74, pt. 125.

36. This committee was formed in January 1938 reportedly because the Red Cross had not taken the initiative to help raise money in the United States, at least not until after the formation of the China Emergency Civilian Relief body chaired by Colonel Theodore Roosevelt Jr. Then the Red Cross launched a national appeal. Colonel Roosevelt, letter to secretary, American Advisory Committee, RG 84, 848–1939. See also RG 74, pt. 125, Shanghai Consulate, Jan. 11, 1938; CWR, Sep 16, 1939.

37. *New York Times,* June 17, 18, 1938.

38. Ibid.

39. Ibid.

40. *China Press,* July 6, 1938.

41. *New York Times,* June 7, 1938.

42. *NCH,* Aug. 3, 1938.

43. *San Francisco Chronicle,* Aug. 1 and 4, 1938.

44. *NCDN,* July 22, 1938.

45. *Shen bao,* Dec. 10, 1937.

46. Consul General C. E. Gauss to State Department, Jan. 17, 1938, U.S. Department of State, General Records, 893.48/1392. Gauss noted that the most effective relief work was being done in Shanghai. Relief areas included the lower Yangzi Valley; Henan, Hubei, and Hunan as a primary refugee zone; and Shaanxi, Sichuan, Guizhou, Yunnan, and Canton, comprising a secondary zone. Shanxi, Chahar, and Suiyuan were inaccessible but in great need.

47. Dec. 16, 1938, RG 74, pt. 125. Wherever certain, U.S. dollar currency is indicated.

48. Ernest Swift to secretary of state, May 27, 1938, U.S. Department of State, General Records, 893.48/1615.

49. JMFA, Tokyo Archives, "Jakino Shimpu no yukue fumei jiken," pp. 0007–0008.

50. *China Weekly Review,* July 30, 1938; *NCDN,* July 26 and 27, 1938.

51. JMFA, Tokyo Archives, "Jakino Shimpu no yukue fumei jiken," p. 0007.

52. *NCDN,* July 29, 1938.

53. JMFA, Tokyo Archives, "Jakino Shimpu no yukue fumei jiken," p. 0008; *NCDN,* July 30, 1938.

54. *NCH,* Aug. 3, 1938.

55. *China Press,* July 30, 1938.

CHAPTER SEVEN

1. *Relations de Chine,* Apr. 1938, p. 347. Ou wrote of Jacquint: "L'enterprise du Père Jacquinot a rendu au Christ la plus grande gloire."

2. *Shanghai wenshi ziliao,* no. 51, (1985) p. 178; *Shen bao,* Dec. 6, p. 5.

3. International Relief Committee, Shanghai, Annual Report, pp. 11–15.

4. Pan Dacheng, "Recollection of the Number One Refugee Camp of the Shanghai International Rescue Society," p. 21. The original vice-chairman was the lawyer, Chen Zhigao and the executive director was Ms. Huang Dinghui. Many staff members came from the local salvation societies, a few from the Guomindang and Three-Principles Youth League.

5. When the Zone closed, 20,000 very poor refugees still remained and became homeless. *Shanghai wenshi ziliao,* no. 51, (1985) p. 179.

6. *Shen bao,* Nov. 17, 1938.

7. *NCDN,* Nov. 30, 1937, lists Chiang Tse-tsing, Shen Sao-ming, Kiang Tsao-wu, Tai Chong-lin, King Chong-lian, and Hsu Hung-kong as area leaders; see also, *Xinmin wanbao,* June 18, 2005, which reports recollections of those directly involved.

8. International Relief Committee, Shanghai Refuge Relief Work, Final Report, data as of Dec. 1937, p. 53. These refugees were from Chapei, Paoshan, Tangtsepoo, Nanshi, Tootung, Tazang, Hongkew, Kiangwan, and Wusung.

9. Ibid.

10. Ibid.

11. *NCDN,* Nov. 27, 1937.

12. Booker, *News Is My Job,* p. 303.

13. Finch, *Shanghai and Beyond,* p. 272.

14. *Shen bao,* Nov. 24, 1937.

15. *Chinese Recorder,* Feb. 1938, pp. 67–68.

16. *Chinese Recorder,* Feb. 1938, pp. 67–70; *Shen bao,* Nov. 29, 1937.

17. *Shen bao,* Dec. 6, 1937; "Zone Jacquinot," report no. 217, nternational Committee of the Red Cross, Mar. 15, 1938, p. 1–6.

18. *Shen bao,* Dec. 14, 1938.

19. Ibid., *Nov.* 24, 1937.

20. Ibid., Nov. 27, Dec. 10, 1937.

21. *Shen bao,* Dec. 3, 1937.

22. Shanghai Municipal Police Files, D7623.
23. *Gemingshi ziliao*, p. 65.
24. *Xinmin wanbao*, June 18, 2005.
25. *Shen bao*, Nov. 18, 23, 1937.
26. *Relations de Chine*, Apr. 1938, p. 341.
27. *China Press*, June 23, 1938.
28. "A Shanghai Refugee Camp," Oliver Papers, p. 4.
29. *China Press*, Nov. 19, 20, 1937.
30. *Shen bao*, Nov. 22, 1937.
31. *NCDN*, Apr. 29, 1939.
32. *Journal de Shanghai*, Nov. 14, 1937.

CHAPTER EIGHT

1. *Shanghai wenshi ziliao*, no. 51, p. 183.
2. Ambassador Henri Cosmé, telegrams to Paris, June 5, 1940 (#399), and Chongqing, June 19, 1940 (#454). Archives of the Ministry of Foreign Affairs, Nantes, Archives rapatriés du consulat de France à Pékin, ser. A, box 81.
3. Cosmé, telegram, June 5, 1940, #399.
4. *NCH*, June 19, 1940.
5. *San Francisco Chronicle*, Aug. 1, 1940. Jacquinot stopped briefly in San Francisco, where he stayed at the University of San Francisco, and the press explained and praised his work in Shanghai.
6. "Compte-rendu de la réunion pour la protection de Paris" (marked Confidential), 2 pp., n.d., JA. Events mentioned in the text, however, suggest a date around June 1941. This conclusion is based mainly on mention of the "last Vichy Conference" on related issues meeting on May 24 at the Park Hotel.
7. Ibid.
8. *Revue internationale de la Croix-Rouge*, no. 254 (Feb. 1940) Library of Congress.
9. *Hospital Localities and Safety Zones*, International Committee of the Red Cross, p. 15.
10. Circular no. 356 dated Apr. 20, 1939, sent to government ministers and all member societies of the Red Cross. *Revue internationale de la Croix-Rouge, no. 249* (Sept. 1939) p. 763, Library of Congress. The International Committee of the Red Cross was started in Geneva in 1863 by Henri Durant. By 1919, it had member societies in sixty-three nations coordinating the many services and resources available to them as a result of their status. By 1939, it counted 20 million members.
11. *Revue internationale de la Croix-Rouge,*no. 244 (Apr. 1939) p. 344, Library of Congress.

12. Ibid., no. 290 (Feb. 1943): 145; no. 299 (Nov. 1943): 902, Library of Congress.

13. "Compte-rendu de la réunion pour la protection de Paris," JA.

14. Between 1937 and 1940, U.S. assistance to China amounted to U.S. $1,328,940. The money was in addition to medicine, such as quinine, and ambulances and clothing. After the fall of Hankou in late 1938, the Chinese Red Cross, which had earlier worked in hospitals in rear areas, sent ambulances to the front lines. Then, changing military tactics, small groups such as stretcher bearers went to identified places where they were needed. *Revue internationale de la Croix-Rouge* Apr. 1941, p. 338; Nov. 1941, p. 948; Jan. 1942,

15. "Le Père Jacquinot de Besange," p. 5, JA.

16. Ibid., p. 4.

17. JA. The French original is:

> *Au soir de la vie*
>
> Chaque jour le radieux été
> S'embrume le soir et s'endeuille;
> La fleur s'épanouit puis s'effeuille.
> Que reste-t-il, mon Dieu, d'avoir été?
>
> Toi, mon Dieu, c'est tout ce qui reste
> Et mon pauvre coeur étonné
> Qu'à Toi seul j'ai si fort donné,
> Tout mon amour sans cesse attesté
>
> De la Source j'ai saisi l'onde,
> De ma vie j'ai filtré longtemps
> Les ans, oh! tristesse profonde.
> Et maintenant Dieu seul m'attend.

18. "Spiritual Help and Catholic Charity," Comité international de l'Aumônerie Catholique, (pamphlet) n.d., p. 2.

19. "Rapport du R. P. Jacquinot sur son voyage en Angleterre et en Irlande," unpublished report, JA, Mar. 31, 1945 (4 pp.).

20. Ibid., p. 2.

21. Ibid., p. 4. De Valera succeeded in gaining complete independence for the Irish Free State in 1937.

22. Nonciature apostolique de France, *Ordre de mission*, no. 284 (Feb. 1945) JA.

23. "La Situation actuelle du Comité international de l'Aumônerie Catholique," June 10, 1945, JA.

24. A very detailed seven-page report with the title "Le Catholicisme aux

Etats-Unis" is found in Jacquinot's file in the Jesuit Archives. However, it is not indicated whether he is the author.

25. He met with the apostolic nuncio, the bishops of Fribourg, Lausanne, and Geneva, and the president of the Swiss Committee of Catholic Charities. The meeting was also likely an opportunity for these key people to "interview" Jacquinot for even greater responsibilities. Nonciature apostolique de France, *Ordre de mission,* no. 284, (Feb 1945) JA.

26. Secretary-general, Comité international de l'Aumônerie Catholique, Paris, letter to Jacquinot, Nov. 23, 1945, JA.

27. The discussion here of Jacquinot's last days is based on a detailed, four-page report dated Oct. 5, 1946, written by an unidentified Jesuit colleague from the French city of Paray-le-Monial, the site of a Jesuit Community. Other material suggests that this may have been written by Father Nicot.

28. Jacquinot's file in the Jesuit Archives contains two very detailed, unsigned reports, both probably written by him: "Observations sur la situation dans la région de Breslau" (marked "Secret"), dealing with the tragic destruction in several villages, confusion regarding boundaries between states, and the many refugee issues; and "Les transports de population en Europe centrale."

29. *La Croix,* Sept. 15, 1946; *Le Figaro,* Sept. 13, 1946; *Epoque,* Sept. 14, 1946.

30. "Mort de Père Jacquinot," n.d., JA.

31. Extensive discussion of the background and procedures for developing the legislation is found in International Committee of the Red Cross, *Hospital Localities and Safety Zones* (Geneva, 1962).

32. The Geneva Convention of August 12, 1949, at www.icrc.org/ihl.nsf (accessed September 15, 2007).

33. Commentary (IV) Relative to the Protection of Victims of International Armed Conflicts, at www.icrc.org/ihl.nsf (accessed September 15, 2007).

34. International Committee of the Red Cross, *Hospitals Localities and Safety Zones,* p. 23.

35. Protocol I, June 8, 1977, at www.icrc.org/ihl.nsf (accessed September 15, 2007).

Epilogue

1. U.N. safes zones have included the "open relief centers" established in Sri Lanka (1990–96), the "save haven and no-fly zone" in northern Iraq, six "safe areas" in Bosnia and Herzegovina (1993–95), and the "secure humanitarian area" in western Rwanda (1994).

Bibliography

ARCHIVES AND PAPERS

Woodstock Library, Georgetown University, Washington, D.C.
Society of Jesus, Catalogus Provinciae Franciae, 1904–46.

Jesuit Archives, Vanves, France
Father Robert Jacquinot de Besange: letters, poems, reports, memoranda, photographs, newspapers, and other documentation
Comité International de l'Aumônerie Catholique, letters to Jacquinot, 1945.
"Le Père Jaquinot de Besange" (undated document)
Lieu de Genéve documentation
Lettres de Jersey, Scolasticate of Jersey (the Channel Islands), 1882–1938 (27 vols.), vols. 1937–38.
Nonciature apostolique de France, *Ordre de mission,* no. 284 (Feb. 1945)
Bulletin de l'Université l'Aurore, no. 3, 1946
Compagnie, no. 8
Études, November 1946
Relations de Chine, 1938 (various issues)

Archives of the French Ministry of Foreign Affairs, Nantes, France
Archives rapatriés du consulat de France à Changhai, ser. A, files 83–91
Archives rapatriés du consulat de France à Pékin, ser. A, file 81, "Changhai, Jacquinot"
Correspondence between Ministry of Foreign Affairs, Paris, and Shanghai, ser. C, files 123–24
Correspondence between Shanghai and Ministry of Foreign Affairs, Paris, ser. C, file 61

Jesuit Archives, Shanghai Municipal Library, Xujiahui, Shanghai, China

Journal de Shanghai, 1930–40 (various issues)
Photograph collections
Wenshi ziliao, vols. 25–26
Historical material on the Zikawei Jesuit complex
Annual Reports, International Relief Committee, Shanghai, 1937–1940

United Nations Library, Geneva, Switzerland

"Et en Chine doit l'emporter: le Père Jacquinot defend à Shanghai au nom del la
   Chrétienté les valeurs humaines," *Tribune des Nations* (Paris), February 3, 1938

*International Red Cross Headquarters, Geneva, Switzerland, documents and
letters*

Diplomatic Conference for Establishing International Convention, *The Geneva
   Convention of August 12, 1949*
International Relief Committee, Shanghai. Annual Reports, 1937 and 1938
International Committee of the Red Cross. *Hospital Localities and Safety Zones.*
   Geneva, 1952
International Humanitarian Law. *Draft International Convention on the Condition
   and Protection of Civilians.* Tokyo, 1934
Dr. Calme, China delegate to the International Committee of the Red Cross,
   "Zone Jacquinot," Report no. 217, Shanghai, March 15, 1938

Shanghai Municipal Archives

Conseil d'Administration municipale de la Concession français à Changhai
   Comptes rendus / Budgets, 1922–43
   Bulletin Municipal, 1922–43
Shanghai Municipal Council
   Municipal Gazette of the Council for the Foreign Settlement of Shanghai,
      1925–43
   Minute Books, 1933–43
   Annual *Reports and Budgets, 1933–43*

Japanese National Diet Library

"Shina Jihen ni kansuru kakkoku shimbun ronchō gaiyō tsuzuri" (Summary of
   Foreign Newspaper Commentaries After April 1, 1938, Concerning the China
   Incident). cabinet document, May 28, 1938, no. 00025100

Japanese Ministry of Foreign Affairs, Library of Congress Microfilm Archives

"Dai Sangoku no ken'eki oyobi dai sangoku-jin no seimei zaisan hogo mondai" ([Draft] Administrative Report on the Protection of Third Country Nationals, Their Interests and Property). S 1.1.1.0–27. Reprinted as *Gaimushō. Shitsumu hōkuku: Tōa kyoku* (Reprints of 1937 Work Report, East Asia Bureau). Tokyo: Kuresu Shuppan, 1993

Japanese Ministry of Foreign Affairs (cited as JMFA), Tokyo Archives

"Jakino Shimpu no yukue fumei jiken" (The Incident Concerning the Disappearance of Father Jacquinot). A110.30–11–2 (K3.6.11)

U.S. Library of Congress, Manuscripts

Nelson T. Johnson Papers. Correspondence with Stanley Hornbeck; memos, vols. 31–32; box 34: review of recent events in China, May 1938
Public papers and addresses of Franklin D. Roosevelt, vols. 6–8

U.S. National Archives and Records Administration

Central Intelligence Agency File, RG 263, Shanghai Municipal Police Files
Records of the Office of the Judge Advocate General, U.S. Army War Crimes Branch
Department of State, General Records, RG 59, decimal files, 811.4611 France; 793.94, 893.48–893.55, China
Department of State, Records of Foreign Service Posts, RG 84, Shanghai Consulate Files
Correspondences: U.S. Consulate General, Shanghai, 1938, RG 74, part 125, 842–850
Red Machine, RG 457, box 2–3, November 1937–September 1938
Office of Strategic Services Archives. Military Records Branch. "History of the Nazi Party in China," RG 226, box 10, folder 86
"Report of the Nanking International Relief Committee, November 1937 to April 30, 1939"
The Story of the Jacquinot Zone, Shanghai, China. 48 pp. Shanghai: Kelly & Walsh, 1939. RG 59, 811,4611 France/114
Universal Newspaper Newsreels, DNS.351 1-8DNS-759

University of South Carolina Film Library

"First Pictures of the Fall of Shanghai to Canton Reds," April 1927, MVTN B8173–8177. "Sino Japanese Conflict," April 5, 1932, MVTN 14–348

University of British Columbia
La Zone Jacquinot: Changhai, 1937–1939. 81 pp. Shanghai: n.p., n.d.

NEWSPAPERS AND OTHER PERIODICALS

Catholic Review Shanghai
China Press
China Weekly Review
Journal de Shanghai
Herald of Asia
Minzhu yu fazhi shibao (Feb. 5, 2006)
North China Daily News
North China Herald
Oriental Affairs
Rape of Nanking. Video recording.
   New York: A&E Television Networks, 1999.

Relations de Chine
Revue internationale de la Croix-Rouge
   (1939–45)
Shanghai Evening Post and Mercury
Shanghai Times
Shen bao
Xinmin wanbao
Catholic World
Chinese Recorder
Commonweal
New York Times
Sign

OTHER SOURCES

Abend, Hallet. *My Life in China, 1926–41.* New York: Harcourt, Brace & Co., 1943.
———. *Treaty Ports.* Garden City, N.Y.: Doubleday, 1944.
All About Shanghai: A Standard Guidebook. Hong Kong: Oxford University Press, 1983.
Amano, Keitarō. *Dai tōa shiryō sōran* [Directory of Materials on Greater East Asia]. Tokyo: Daigadō, 1994.
American National Red Cross. *Annual Report of the American Red Cross for 1923.*
Asahi Shimbun sha. Newsreel footage. Library of Congress, 1937–38, nos. 190, 207, 228, 312, 552.
Association des Lieux de Genève, ed. *La guerre moderne et la protection des civils.* Geneva, 1943.
Arturo, José. "Ha muerto el P. Robert Jacquinot, S.J. Un heroe gigantero en las misiones." *Siglo de las misiones* 33 (1946): 455–56.
Bailey, Gauvin Alexander. *Art on the Jesuit Missions in Asia and Latin America, 1542–1773.* Toronto: University of Toronto Press, 1999.
Ballard, J. G. *Empire of the Sun: A Novel.* New York: Simon & Schuster, 1984.
Barber, Noel. *The Fall of Shanghai.* New York: Coward, McCann, & Geoghegan, 1979.
Baum, Vicki. *Shanghai '37.* New York: Oxford University Press, 1986.

Bays, Daniel H., ed. *Christianity in China: from the Eighteenth Century to the Present*. Stanford: Stanford University Press, 1996.

Bergere, Marie-Claire. "'The Other China': Shanghai from 1919–1949." In *Shanghai: Revolution and Development in an Asian Metropolis*, ed Christopher Howe, pp. 1–34. Cambridge: Cambridge University Press, 1981.

———. *The Golden Age of the Chinese Bourgeoisie, 1911–1937*. New York: Cambridge University Press, 1989.

———. *Sun Yat-sen*. Stanford: Stanford University Press, 1999.

Bibliotheca missionum. Edited by Robert Streit O.M.I., Johannes Dindinger O.M.I., et al. Freiburg: Herder, 1951–74.

Bickers, Robert A. *Britain in China: Community, Culture and Colonialism, 1900–1949*. Manchester: University of Manchester Press, 1999.

———. *Empire Made Me: An Englishman Adrift in Shanghai*. London: Allen Lane, 2003.

Booker, Edna Lee. *News Is my Job: A Correspondent in War-Torn China*. New York: Macmillan, 1940.

Boyle, John Hunter. *China and Japan at War, 1937–1945: The Politics of Collaboration*. Stanford: Stanford University Press, 1972.

Brook, Timothy. *Collaboration: Japanese Agents and Local Elites in Wartime China*. Cambridge, Mass,: Harvard University Press, 2005.

———, ed., *Documents on the Rape of Nanking*. Ann Arbor: University of Michigan, 1999.

Brossollet, Guy. *Les Français de Shanghai, 1849–1949*. Paris: Belin, 1999.

Bruce, George C. *Shanghai's Undeclared War*. Shanghai: Mercury Press 1937.

Caldwell, Bo. *The Distant Land of my Father*. San Francisco: Chronicle Books, 2001.

Candlin, Enid Saunders. *The Breach in the Wall: A Memoir of the Old China*. New York: Macmillan, 1973.

Carey, Arch. *The War Years at Shanghai, 1941–45–48*. New York: Vantage Press, 1967.

Chamberlin, William Henry. "Asia's Irrepressible Conflict: A Distinguished Correspondent Analyzes the Background of the Present Battles." *Current History*, October 1937.

Chang, Iris. *The Rape of Nanking: The Forgotten Holocaust of World War II*. New York: Basic Books, 1997.

Chang, Kia-Ngau. *The Inflationary Spiral: The Experience in China, 1939–1950*. Cambridge, Mass: The Technology Press of Massachusetts Institute of Technology; New York: John Wiley & Sons, 1958.

Charles, Ronan, and Bonnie Oh, eds. *East Meets West: The Jesuits in China, 1582–1773*. Chicago: Loyola University Press, 1988.

Chen, Joseph T. *The May Fourth Movement in Shanghai: The Making of a Social Movement in Modern China.* Leiden: E. J. Brill, 1971.

Ch'i Hsi-sheng. *Nationalist China at War: Military Defeats and Political Collapse, 1937–1945.* Ann Arbor: University of Michigan Press, 1982.

China, Republic of. *Report of the National Flood Relief Commission, 1931–1932.* Shanghai, 1933.

Chou, Shun-hsin. *The Chinese Inflation, 1937–1949.* New York: Columbia University Press, 1963.

Clifford, Nicholas R. *Spoilt Children of Empire: Westerners in Shanghai and the Chinese Revolution of the 1920s.* Middlebury, Vt.: Middlebury College Press, 1991.

Coble, Parks M. *Facing Japan: Chinese Politics and Japanese Imperialism, 1931–1937.* Cambridge, Mass.: Council on East Asian Studies, Harvard University, 1991.

———. *Chinese Capitalists in Japan's New Order: The Occupied Lower Yangzi, 1937–1945.* Berkeley: University of California Press, 2003.

Cohen, Paul A. *History in Three Keys: The Boxers as Event, Experience, and Myth.* New York: Columbia University Press, 1997.

Compagnie de Jésus. *Lettres édifiantes et curieuses écrites des missions étrangères.* Paris: Nicolas Le Clerc, 1707–76. New ed. 14 vols. Lyon: J. Vernarel, 1819.

Cronin, Victor. *The Wise Man from the West.* New York: Dutton, 1955.

Darwent, E. C. *Shanghai: A Handbook for Travellers and Residents.* Shanghai: Kelly & Walsh, 1920.

Deacon, Richard. *Kempei Tai: The Japanese Secret Service Then and Now.* New York: Beaufort Books, 1983.

Deng, Ming, ed. *Survey of Shanghai, 1980s–1940s: Shanghai bainian lueying.* Shanghai: Shanghai People's Fine Arts Publishing House, 1993.

Des Gouttes, Paul. "Les 75 premières années de la Convention de Genève." *Revue Internationale de la Croix-Rouge* 21 (July–December 1939).

Diccionario histórico de la Compañia de Jesús. 4 vols. Rome: Institutum Historicum; Madrid : Universidad Pontificia Comillas, 2001.

Dictionnaire de biographie française. Vol. 18: *Humann-Lacombe.* Paris: Letouzey & Ané, 1989–94.

Dictionnaire du monde religieux dans la France contemporaine. Edited by Jean-Marie Mayeur and Yves-Marie Hilaire. Vol. 1: *Les Jésuites.* Paris: Beauchesne, 1985.

Dirksen, Herbert von. *Moscow, Tokyo, London: Twenty Years of German Foreign Policy.* Norman: University of Oklahoma Press, 1952.

Donnelly, Francis P., S.J., *Principles of Jesuit Education in Practice.* New York: P. J. Kenedy & Sons, 1934.

Duteil, Jean-Pierre. *Le mandat du ciel: Le rôle des jésuites en Chine, de la mort de François-Xavier à la dissolution de la Compagnie de Jésus, 1552–1774.* Lille: A.N.R.T, Université de Lille III, 1993. Paris: Editions Arguments, 1994.

Duus, Peter, Ramon H. Myers, and Mark R. Peattie, eds. *The Japanese Informal Empire in China, 1895–1937.* Princeton: Princeton University Press, 1989.

Eastman, Lloyd E. *Seeds of Destruction: Nationalist China in War and Revolution, 1937–1949.* Stanford: Stanford University Press, 1984.

Elvin, Mark. "The Administration of Shanghai." In *The Chinese City between Two Worlds,* ed. Mark Elvin and G. William Skinner, pp. 239–62. Stanford: Stanford University Press, 1974.

Fairbanks, John King. *Trade and Diplomacy on the China Coast: The Opening of the Treaty Ports, 1842–1854.* Stanford: Stanford University Press, 1969.

Feetham, Richard. *Report of the Honorable Richard Feetham, C.M.G., Judge of the Supreme Court of the Union of South Africa to the Shanghai Municipal Council.* 3 vols. Shanghai: North China Daily News and Herald, 1931.

Feng Yi, "Elites locales et solidarities régionales: L'aide aux réfugiés à Shanghai (1937–1940)." *Études chinoises* 15, nos. 1–2 (Spring–Autumn 1996).

Finch, Percy. *Shanghai and Beyond.* New York: Scribner, 1953.

Fighting Around Shanghai. Tokyo: Herald Press, 1932.

Fitch, George A. *My Eighty Years in China.* Private printing, 1974.

Fogel, Joshua A., ed. *The Nanjing Massacre in History and Historiography.* Berkeley: University of California Press, 2000.

Fu, Poshek. *Passivity, Resistance, and Collaboration: Intellectual Choices in Occupied Shanghai, 1937–1945.* Stanford: Stanford University Press, 1993.

Fujiwara, Akira. *Nankin daigyakusatsu* [Nanjing Massacre]. Tokyo: Iwanami Shoten, 1988.

Gernet, Jacques. *China and the Christian Impact: A Conflict of Cultures.* New York: Cambridge University Press, 1985.

Glines, Carroll V. *The Doolittle Raid: America's Daring First Strike Against Japan.* New York: Orion Books, 1988.

Gongbuju dongshihui huiyilu [Minutes of the Directors' meetings, Shanghai Municipal Council], 29 vols. Shanghai: Shanghai guji chubanshe, 2001.

Goodman, Bryna. *Native Place, City, and Nation: Regional Networks and Identities in Shanghai, 1853–1937.* Berkeley: University of California Press, 1995.

Goto-Shibata, Harumi. *Japan and Britain in Shanghai, 1925–31.* New York: St. Martin's Press, 1995.

Le Guerre Moderne et la Protection des Civils, Secrétariat Général des Lieux de Genève. Genève: Château Banquet, 1943.

Hahn, Emily. *China to Me: A Partial Autobiography.* Garden City, N.Y.: Doubleday, Doran, 1944.

Hauser, Ernest O. *Shanghai: City for Sale.* New York: Harcourt, Brace, 1940.

Hayward, Victor E. W. *Christians and China.* Belfast: Christian Journals Limited, 1974.

He Shengsui and Chen Maiqing. *Lunxian tongshi* [The grieved history of the besieged land]. Shanghai: Fudan University Press, 1999.

Henriot, Christian. *Belles de Shanghai: Prostitution et sexualité en Chine aux XIXe–XXE siècles.* Paris: CNRS, 1997.

————. *Shanghai, 1927–1937: Municipal Power, Locality, and Modernization.* Translated by Noel Castelino. Berkeley: University of California Press, 1993.

Henriot, Christian, and Yeh Wen-hsin, eds. *In the Shadow of the Rising Sun: Shanghai Under Japanese Occupation.* Cambridge: Cambridge University Press, 2006.

Herald of Asia, nos. 6–8. Tokyo: Herald Press.

Hirota Kōki Denki Kankōkai [Committee for the publication of Hirota Kōki's biography], comp. *Hirota Kōki.* Fukuoka: Ashi Shobō, 1996.

Honda, Katsuichi. *The Nanjing Massacre: A Japanese Journalist Confronts Japan's National Shame.* Armonk, N.Y.: M. E. Sharpe, 1999.

Honig, Emily. *Creating Chinese Ethnicity: Subei People in Shanghai, 1850–1980.* New Haven, Conn.: Yale University Press, 1992.

Hicks, George. *The Comfort Women: Japan's Brutal Regime of Enforced Prostitution in the Second World War.* New York: Norton, 1994.

Hsia, Ching-lin. *The Status of Shanghai: A Historical Review of the International Settlement.* Shanghai: Kelly & Walsh, 1929.

Hsü Shu-hsi. *A Digest of Japanese War Conduct.* Shanghai: Kelly & Walsh, 1939.

————. *Documents of the Nanking Safety Zone.* Shanghai: Kelly & Walsh, 1939.

————. *Japan and Shanghai.* Shanghai: Kelly & Walsh, 1938.

Hu Hua-ling. *American Goddess at the Rape of Nanking: The Courage of Minnie Vautrin.* Carbondale: Southern Illinois University Press, 2000.

Huebner, Jon W. "Old Shanghai Revisited," *American Asian Review* 5, no. 3 (Fall 1987): 84–104.

Hunter, Janet E., comp. *Concise Dictionary of Modern Japanese History.* Berkeley: University of California Press, 1984.

Hutchison, William R. *Errand to the World: American Protestant Thought and Foreign Mission.* Chicago: University of Chicago Press, 1987.

International Military Tribunal for the Far East. *The Tokyo War Crimes Trial.* Edited by R. John Pritchard and Sonia Magbanua Zaide. New York: Garland, 1981.

Iriye, Akita. *Power and Culture: The Japanese-American War, 1941–1945.* Cambridge, Mass.: Harvard University Press, 1981.

Ishii, Vicount Kikujiro. "History Repeats Itself." *Contemporary Japan: A Review of Japanese Affairs* 7, no. 2 (September 1938): 228–36.

Japan. Ministry of Foreign Affairs. *Gaimushō. Shitsumu hōkuku: Tōa kyoku* (Reprints of 1937 Work Report, East Asia Bureau). Tokyo: Kuresu Shuppan, 1993.

Japonicus (sic). "Les Zones Jacquinot." *Lettres de Jersey*, vol. 1937–1938, pp. 93–106.

Johnson, Linda Cooke. *Shanghai: From Market Town to Treaty Port, 1074–1858.* Stanford: Stanford University Press, 1995.

———. "Shanghai: Emerging Jiangnan Port, 1683–1840." In *Cities of Jiangnan in Late Imperial China*, ed. Linda Cooke Johnson, pp. 151–81. Albany: State University of New York Press, 1993.

Johnston, Tess, and Deke Erh. *A Last Look: Western Architecture in Old Shanghai.* Hong Kong: Old China Hand Press, 1993.

Johnstone, William C., Jr. *The Shanghai Problem.* Stanford: Stanford University Press, 1937.

Jordan, Donald A. *China's Trial by Fire: The Shanghai War of 1932.* Ann Arbor: University of Michigan Press, 2001.

Kengelbacher, Peter. *Shanghai 1937: Photographs of Karl Kengelbacher,* www.japan. guide.com/a/shanghai (accessed October 1, 2007)

Kirby, William C. *Germany and Republican China.* Stanford: Stanford University Press, 1984.

———. "The Internationalization of China: Foreign Relations at Home and Abroad in the Republican Era." *China Quarterly*, no. 150 (June 1997): 433–58.

Kounin, I. I. *Eighty-Five Years of the Shanghai Volunteer Corps.* Shanghai: Cosmopolitan Press, 1938.

Ladany, Laszlo. *The Catholic Church in China.* New York: Freedom House, 1987.

Lary, Diana, and Stephen MacKinnon, eds. *Scars of War: The Impact of Warfare on Modern China.* Vancouver: University of British Columbia Press, 2001.

Leck, Greg. *Captives of Empire: The Japanese Internment of Allied Civilians in China, 1941- 1945.* Bangor, Pa.: Shandy Press, 2006.

Lee, Elizabeth. *A Letter to My Aunt.* New York: Carlton Press, 1981.

Li, Fei Fei, Robert Sabella, and David Liu, eds. *Nanking 1937: Memory and Healing.* Armonk, N.Y.: M. E. Sharpe, 2002.

Liu, F. F. *A Military History of Modern China, 1924–1949.* Westport, Conn: Greenwood Press, 1956.

Lu Suping. *They Were in Nanjing: The Nanjing Massacre Witnessed by American and British Nations.* Hong Kong: Hong Kong University Press, 2004.

Lutz, Jessie. *Chinese Politics and Christian Missions: The Anti-Christian Movements of 1920–1928.* Notre Dame, Ind.: Cross Cultural Publications, 1988.

MacKinnon, Stephen. "The Tragedy of Wuhan, 1938." *Modern Asian Studies* 30, no. 4 (1966): 931–43.

Madsen, Richard. *China's Catholics: Tragedy and Hope in an Emerging Civil Society.* Berkeley: University of California Press, 1998.

Malcom-Kluge, Mary. *Highlights of a Life.* Paris: 1997.

Mancall, Mark. *China at the Center: 300 Years of Foreign Policy.* New York: Free Press, 1984.

Maruyama Masao. "Theory and Psychology of Ultranationalism." *Japan Echo,* special issue, 1997.

Martin, Arthur W., Jr. "Autobiography." Unpublished manuscript.

Martin, Brian G. *The Shanghai Green Gang: Politics and Organized Crime, 1919–1937.* Berkeley: University of California Press, 1996.

Matsui Iwane. *Matsui Iwane taishō senjin nikki* [General Matsui Iwane's campaign diary]. In *Nanking senshi shiryō-shū* II [Collection of Nanjing military campaign materials] Tokyo: Kaikōsha, 1993.

Mayeur, Jean-Marie and Yves-Marie Hilaire. *Dictionnaire du Monde Religieux dans la France Contemporaine,* vol. 1. Paris: Beauchesne, 1985.

Meehan, John D., S.J. "The Savior of Shanghai: Robert Jacquinot, S.J., and His Safety Zone in a City at War, 1937." *Company,* Spring 2006, pp. 16–21.

———. "Un îlot de refuge: la 'Zone Jacquinot' et la guerre à Shanghai, 1937." Unpublished paper. n.d.

Mendizábal, P. Rufo, S.J. *Catalogus Defunctorum in renata Societate Iesu, 1814–1970.* Rome, Curia P. Gen, 1972.

Meskill, Johanna Menzel. *Hitler & Japan: The Hollow Alliance.* New York: Atherton Press, 1966.

Millard, Thomas. *China, Where It Is Today and Why.* Shanghai: Kelly & Walsh, 1928.

Miller, G. E. *Shanghai: Paradise of Adventures.* New York: Orsay Publishing House, 1937.

Minamiki, George, S.J. *The Chinese Rites Controversy from Its Beginning to Modern Times.* Chicago: Loyola University Press, 1985.

Mungello, David E. *The Great Encounter of China and the West, 1500–1800.* Lanham, Md.: Rowman & Littlefield, 2005.

———. *The Forgotten Christians of Hangzhou.* Honolulu: University of Hawaii Press, 1994.

———. *Curious Land: Jesuit Accommodation and the Origins of Sinology.* Honolulu: University of Hawaii Press, 1989.

Murphy, Rhoads. *Shanghai: Key to Modern China.* Cambridge, Mass: Harvard University Press, 1953.

Nankin Senshi Shiyōshū: II [Collection of materials concerning Nanjing military operations]. Tokyo: Kaikōsha, 1993.

Negroponte, John D. "Protection of Humanitarian Personnel in Conflict Zones." Statement in the United National Security Council, August 26, 2003.

Nish, Ian Hill. *The Origins of the Russo-Japanese War.* London: Longman, 1985.

"An Overview of Relations Between China and Japan, 1895–1945." *China Quarterly*, no. 124 December 1990): 601–23.

The Nanking Atrocities (Online Documentary). University of Missouri-Columbia University, 2000. www.nankingatrocities.net (accessed August 28, 2007).

Ogata, Sadako. *The Turbulent Decade: Confronting the Refugee Crisis of the 1990s.* New York: Norton, 2005.

Oliver, Jay C. "Shanghai Chinese YMCA Refugee work." Presentation for Christian Broadcasting Station, April 14, 1938.

Oliver Papers, University of Oregon, Knight Library. Pan, Ling. *In Search of Old Shanghai*. Hong Kong: Joint Publishing Company, 1982.

————. *Old Shanghai: Gangsters in Paradise*. Hong Kong: Heinemann Asia, 1984.

Pan, Lynn. *Shanghai: A Century of Change in Photographs, 1843–1949: The End of an Era.* New York: New Amsterdam Books, 1990.

Patent, Gregory. *Shanghai Passage*. New York: Clarion Books, 1990.

Peattie, Mark R. "Japanese Treaty Port Settlements in China, 1895–1937." In *The Japanese Informal Empire in China*, ed. Peter Duus, Ramon H. Myers, and Mark R. Peattie, pp. 166–209. Princeton: Princeton University Press, 1989.

Perruchoud, Richard. *Les résolutions des conférences internationales de la Croix-Rouge*. Geneva: Institut Henry-Dunant, 1979.

Pinot, Virgile. *La Chine et la formation de l'esprit philosophique in France, 1640–1740.* 1932. Reprint. Geneva: Slatkine, 1971.

Pott, F. L. Hawks. *A Short History of Shanghai*. Shanghai: Kelly & Walsh, 1937.

Powell, John B. *My Twenty-Five Years in China*. New York: Macmillan, 1945.

Presseisen, Ernst L. *Germany and Japan: A Study in Totalitarian Diplomacy, 1933–1941.* The Hague: Martinus Nijhoff, 1958.

Rabe, John. *The Good Man of Nanking: The Diaries of John Rabe*. New York: Knopf, 1998.

Rape of Nanking. Video recording. New York: A&E Television Networks, 1999.

Ricci, Matteo. *China in the Sixteenth Century: The Journals of Matthew Ricci: 1583–1610.* New York: Random House, 1953.

Rigby, Richard W. *The May 30 Movement: Events and Themes*. Canberra: Australian National University Press, 1980.

Ristaino, Marcia R. *China's Art of Revolution: The Mobilization of Discontent, 1927 and 1928.* Durham, N.C.: Duke University Press, 1987.

————. *Port of Last Resort: The Diaspora Communities of Shanghai*. Stanford: Stanford University Press, 2001.

Rivière, Claude. *En Chine avec Teilhard: Lettres inédites de P. Teilhard de Chardin.* Paris: Seuil, 1968.

Roberts, Adam. "The Role of Humanitarian Issues in International Politics in the 1990s." *International Review of the Red Cross*, no. 833 (1999).

Roosevelt, Franklin D. "Quarantine Speech." October 5, 1937. www.vlib.us/amdocs/texts/fdrquarn.html (accessed August 28, 2007).

Rosso, Antonio Sisto. *Apostolic Legations to China of the Eighteenth Century.* South Pasadena, Calif.: P. D. and I. Perkins, 1948.

Rowbotham, Arnold. *Missionary and Mandarin: The Jesuits at the Court of China.* New York: Russell & Russell, 1966.

Rowe, William T. *Hankow: Conflict and Community in a Chinese City, 1796–1895.* Stanford: Stanford University Press, 1989.

Schrecker, John E. *Imperialism and Chinese Nationalism: Germany in Shantung.* Cambridge, Mass.: Harvard University Press, 1971.

Sebes, Joseph, S.J. *The Jesuits and the Sino-Russian Treaty of Nerchinsk (1689).* Rome: Institutum Historicum S.I., 1961.

Sergeant, Harriet. *Shanghai: Collision Point of Cultures, 1918–1939.* New York: Crown, 1990.

Shanghai Affair. Tokyo: Herald Press, 1932.

Shanghaishi nianjian [Shanghai yearbook]. Shanghai: 1935.

Shiroyama Saburo. *War Criminal: The Life and Death of Hirota Kōki.* Translated by John Bester. Tokyo: Kodansha International, 1977.

Silva, Frederic A. *Todo o nosso passado: os filhos de Macau, sua história e herança/ All Our Yesterdays: The Sons of Macao, Their History and Heritage.* Translated by Maria Alice Morais Jorge and Cecília Jorge. Macao: Livros do Oriente, 1996.

Simpson, John Hope. *Refugees: Preliminary Report of a Problem.* London: Royal Institute of International Affairs, 1938.

———. *The Refugee Problem: Report of a Survey.* London: Oxford University Press, 1939.

Smedley, Agnes. *Battle Hymn of China.* New York: Knopf, 1943.

Smythe, Lewis S. C. *War Damage in the Nanking Area, December 1937 to March 1938.* Nanking: Nanking International Relief Committee, 1938.

Steele, A. T. *Shanghai and Manchuria, 1932: Recollections of a War Correspondent.* Tempe: Center for Asian Studies, Arizona State University, 1977.

Story of the Jacquinot Zone, Shanghai China. Shanghai: Kelly & Walsh, 1939. Copy in RG 59, 811,4611 France/114.

Stranahan, Patricia. *Underground: The Shanghai Communist Party and the Politics of Survival, 1927–1927.* Lanham, Md.: Rowman & Littlefield, 1998.

———. "Radicalization of Refugees," *Modern China* 26, no. 2 (April 2000): 166–93.

Streit, R. *Bibliotheca Missionum.* Aachen, 1916.

Sun, You-Li. *China and the Origins of the Pacific War, 1931–1941.* New York: St. Martin's Press, 1993.

Sun Zhaiwei, ed. *Nanjing datusha* [The Nanjing Massacre].Beijing: Beijing chubanshe, 1997.

Tang, Edmond, and Jean-Paul Wiest, eds. *The Catholic Church in Modern China.* Maryknoll, N.Y.: Orbis Books, 1993.

Tata, Sam (photographer). *Shanghai 1949: The End of an Era.* Introduction by Ian McLachlan. New York: New Amsterdam Books, 1990.

Teilhard de Chardin, Pierre. *Le phénomène humain.* Paris: Seuil, 1955. Translated by Bernard Wall as *The Phenomenon of Man* (New York: Harper & Row, 1959).

Thomas, Hugh. *The Spanish Civil War.* New York: Harper & Row, 1977.

Thomson, David. *Democracy in France Since 1870.* New York: Oxford University Press, 1964.

Timperley, J. S. *What War Means:The Japanese Terror in China: A Documentary Record.* London: Gollancz, 1938.

Uhalley, Stephen, and Xiaoxin Wu, eds. *China and Christianity: Burdened Past Hopeful Future.* Armonk, N.Y.: M. E. Sharpe, 2001.

United Nations. *Report of the Secretary-General on Protection for Humanitarian Assistance to Refugees and Others in Conflict Situations.* S/1998/883. September 22, 1998. http://daccessdds.un.org/doc/UNDOC/GEN/N98/276/77/PDF/ N9827677.pdf?OpenElement (accessed August 28, 2007).

United States. Department of State. *Papers Relating to the Foreign Relations of the United States: Japan, 1931–1941.* 2 vols. Washington, D.C.: GPO, 1943.

————. *Foreign Relations of the United States: Diplomatic Papers, 1940.* 5 vols. Washington, D.C.: GPO, 1955–61.

Uyehara, Cecil H. *Checklist of Archives in the Japanese Ministry of Foreign Affairs, Tokyo, Japan, 1868–1945.* Washington, D.C.: Library of Congress, 1954.

Van de Ven, Hans J. *War and Nationalism in Shanghai, 1925–1945.* New York: Routledge- Curzon, 2003.

Wakeman, Frederic, Jr. *Policing Shanghai, 1927–1937.* Berkeley: University of California Press, 1995.

————. *The Shanghai Badlands: Wartime Terrorism and Urban Crime, 1937–41.* Cambridge: Cambridge University Press, 1996.

Wakeman, Frederic, Jr., and Wen-hsin Yeh, eds. *Shanghai Sojourners.* Berkeley, Calif.: Institute of East Asian Studies, 1992.

Wasserstein, Bernard. *Secret War in Shanghai: Treachery, Subversion and Collaboration in the Second World War.* London: Profile Books, 1998.

Wei, Betty Peh-t'i. *Shanghai: Crucible of Modern China.* Hong Kong: Oxford University Press, 1987.

Who's Who in China. 5th ed. Shanghai: China Weekly Review, 1936.

Who's Who in China. Supplement to the 5th ed. Shanghai: China Weekly Review, 1940.

Whyte, William Foote. *Street Corner Society: The Social Structure of an Italian Slum.* Chicago: University of Chicago Press, 1943.

Wiest, Jean-Paul. *The Maryknoll in China: A History, 1918–1955.* Maryknoll, N.Y.: Orbis Books, 1997.

Wright, Gordon. *France in Modern Times: From the Enlightenment to the Present.* 5th ed. New York: Norton, 1995.

Xu Chi. "Qichuang de Shanghai." In *Jieho de Shanghai.* Shanghai: Zhanshi chubanshe, 1938.

Yamamoto, Masahiro. *Nanking: Anatomy of an Atrocity.* Westport, Conn.: Praeger, 2000.

———. "A Tale of Two Atrocities: American Historiography of the 'Rape of Nanking' in Comparison with the Case of James Bacque's *Other Losses.*" *Virginia Review of Asian Studies* 11 (Fall 2000).

Yang, Daqing. "The Challenges of the Nanjing Massacre: Reflections on Historical Inquiry." In *The Nanjing Massacre in History and Historiography,* ed. Joshua A. Fogel. Berkeley: University of California Press, 2000.

Ye, Xiaoqing. "Shanghai Before Nationalism." *East Asian History,* no. 3 (June 1991): 33–52.

Yeh, Wen-hsin. "Shanghai Modernity: Commerce and Culture in a Republican City." *China Quarterly,* no. 150 (1997): 375–94.

———, ed. *Wartime Shanghai.* New York: Routledge, 1998.

Yin, James. *The Rape of Nanking: An Undeniable History in Photographs.* Edited by Ron Dorfman and Shi Yong. Chicago: Innovative Publishing Group, 1996.

Yip, Ka-che. *Religion, Nationalism, and Chinese Students: The Anti-Christian Movement of 1922–1927.* Bellingham: Center for East Asian Studies, Western Washington University, 1980.

———. *Health and Reconstruction in Nationalist China: the Development of Modern Health Services, 1928–1937.* Ann Arbor, Mich.: Association for Asian Studies, 1995.

Zhao Puchu. "Danzhan chuqi de Shanghai Nanmin gongzuo" [Work with Shanghai Refugees During the Early Period of the Sino-Japanese War]. *Lishi yanjiu ziliao,* no. 4 (1986): 31–50.

La Zone Jacquinot: Changhai, 1937–1939. 81pp. Shanghai: n.p., n.d. Copy in University of British Columbia Library.

INTERVIEWS

Bryan, Gertrude. Interview, February 11, 1989, Arlington, Va.

Fuchs, Wather. Interview, Cologne, Germany, 1963.

Hu Wen-an and Peggy Hu. Interview, February 26, 1995, Bethesda, Md.

Ishiguro Kenji. Interview, September 11, 1996, Washington, D.C.

Monnot, Fernande. Telephone interview, March 5, 2006.

de Stackelberg, Baroness Garnett. Telephone interview, March 23, 1989.

Willens, Liliane. Interview, August 5, 2005, Washington, D.C.

Witt, Pauline. Interview, January 2–3, 2007, Walnut Creek, Calif.

Index

The authorized representative in the EU for product safety and compliance is:
Mare Nostrum Group
B.V Doelen 72
4831 GR Breda
The Netherlands

www.ingramcontent.com/pod-product-compliance
Lightning Source LLC
Chambersburg PA
CBHW030411100426
42812CB00028B/2911/J